Virtual LANs

Construction, Implementation, and Management

Gilbert Held

WILEY COMPUTER PUBLISHING

John Wiley & Sons, Inc.

New York • Chichester • Weinheim
• Brisbane • Singapore • Toronto

Executive Publisher: Katherine Schowalter
Editor: Theresa Hudson
Associate Managing Editor: Angela Murphy
Text Design & Composition: Publishers Design & Production Services, Inc.

Designations used by companies to distinguish their products are often claimed as trademarks. In all instances where John Wiley & Sons, Inc., is aware of a claim, the product names appear in initial capital or ALL CAPITAL LETTERS. Readers, however, should contact the appropriate companies for more complete information regarding trademarks and registration.

This text is printed on acid-free paper.

This publication is designed to provide accurate and authoritative information in regard to the subject matter covered. It is sold with the understanding that the publisher is not engaged in rendering legal, accounting, or other professional service. If legal advice or other expert assistance is required, the services of a competent professional person should be sought.

Library of Congress Cataloging-in-Publication Data

Held, Gilbert.
    Virtual LANs : construction, implementation, and management / Gilbert Held.
        p. cm.
    Includes index.
    ISBN 0-471-17732-6 (pbk. : alk. paper)
    1. Local area networks (Computer networks)   2. Virtual computer systems.   I. Title.
    TK5105.7.H44474 1997
    004.6′8—dc21   96-52022

Printed in the United States of America
10 9 8 7 6 5 4 3 2 1

Contents

Preface   **xiii**

1   INTRODUCTION TO VLANS   **1**

vLAN Overview   1
   Construction Basics   2
      Implicit versus Explicit Tagging   2
      Using Implicit Tagging   3
Rationale for Use   5
   Supporting Virtual Organizations   5
   LAN Administration   6
   More Efficient Bandwidth Utilization   7
   Improved Security   7
Network Issues   8
   Multivendor Product Compatibility   8
   Interdomain Communications   9
   vLAN Awareness   9
   Priority Specification   9
   IP Multicast Address Support   10
   Nonclassified Frame Support   10
   Inactive vLAN Table Entry Processing   10
Chapter Preview   11
   Networking Standards   12
   Frame and Cell Operations   12

Network Layer Operations	12
LAN Equipment Operations	12
vLAN Construction Basics	13
Standards	13
Virtual Networking	13

2 NETWORKING STANDARDS — **15**

Standards Organizations	16
National Standards Organizations	16
ANSI	17
IEEE	18
International Standards Organizations	18
ITU-T	18
ISO	19
The ISO Reference Model	19
Layered Architecture	21
OSI Layers	21
Layer 1—The Physical Layer	23
Layer 2—The Data Link Layer	23
Layer 3—The Network Layer	24
Layer 4—The Transport Layer	25
Layer 5—The Session Layer	25
Layer 6—The Presentation Layer	25
Layer 7—The Application Layer	26
Data Flow	26
IEEE 802 Standards	27
802 Committees	28
Data Link Subdivision	30
Medium Access Control	31
Logical Link Control	32
Additional Sublayering	33
LAN Frame Header	35

3 FRAME AND CELL OPERATIONS — **37**

Ethernet Frame Composition	38
Preamble Field	40
Start-of-Frame Delimiter Field	40
Destination Address Field	41
I/G Subfield	42
U/L Subfield	42
Universally versus Locally Administered Addressing	42
Source Address Field	44

Type Field   44
Length Field   45
Data Field   46
Frame Check Sequence Field   46
Ethernet Media Access Control   47
  Functions   47
    Transmit Media Access Management   48
    Service Primitives   54
    Primitive Operations   55
Ethernet Logical Link Control   56
  The LLC Protocol Data Unit   56
  Ethernet_SNAP Frame   58
  NetWare Ethernet_802.3 Frame   59
  Receiver Frame Determination   60
  Types of Service   61
    Type 1   61
    Type 2   62
    Type 3   63
  Classes of Service   63
  Service Primitives   63
Fast Ethernet   64
  Encoding   64
  Start-of-Stream Delimiter   65
  End-of-Stream Delimiter   65
Token Ring Frame Operations   65
  Transmission Formats   66
  Starting/Ending Delimiters   68
    Differential Manchester Encoding   68
    Nondata Symbols   69
  Access Control Field   71
    The Monitor Bit   74
    The Active Monitor   75
  Frame Control Field   76
  Destination Address Field   77
    Universally Administered Address   77
    Locally Administered Address   78
    Functional Address Indicator   79
    Address Values   79
  Source Address Field   81
  Routing Information Field   82
  Information Field   82
  Frame Check Sequence   84

Frame Status Field	84
Token Ring Medium Access Control	85
Vectors and Subvectors	85
MAC Control	86
Purge Frame	88
Beacon Frame	88
Duplicate Address Test Frame	89
Station Insertion	89
Token Ring Logical Link Control	91
Service Access Points	92
Types and Classes of Service	93
FDDI	93
Network Advantages	94
Operating Rate	94
Reliability	94
Use of Optical Media	95
Hardware Components, Network Topology, and Access	95
Optical Transmitters	95
Optical Receiver	96
Fiber Optic Cable	96
Power Loss	97
Connectors	97
Network Topology	98
Counter-Rotating Rings	98
Token Use	98
Network Access	99
Dual Attached Station	99
Single Attached Station	100
Data Encoding	101
NRZI Signaling	102
4B/5B Encoding	103
Frame Formats	103
FDDI Token	105
FDDI Frame	106
FDDI_802.2	107
FDDI_SNAP	108
Bandwidth Allocation	108
Classes of Traffic	110
Timers	110
Synchronous Transmission	111
Asynchronous Transmission	112
Transmission Example	113

ATM   113
  Benefits   113
    Scalability   115
    Transparency   116
    Traffic Classification   116
  The ATM Protocol Stack   116
    ATM Adaptation Layer   116
    ATM Layer   117
    Physical Layer   118
  ATM Operation   118
    ATM Network Interface Cards   119
    LAN Switch   119
    ATM Router   119
    ATM Switch   120
    ATM Service Processor   121
  Network Interfaces   121
    User-to-Network Interface   121
    Network-to-Node Interface   122
  ATM Cell Header   122
    Generic Flow Control Field   123
    Virtual Path Identifier Field   123
    Virtual Circuit Identifier Field   124
    Payload Type Identifier Field   125
    Cell Loss Priority Field   125
    Header Error Check Field   125
  ATM Connections and Cell Switching   125
    Connections   126
    Cell Switching   126
    Types of Switches   126
    Using Connection Identifiers   127
  LAN Emulation   128

4 **NETWORK LAYER OPERATIONS**   **133**
   NetWare IPX/SPX and Related Protocols   133
     IPX   134
       Checksum Field   134
       Length Field   134
       Transport Control Field   134
       Packet Type Field   134
       Destination Network Field   136
       Destination Node Field   136
       Destination Socket Field   136

Source Network Field	136
Source Node and Source Socket Fields	137
IPX Data Field Composition	137
SPX	139
Connection Control Field	139
Datastream Type Field	139
Source and Destination Connection ID Fields	140
Sequence Number Field	140
Acknowledgment Number Field	140
Allocation Number Field	141
SAP and RIP	141
SAP Operation	141
SAP Fields	142
RIP Operation	142
Performance Issues	143
TCP/IP	143
Datagrams versus Virtual Circuits	144
ICMP and ARP	145
TCP	145
UDP	147
IP	148
Domain Name Service	154
Name Server	156
5 LAN EQUIPMENT OPERATIONS	**159**
Bridges	159
Operational Overview	159
Filtering and Forwarding	161
Types	162
Bridge Table Operations	163
Frame Conversion	163
Address/Routing Table Construction	164
Spanning Tree Protocol	167
Operation	167
Source Routing	172
The RIF Field	173
Operation Example	174
Advantages	176
Disadvantages	176
Source Routing Transparent Bridges	177
Operation	178
Advantages	178

Translating Operations   178
Bridge Utilization   181
    Serial and Sequential Bridging   181
    Parallel Bridging   183
    Star Bridging   183
    Backbone Bridging   184
Intelligent Switches   184
    Conventional Hub Bottlenecks   186
        Ethernet Hub Operation   186
        Token Ring Hub Operation   188
        Bottleneck Creation   189
    Switching Operations   190
        Bridge Switching   190
        The Switching Hub   191
    Switching Techniques   195
        Cross-Point Switching   195
        Store-and-Forward   196
        Hybrid   199
        Port-Based Switching   199
        Segment-Based Switching   201
    Switching Architecture   203
    High-Speed Port Operation   204
        Full-Duplex Ethernet and Token Ring 204
        Fat Pipe   206
        100BASE-T   207
        FDDI and ATM Connections   208
        Flow Control   209
    Token Ring Switching   210
        Port Switching   210
        Switching Techniques   212
    Network Utilization   212
        Network Redistribution   213
        Server Segmentation   214
        Network Segmentation   214
        Backbone Replacement   215
Routers   218
    Basic Operation and Use of Routing Tables   218
    Networking Capability   220
    Communication, Transport, and Routing Protocols   221
        Communication Protocol   222
        Routing Protocol   222
        Transport Protocol   222

Types of Routing Protocols   223
    Interior Domain   224
    Exterior Domain   224
Protocol Operation   224
    Vector Distance Protocol   224
    Link State Protocols   227
Filtering   228
    Filtering Expressions   230
    Filtering Examples   230

6   VLAN CONSTRUCTION BASICS   233
Port-Grouping vLANs   233
  Using Intelligent Wiring Hubs   234
    Operation   234
    vLAN Creation   234
    Advantages   235
    Disadvantages   236
  Using LAN Switches   237
    Operation   237
    Advantages   238
    Disadvantages   239
    Supporting Inter-vLAN Communications   239
MAC-Based Switching   240
  Operational Example   241
  Advantages   243
    Flexibility   243
    Bandwidth and Expandability   243
  Disadvantages   244
    MAC Address Lists   245
    Interswitch Communications   246
    Router Restrictions   246
    Configuration and Support   248
Layer-3-Based vLANs   249
  Subnet-Based vLANs   249
    Advantages   250
    Disadvantages   251
  Protocol-Based vLANs   251
    Advantages   252
    Disadvantages   254
Rule-Based vLANs   254
  Capabilities   254
  Multicast Support   255

Advantages 256
Disadvantages 256
Comparing vLAN Creation Features 257
Connectivity Beyond the Workgroup 258
Ease of Station Assignment 258
Flexibility 258
Improving Workgroup Bandwidth 258
Multicast Support 259
Multiple vLANs per Port 259
Security 259
vLAN Spanning 260

7 **STANDARDS** 261
De facto Standards 262
The ISL Protocol 262
Overview 262
Frame Flow 263
Frame Composition 263
Configuration Example 267
The 802.10 Security Protocol 269
The 802.10 Frame 270
Cisco Systems Frame Modification 272
De jure Standards 273
LAN Emulation 273
Rationale for the Process 273
Operation 274
IP over ATM Address Resolution 277
IEEE 802.1Q 277
Architecture 278
Frame Tagging 279
Proposed vLAN Tagging 280
Frame Formats 281
The Continuing Effort 283

8 **VIRTUAL NETWORKING** 285
Rationale 286
Reliability 286
Economics 288
Applications 289
Voice and Fax 289
Micom's V/IP 290
Local Virtual Networking 291

Inter-vLAN, Intraswitch Communications 292
    Creative Communications 292
    Using a Router 293
Inter-vLAN, Interswitch Communications 295
    Creative Communications 295
    Using a Router 295
    Backbone Switching 297
    ATM Considerations 298
Using the Internet 301
    Security Considerations 301
      The Basic Firewall 301
      Encryption 310
      Authentication 311
      Proxy Services 313
    Testing Considerations 314
    Performance Issues 315

Index **317**

Preface

Imagine a virtual organization in which employees are assigned to work on different projects regardless of their geographical location. In the past, the logistics required to support a virtual organization were daunting, requiring network managers and administrators to spend a considerable amount of effort to support new groups of users formed on a temporary basis to work on a specific project. Today, the new fields of communications known as virtual local area networks, or *vLANs*, and their interconnection via *virtual networking*, provide network managers and administrators with the ability to tailor logically developed networks across their physical infrastructure to support the dynamic communications requirements of their organizations.

Similar to most communications-related technologies in their early stage of development, both vLANs and virtual networking still need to be standardized. Although the Institute of Electrical and Electronic Engineers (IEEE) has a group that is developing a virtual LAN standard, many issues remain to be tackled, and a uniform series of standards agreeable to all equipment vendors may take several years or more to reach an implementation stage. In the interim, for many organizations it is more important to support projects with existing off-the-shelf products than to hold projects in abeyance until standards-compliant products are obtainable. Thus, this book is focused upon the construction and operation of virtual LANs based upon various vendor-proprietary techniques as well as the emerging IEEE standard. In doing so, this book provides you with detailed information concerning the OSI Reference Model, different LAN frame and cell formats, and the operation of bridges, switches, and routers, all of which are important for understanding how virtual LANs are constructed as well as for understanding vLAN interoperability and network management–related issues.

While vLANs are an important emerging technology, there is another equally crucial emerging technique that *links* both conventional and virtual LANs. That technology is known as virtual networking and is also the focus of this book. Through virtual networking it becomes possible to replace corporate private networks with transmission facilities obtained from Internet service providers, in effect creating an intranet on the Internet. By examining the advantages and disadvantages of this emerging networking technique, you can decide if the potential economic savings and enhanced network reliability derived from virtual networking are sufficient to overcome some performance limitations and security issues also associated with this technology.

As a professional author, I highly value reader comments. You can send me your comments and suggestions concerning the addition or deletion of material for a possible future edition of this book via my publisher, whose address is listed on the back cover of this book.

ACKNOWLEDGMENTS

The preparation of a manuscript and its resulting publication as a book is a team effort, requiring the work of many people. As an old fashioned author who uses pen and paper (after having airlines request him to turn off his laptop computer), I am indebted to Mrs. Linda Hayes. Linda has a unique ability to decipher my handwriting as well as produce the professional manuscript rightly required by a publisher. Concerning the publisher, I would like to thank Terri Hudson for backing this project as well as Angela Murphy and the production department of John Wiley & Sons for their effort in producing this book. Last, but not least, I would like to thank my family for their patience and understanding during those long evenings and weekends when I sequestered myself to write this book.

Introduction
to vLANs

In this introductory chapter we will focus our attention upon the basics, attempting to answer most questions that readers previewing a new technology typically have. We will examine what constitutes a virtual LAN, or vLAN, the benefits and rationale associated with its use, how it is constructed, and some of the key issues associated with its construction. To accomplish those tasks we will first obtain a general overview of virtual LANs, leaving it for succeeding chapters to obtain detailed information concerning the construction, operation, and management of this relatively new technology. In concluding this chapter we will briefly preview succeeding chapters. This will enable you to determine if you should directly turn your attention to a specific chapter to obtain information on a particular topic, or if you should elect to read this book in chapter sequence.

VLAN OVERVIEW

A virtual LAN can be considered to represent a broadcast domain. This means that a transmission generated by one station on a vLAN is received only by those stations predefined by certain criteria to be in the domain.

Construction Basics

A vLAN is constructed by the logical grouping of two or more network nodes on a physical topology. To accomplish this logical grouping you must use a *vLAN-aware* switching device. Those devices can include intelligent switches, which essentially perform bridging and operate at the media access control (MAC) layer, or routers, which operate at the network layer, or layer 3, of the Open Systems Interconnection (OSI) Reference Model. Although a switching device is required to develop a vLAN, in actuality it is the software used by the device that provides vLAN capability. That is, a vLAN represents a subnetwork or broadcast domain defined by software and not by the physical topology of a network. Instead, the physical topology of a network serves as a constraint for the software-based grouping of nodes into a logically defined network.

Implicit versus Explicit Tagging

The actual criteria used to define the logical grouping of nodes into a vLAN can be based upon implicit or explicit tagging. Implicit tagging, which in effect eliminates the use of a special tagging field inserted into frames or packets, can be based upon MAC address, port number of a switch used by a node, protocol, or another parameter that nodes can be logically grouped into. Since many vendors offering vLAN products use different construction techniques, interoperability between vendors may be difficult, if not impossible. In comparison, explicit tagging requires the addition of a field into a frame or packet header. This action can result in incompatibilities with certain types of vendor equipment as the extension of the length of a frame or packet beyond its maximum can result in the inability of such equipment to handle such frames or packets. Because of these factors, the differences between implicit and explicit tagging can be illustrated by the proverbial statement "between a rock and a hard place." Although standards can be expected to resolve many interoperability problems, network managers and administrators may not have the luxury of time to wait until such standards are developed. Instead, you may wish to use existing equipment to develop vLANs to satisfy current and evolving organizational requirements. In later chapters in this book, I will provide detailed information necessary to assist you in selecting an appropriate vLAN construction technique. However, to provide you with an illustration of the actual construction of several vLANs, as well as to obtain the basics for discussing advantages associated with vLANs, I will illustrate the use of implicit tagging based upon switch ports.

Using Implicit Tagging

Figure 1.1 illustrates a simple eight-port Ethernet port-switching hub used to support two servers and six network nodes. The port-switching hub functions as a matrix switch, providing the ability to route a frame received on any port to any other port.

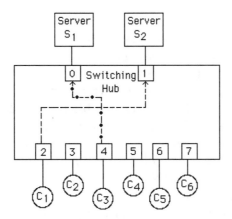

Legend S_1, S_2 servers
$C_1, \ldots C_6$ client workstations
$\boxed{n}$ switch port n

In a client–server communications environment, the use of a port switching hub enhances bandwidth utilization due to the support of simultaneous cross-connections. In this example, ports 2 and 1 and 4 and 0 are cross-connected.

Figure 1.1 Using an Ethernet port-switching hub.

For simplicity, let us assume that the ports are labeled 0 through 7, with ports 0 and 1 used to connect two servers to the switch and ports 2 through 7 used to connect six client workstations to the switch. As indicated in Figure 1.1, the servers are labeled S_1 and S_2, while the client workstations are labeled C_1 through C_6.

In a typical client-server communications environment the switch illustrated in Figure 1.1 would allow up to two simultaneous client-server communications to occur, in effect doubling available bandwidth through the switch in comparison to the use of a "flat" network in which all workstations contend for access to the network along with each server. The two dash lines in Figure 1.1 indicate two possible simultaneous client-server cross connections or communications.

To illustrate the creation of a virtual LAN, let us assume that the organization using the switch shown in Figure 1.1 consists of employees working in the sales and administrative departments. Let us further assume that server S_1 and clients C_1, C_2, C_3, and C_4 are associated with employees in the sales department, while server S_2 and clients C_5 and C_6 are associated with the administrative department. Through the use of a vLAN-capable switch that can associate ports with virtual LAN membership, you could logically establish two vLANs. Figure 1.2 illustrates the establishment of those vLANs based upon the association of ports to membership in each virtual LAN. Here the use of port address provides an implicit tagging method for the creation of the two vLANs.

In examining Figure 1.2, note that each vLAN represents a logical grouping of ports on top of the physical topology of the network. Thus, the network previously illustrated in Figure 1.1 has been segmented by the connection of client workstations and servers to different ports on a switching hub. In this example there are two segments that represent independent broadcast domains. That is, frames transmitted by a workstation or server on one domain remain constrained to that domain. Now that we have a basic level of knowledge concerning one method used to establish virtual LANs, let's use that construction method to discuss some of the advantages associated with the use of vLANs.

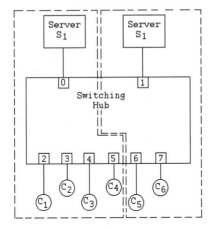

Legend:

S$_1$, S$_2$ servers
C$_1$. . . C$_6$ client workstations
$\boxed{n}$ port switch

Figure 1.2   Establishing vLANs based upon the use of switch ports.

RATIONALE FOR USE

There are four key reasons that can be considered as the driving force behind the development of vLANs and virtual networking. Those reasons include the necessity to support virtual organizations, the ability to simplify LAN administration, more efficient utilization of network bandwidth, and enhanced network security. Let us examine each in turn.

Supporting Virtual Organizations

A virtual organization is commonly defined as an organization without walls. What this definition means is that an organization can select its "best and brightest" employees to work on a specific project without regard to their physical location.

Prior to the development of vLANs, the primary method used to support the virtual networking requirements of virtual organizations was commonly limited to fax, telephone, and electronic mail. While those methods are still commonly used and more than likely will continue to be used in the future, vLANs provide a mechanism to establish a subnetwork of users and servers dedicated to the support of a specific project or group of projects. Through the use of a virtual LAN, employees can be easily added or dropped from a project, as well as obtain the ability to share access to a projects database. Thus, another reason for the desire of many organizations to obtain a virtual LAN capability concerns LAN administration.

LAN Administration

The use of equipment that supports virtual LANs can significantly simplify administrative costs associated with network additions, moves, and changes. For example, assume the employee that uses client workstation C_4 is reassigned from working in the sales department to a virtual organization group working in the administrative department. Through the use of an administrator console, the reassignment of workstation C_4 can be made without having to physically modify the workstation, alter cabling, or perform another physical activity.

Figure 1.3 illustrates the effect of reassigning workstation

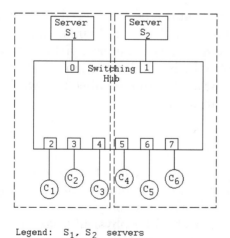

Legend: S_1, S_2 servers

C_1 . . . C_6 workstations

$\boxed{n}$ switch port n

Figure 1.3 Altering vLAN membership.

C$_4$ from the sales to the administrative department. In many cases, the actual effort required to accomplish moves and changes using a vLAN-capable device is as simple as a Windows drag-and-drop operation that can be accomplished in a few seconds. With the typical cost associated with physically moving workstations and recabling operations ranging between $500 and $1,000, a dynamic organization can severely tax the conventional method of network support as well as represent a considerable expense.

More Efficient Bandwidth Utilization

As previously noted, vLANs are created by logically segmenting a network into broadcast domains. For example, in Figures 1.2 and 1.3 two broadcast domains were created to represent logical groupings of network nodes. Once such logical groups are created, frames or packets transmitted by a member of one group are switched only among ports that are designated as belonging to the same virtual LAN. This results in network traffic originating within one logically created vLAN being contained within that network and results in a more efficient use of bandwidth. In addition, instead of broadcast traffic propagating throughout the physical infrastructure, such traffic is restricted to the "broadcast domains" that represent each virtually created segment. Such broadcast traffic commonly originates from servers that advertise their presence and capability to other network devices. One common example of the generation of broadcast traffic is Novell Inc.'s Service Advertisement Protocol (SAP) in which network servers advertise their presence and the type of service they provide by broadcasting a SAP packet every 60 seconds. By limiting broadcast packets or frames to a "broadcast domain" instead of transmitting that traffic to all network stations, network bandwidth is more efficiently used.

Improved Security

Although a vLAN is not a security device, nor should it be considered as one, it does improve security. The reason for this is the fact that transmissions are limited to broadcast domains.

For example, consider Figure 1.3, which illustrates the previously discussed altered pair of vLANs. If user C_1 transmits a request to any administration department employee, the request cannot move beyond physical ports 0, 2, 3, and 4. This means that nodes outside the domain will not be capable of receiving traffic generated on the other domain. It also means that a virtual organization whose members are located in different geographical areas and are working on a confidential project can rest assured that their traffic will not be visible outside of their virtual workgroup.

NETWORK ISSUES

While virtual LANs provide the potential to satisfy the dynamic networking requirements of many organizations, their construction, operation, and utilization is not problem free. In fact, there are a number of key issues network managers and administrators must consider prior to developing a virtual networking infrastructure. Table 1.1 lists seven of those issues that need to be addressed.

Multivendor Product Compatibility

Today there are a number of methods used by vendors to form vLANs, with such methods differing among vendors, as well as across equipment product lines manufactured by the same vendor. For example, some vendor products create vLANs based upon different implicit tagging methods, such as port assign-

Table 1.1 Virtual Networking Issues

Multivendor product compatibility
Interdomain communications
vLAN-aware versus vLAN-unaware operations
Priority specification
IP Multicast address support
Nonclassified frame support
Inactive vLAN table processing

---

ment, protocol, or MAC address. In comparison, other vendor products use proprietary explicit tagging techniques. If you select one vendor product, will that product correctly work with other vendor products? If your organization's vLAN requirements expand and you decide to obtain a different series of products from the vendor currently providing vLAN support, will those new products interoperate with your existing equipment? Those are two of several questions concerning equipment compatibility you may wish to investigate.

Interdomain Communications

We have noted that a vLAN can be defined as a broadcast domain and that frames or packets originated by a station assigned to that domain remain on that domain. Using our previously developed example of the construction of two vLANs representing sales and administration department employees, illustrated in Figure 1.3, what happens when a member of one vLAN needs to communicate with a client or server associated with the other vLAN? Or, phrasing the question another way, how does one obtain interdomain communications capability when the basic design goal of a vLAN restricts communications to particular domains? This is another key question for which network managers and administrators may require an answer, and on which we will focus our attention later in this book.

vLAN Awareness

Most networks consist of a mixture of equipment acquired over a period of time. This means that some equipment may be *vLAN-aware*, while other equipment may be *vLAN-unaware*. How vLAN-aware and vLAN-unaware equipment will interoperate is another important question that deserves consideration.

Priority Specification

Unlike humans, all frames are not created equal. Some frames may require a higher priority than other frames, especially when asynchronous transfer mode (ATM) cells are transported, since different qualities of service (QOS) can be associated with that protocol. Currently, vLAN equipment is conspicuous by its absence of a priority mechanism. While this is commendable for a workers' paradise where all people are created equal, this situation may not be suitable as the traffic load handled by vLAN equipment grows. Thus, the method used to specify priorities over vLANs may deserve investigation.

IP Multicast Address Support

An Internet protocol (IP) multicast address is used to enable a single packet to be passed to selected destinations. Since an IP multicast address could require access to different vLANs, the support of IP multicast addresses can be considered to represent a specially focused version of the previously discussed interdomain communications issue; that is, how will vLAN-compliant switches support IP multicast transmission across vLAN domain boundaries?

Nonclassified Frame Support

In a mixed networking environment, it is reasonable to expect many nodes to be classified into one or more vLAN broadcast domains, while other nodes are not classified as a member of a particular vLAN. What does a vLAN-compatible device do with nonclassified packets? Will there be a "default vLAN" onto which such packets are tossed? Will those packets be handled in a different manner and, if so, how? Again, these questions relate to vLAN issues that require investigation.

Inactive vLAN Table Entry Processing

As we will discuss later in this book, the construction of vLANs via the use of switches is often based upon the creation of tables. Most switches simply represent sophisticated bridges, and many types of bridges flush table entries after a period of inactivity. Although table flushing can be an important feature of conventional bridges and switches, its extension to vLANs may or may not be suitable, according to your networking environ-ment. For example, an implicit tagging method used by a seg-ment-sharing switch would be appropriate due to the necessity to support a large number of nodes per segment. In comparison, an implicit tagging method used by a port-based switch would have no need to flush table entries and any flushing could cause havoc to predefined vLAN criteria. Concerning table flushing, how this is accomplished might represent another item to con-sider. Will switches depend on timers or on another mechanism, such as a management platform, to flush out aged and inactive vLAN entries? Once again, these are questions that standards may resolve.

Although there are a large number of issues that remain to be resolved, for many organizations the functionality and capa-bility of vLANs overrides concern about those issues. While stan-dards may address most, if not all, of the previously described issues, they should be viewed as helpful information to assist you in considering whether to implement a vLAN capability, and not as a firm barrier to vLAN implementation. For most organiza-tions many of those issues may not be applicable, while for other organizations the selection of appropriate vendor equipment that is software upgradable may allow vLAN construction to pro-ceed even while some issues remain to be resolved.

CHAPTER PREVIEW

Now that we have an appreciation for the benefits, basic method of operation, and issues associated with vLANs, let's turn our attention to previewing succeeding chapters in this book. In doing so you can note the relevance of specific chapters to your information requirements, which may facilitate your ability to rapidly acquire the information you need. For other readers who may not be very familiar with LANs, it is suggested that you read succeeding chapters in the order they are presented. Since information presented in each succeeding chapter builds upon the information presented in preceding chapters, this will enable you to obtain the maximum benefit from this book.

Networking Standards

In Chapter 2 we will focus our attention upon network standards to include the International Standards Organization Open Systems Interconnection (OSI) Reference Model and its applicability to LAN and wide area network (WAN) operations. Doing so will provide us with a foundation of knowledge concerning how communication protocols operate at different network layers, and will form the basis for discussing standardization issues, frame formats, and equipment operation.

Frame and Cell Operations

Chapter 3 provides information concerning frame, packet, and cell formats of different transport mechanisms. As we will note later, the terms *frame* and *packet* many times can be used synonymously, although in certain situations they represent distinct entities. Concerning cells, since that term is primarily associated with ATM, we will use that term throughout this book to reference the transport of information via ATM. For readers unfamiliar with the operation of different types of LANs, Chapter 3 provides a detailed explanation of the composition of various types of LAN frames and cells. By focusing upon describing the format and field composition of frames and cells, Chapter 3 will provide information useful in understanding how key LAN equipment operates.

Network Layer Operations

Interdomain communications, IP multicast address support, and other vLAN operations depend upon network layer operations. Thus, in Chapter 4 we will turn our attention to this topic, obtaining an overview of TCP/IP, IP addressing, and NetWare's IPX/SPX.

LAN Equipment Operations

In Chapter 5 we turn our attention to the operation of bridges, routers, and switches. Information presented in this chapter builds upon the explanation of frame and cell formats presented in Chapter 3 and network layer operations presented in Chapter 4.

vLAN Construction Basics

Once we examine the OSI Reference Model, understand data link and network layer operations, and have an appreciation for the operation of bridges, switches, and routers, we have obtained the foundation necessary to focus our attention upon different vLAN constructions methods. In Chapter 6 we will examine the use of switches and routers to construct vLANs, as well as the use of implicit tagging methods.

Standards

After we understand the various methods by which vLANs can be constructed and their operational capabilities, we will turn our attention to standards. Chapter 7 will examine both present de facto and developing de jure standards and interoperability considerations.

Virtual Networking

In concluding this book, we will focus attention upon several management issues and note the use of the Simple Network Management Protocol (SNMP) and Remote Monitoring (RMON) to facilitate the management of virtual LANs and virtual networks. Since vLANs represent an emerging technology, the concluding portion of Chapter 8 will include a discussion of emerging trends that can be expected to have an impact upon the operation and utilization of virtual LANs and virtual networking.

Networking
Standards

Standards can be viewed as the "glue" that binds hardware and software from different vendors so they can interoperate. The importance of standards and the work of standards organizations have proved essential for the growth of both local and worldwide communications. In the United States and many other countries, national standards organizations have defined physical and operational characteristics that enable vendors to manufacture equipment compatible with line facilities provided by communications carriers as well as equipment produced by other vendors that may be connected to a local or wide area network. At the international level, standards organizations have promulgated several series of communications-related recommendations. These recommendations, while not mandatory, have become highly influential on a worldwide basis for the development of equipment and facilities and have been adopted by hundreds of public companies and communications carriers.

In addition to national and international standards, a series of de facto standards has evolved through the dominance of a company in a particular area of communications or through the licensing of technology among companies. Such de facto standards, as an example, have facilitated the development of communications software for use on personal computers. Today, consumers can purchase communications software that can control modems manufactured by hundreds of vendors since most modems are now constructed to respond to a core set of uniform control codes.

STANDARDS ORGANIZATIONS

In this chapter we will first focus our attention upon two national and two international standards organizations. The national standards organizations we will briefly discuss in this section are the American National Standards Institute (ANSI) and the Institute of Electrical and Electronic Engineers (IEEE). The work of each organization has been a guiding force in the rapid expansion in the use of local area networks due to a series of standards developed by those organization. In the international area, we will discuss the role of the Consultative Committee for International Telephone and Telegraph (CCITT), now known as the International Telecommunications Union–Telecommunications Standardization (ITU-T) body, and the International Standards Organization (ISO), both of which have developed numerous standards that facilitate the operation of local and wide area networks.

Due to the importance of the ISO's Open Systems Interconnection (OSI) Reference Model and the IEEE's 802 Committee lower layer standards, we will examine each as separate entities in this chapter. Since we must understand the OSI Reference Model prior to examining the effect of the efforts of the IEEE and ANSI upon the lower layers of that model, we will look first at the OSI Reference Model.

National Standards Organizations

The two national standards organizations we will briefly discuss are the American National Standards Institute and the Institute of Electrical and Electronic Engineers. Both ANSI and the IEEE work in conjunction with the ISO to standardize LAN technology.

The ISO delegated the standardization of local area networking technology to ANSI. ANSI in turn delegated lower-speed LAN standards, initially defined as operating rates at and below 50 Mbps, to the IEEE. This resulted in ANSI developing standards for the 100-Mbps Fiber Distributed Data Interface (FDDI), while the IEEE developed standards for Ethernet, Token Ring, and other local area networks. Since the IEEE developed standards for 10-Mbps Ethernet, that organization was tasked with the responsibility for modifications to that local area network technology. This resulted in the IEEE becoming responsible for the standardization of high-speed Ethernet, including isoENET, 100BASE-T, and 100VG-AnyLAN, the latter two representing 100-Mbps local area network operating rates.

Once the IEEE develops and approves a standard it is sent to ANSI for review. If ANSI approves the standard it is then sent to the ISO. Then, the ISO solicits comments from all member countries to ensure the standard will work at the international level, resulting in an IEEE- or ANSI-developed standard becoming an ISO standard.

ANSI

The principal standards-forming body in the United States is the American National Standards Institute (ANSI). Located in New York City, this nonprofit, nongovernmental organization was founded in 1918 and functions as the representative of the United States to the ISO.

ANSI standards are developed through the work of its approximately 300 Standards Committees or from the efforts of associated groups, such as the Electronic Industry Association (EIA). Recognizing the importance of the computer industry, ANSI established its X3 Standards Committee in 1960. That committee consists of 25 Technical Committees, each assigned to develop standards for a specific technical area. One of those Technical Committees is the X3S3 committee, more formally known as the Data Communications Technical Committee, which was responsible for the ANSI X3T9.5 standard that governs FDDI operations and that is now recognized as the ISO 9314 standard.

IEEE

The Institute of Electrical and Electronic Engineers (IEEE) is a U.S.-based engineering society that is very active in the development of data communications standards. In fact, the most prominent developer of local area networking standards is the IEEE, whose subcommittee 802 began its work in 1980 prior to the establishment of a viable market for the technology.

The IEEE Project 802 efforts are concentrated upon the physical interface of equipment and the procedures and functions required to establish, maintain, and release connections among network devices, including defining data formats, error control procedures, and other control activities governing the flow of information. This focus of the IEEE actually represents the two lowest layers of the ISO model, physical and link, which are discussed later in this chapter.

International Standards Organizations

Two important international standards organizations are the International Telecommunications Union–Telecommunications Standardization (ITU-T) body, which was for decades known as the Consultative Committee for International Telephone and Telegraph (CCITT), and the International Standards Organization (ISO). The ITU-T can be considered as a governmental body as it functions under the auspices of an agency of the United Nations. Although the ISO is a nongovernmental agency, its work in the field of data communications is well recognized.

ITU-T

The ITU-T is a group within the International Telecommunications Union (ITU), the latter being a specialized agency of the United Nations headquartered in Geneva, Switzerland. The ITU-T is tasked with direct responsibility for developing data communications standards and consists of 15 Study Groups, each charged with a specific area of responsibility. Although the CCITT was renamed ITU in 1994, it continues to be primarily recognized by its former mnemonic. Thus, in the remainder of this book, we will continue to refer to this standards organization by both its new as well as its commonly recognized initials, although in a few years it is quite possible that that organization's new name will receive a wide degree of recognition.

The work of the ITU-T (CCITT) is performed on a four-year cycle, which is known as a Study Period. At the conclusion of each Study Period, a Plenary Session occurs. During the Plenary Session, the work of the ITU-T (CCITT) during the previous four years is reviewed, proposed recommendations are considered for adoption, and items to be investigated during the next four-year cycle are considered.

The ITU-T's (CCITT's) Tenth Plenary Session met in 1992 and its eleventh session occurred during 1996. Although approval of recommended standards is not intended to be mandatory, ITU-T (CCITT) recommendations have the effect of law in some Western European countries and many of its recommendations have been adopted by both communications carriers and vendors in the United States. Perhaps the best known set of recommendations is its V series, which describes the operation of a large number of modems and different modem features, such as data compression and transmission error detection and correction.

ISO

The International Standards Organization (ISO) is a nongovernmental entity that has consultative status within the UN Economic and Social Council. The goal of the ISO is to "promote the development of standards in the world with a view to facilitating international exchange of goods and services."

The membership of the ISO consists of the national standards organizations of most countries, with approximately 100 countries currently participating in its work.

Perhaps the most notable achievement of the ISO in the field of communications is its development of the seven-layer Open Systems Interconnection (OSI) Reference Model.

The ISO Reference Model

The International Standards Organization (ISO) established a framework for standardizing communications systems called the Open Systems Interconnection (OSI) Reference Model. The

OSI architecture defines the communications process as a set of seven layers, with specific functions isolated and associated with each layer. Each layer, as illustrated in Figure 2.1, covers lower-layer processes, effectively isolating them from higher-layer functions. In this way, each layer performs a set of functions necessary to provide a set of services to the layer above it.

Layer isolation permits the characteristics of a given layer to change without impacting the remainder of the model, provided that the supporting services remain the same. One major advantage of this layered approach is that users can mix and match OSI-conforming communications products to tailor their communications systems to satisfy a particular networking requirement.

The OSI Reference Model, while not completely viable with many current network architectures, offers the potential to directly interconnect networks based upon the use of different vendor equipment. This interconnectivity potential will be of substantial benefit to both users and vendors. For users, interconnectivity will remove the shackles that in many instances tie them to a particular vendor. For vendors, the ability to easily interconnect their products will provide them with access to a larger market. The importance of the OSI model is such that it has been adopted by the ITU-T (CCITT) as Recommendation X.200.

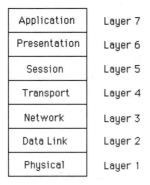

Figure 2.1 ISO Reference Model.

Layered Architecture

As previously discussed, the OSI Reference Model is based upon the establishment of a layered, or partitioned, architecture. This partitioning effort is derived from the scientific process whereby complex problems are subdivided into functional tasks that are easier to implement on an aggregate individual basis than as a whole.

As a result of the application of a partitioning approach to communications network architecture, the communications process was subdivided into seven distinct partitions, called layers. Each layer consists of a set of functions designed to provide a defined series of services which relate to the mission of that layer. For example, the functions associated with the physical connection of equipment to a network are referred to as the physical layer.

With the exception of layers 1 and 7, each layer is bounded by the layers above and below it. Layer 1, the physical layer, can be considered to be bound below by the interconnecting medium over which transmission flows, while layer 7 is the upper layer and has no upper boundary. Within each layer is a group of functions which can be viewed as providing a set of defined services to the layer which bounds it from above, resulting in layer n using the services of layer $n-1$. Thus, the design of a layered architecture enables the characteristics of a particular layer to change without affecting the rest of the system, assuming the services provided by the layer do not change.

OSI Layers

An understanding of the OSI layers is best obtained by first examining a possible network structure that illustrates the components of a typical wide area network. Figure 2.2 illustrates a network structure which is typical only in the sense that it will be used for a discussion of the components upon which networks are constructed.

The circles in Figure 2.2 represent nodes which are points where data enters or exits a network or is switched between two networks connected by one or more paths. Nodes are connected

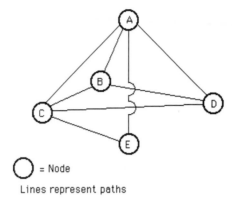

= Node

Lines represent paths

Figure 2.2 Generic network structure.

to other nodes via communications cables or circuits and can be established on any type of communications media, such as cable, microwave, or radio.

From a physical perspective, a node can be based upon the use of one of several types of computers, including a personal computer, minicomputer, mainframe computer, or specialized computer, such as a front-end processor. Connections to network nodes into a wide area network can occur via the use of terminals directly connected to computers, terminals connected to a node via the use of one or more intermediate communications devices, or via paths linking one network to another network. In fact, a workstation on an Ethernet local area network that provides access into a wide area network can be considered a network node. In this situation, the workstation is a node on the LAN as well as a node on the WAN that gains access to the wide area network via the services of a bridge, router, or gateway.

The routes between two nodes, such as C-E-A, C-D-A, C-A, and C-B-A, which could be used to route data between nodes A and C, are information paths. Due to the variability in the flow of information through a wide area network, the shortest path between nodes may not be available for use or may represent a nonefficient path with respect to other paths constructed through intermediate nodes between a source and destination node. A temporary connection established to link two nodes whose route is based upon such parameters as current network activity is known as a *logical connection*. This logical connection represents the use of physical facilities, including paths and node-switching capability on a temporary basis.

The major functions of each of the seven OSI layers are described in the following.

Layer 1—The Physical Layer

At the lowest or most basic level, the physical layer (level 1) is a set of rules that specifies the electrical and physical connection between devices. This level specifies the cable connections and the electrical rules necessary to transfer data between devices. Typically, the physical link corresponds to previously established interface standards, such as the RS-232/V.24 interface, which governs the attachment of data terminal equipment, such as the serial port of personal computers, to data communications equipment, such as modems, at data rates below 19.2 Kbps.

Layer 2—The Data Link Layer

The next layer, which is known as the data link layer (level 2), denotes how a device gains access to the medium specified in the physical layer; it also defines data formats, including the framing of data within transmitted messages, error control procedures, and other link control activities. From defining data formats, including procedures to correct transmission errors, this layer becomes responsible for the reliable delivery of information. Two examples of data link control protocols that can reside in this layer include IBM's Binary Synchronous Communications (BSC) and the ITU-T's (CCITT's) High-level Data Link Control (HDLC).

Since the development of OSI layers was originally targeted toward wide area networking, its applicability to local area networks required a degree of modification. Under the IEEE 802 standards, the data link layer was initially divided into two sublayers—logical link control (LLC) and media access control (MAC). The LLC layer is responsible for generating and interpreting commands which control the flow of data and perform recovery operations in the event of errors. In comparison, the MAC layer is responsible for providing access to the local area network, which enables a station on the network to transmit information.

With the development of high-speed local area networks designed to operate on a variety of media, an additional degree of OSI layer subdivision was required. For example, for Fast Ethernet the data link layer required the addition of a reconciliation layer (RL) to reconcile a medium independent interface (MII) signal added to high-speed Ethernet. Next, the physical layer required a subdivision into three sublayers. One sublayer, known as the physical coding sublayer (PCS) performs data encoding. A physical medium attachment (PMA) sublayer maps messages from the physical coding sublayer to the transmission media, while a medium dependent interface (MDI) specifies the connector for the media used. Later in this chapter we will examine the IEEE 802 subdivision of the data link and physical layers, as well as the operation of each resulting sublayer.

When information is transported at the data link layer, it is common to reference the transport mechanism as a *frame*. In comparison, when data is transported at the network layer, the term *packet* is commonly used to reference the transport mechanism. When data flows exclusively on a LAN, the higher levels of the protocol stack continue to operate on frames and most people continue to reference the transport mechanism as a frame. This frame reference is carried over to a point-to-point wide area network where we can continue to reference frames. However, as the network layer (described next) is used to route frames on a network path formed by linking nodes, the resulting transport is referred to as a packet. (Perhaps network analysts and designers obtain a high degree of job security by making it difficult to determine what is being routed between locations?)

Layer 3—The Network Layer

The network layer (level 3) is responsible for arranging a logical connection between the source and destination nodes on the network, including the selection and management of a route for the flow of information between source and destination based upon the available data paths in the network. Services provided by this layer are associated with the movement of data packets through a network, including addressing, routing, switching, sequencing, and flow control procedures. In a complex network, the source and destination may not be directly connected by a single path, but instead require a path to be established that consists of many subpaths. Thus, routing data through the network onto the correct paths is an important feature of this layer.

Several protocols have been defined for layer 3, including the ITU-T (CCITT) X.25 packet-switching protocol and the ITU-T (CCITT) X.75 gateway protocol. X.25 governs the flow of information through a packet network, while X.75 governs the flow of information between packet networks.

Layer 4—The Transport Layer

The transport layer (level 4) is responsible for guaranteeing that the transfer of information occurs correctly after a route has been established through the network by the network level protocol. Thus, the primary function of this layer is to control the communications session between network nodes once a path has been established by the network control layer. Error control, sequence checking, and other end-to-end data reliability factors are the primary concern of the transport layer, which enable it to provide a reliable end-to-end data transfer capability.

Layer 5—The Session Layer

The session layer (level 5) provides a set of rules for establishing and terminating data streams between nodes in a network. The services that this session layer can provide include establishing and terminating node connections, message flow control, dialogue control, and end-to-end data control.

Layer 6—The Presentation Layer

The presentation layer (level 6) services are concerned with data transformation, formatting, and syntax. One of the primary functions performed by the presentation layer is the conversion of transmitted data into a display format appropriate for a receiving device. This can include any necessary conversion between ASCII and EBCDIC codes. Data encryption and decryption and data compression and decompression are additional examples of the data transformation that could be handled by this layer.

Layer 7—The Application Layer

Finally, the application layer (level 7) acts as a window through which the application gains access to all of the services provided by the model. Examples of functions performed at this level include file transfers, resource sharing, and database access. While the first four layers are fairly well defined, the top three layers may vary considerably, depending upon the network used. Figure 2.3 illustrates the OSI model in schematic format, showing the various levels of the model with respect to a terminal device, such as a personal computer accessing an application on a host computer system.

Data Flow

As data flows within an ISO network, each layer appends appropriate heading information to frames of information flowing

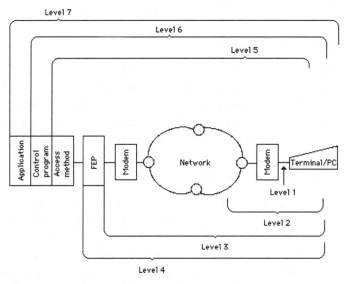

Figure 2.3 OSI model schematic.

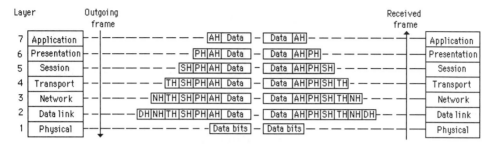

Figure 2.4 Appending and removing frame header information.

within the network while removing the heading information added by a lower layer. In this manner, layer (*n*) interacts with layer (*n–*1) as data flows through an ISO network.

Figure 2.4 illustrates the appending and removal of frame header information as data flows through a network constructed according to the ISO Reference Model. Since each higher level removes the header appended by a lower level, the frame traversing the network arrives in its original form at its destination.

As the reader will surmise from the previous illustrations, the ISO Reference Model is designed to simplify the construction of data networks. This simplification is due to the eventual standardization of methods and procedures to append appropriate heading information to frames flowing through a network, permitting data to be routed to its appropriate destination following a uniform procedure.

IEEE 802 STANDARDS

The Institute of Electrical and Electronic Engineers (IEEE) Committee 802 was formed at the beginning of the 1980s to develop standards for emerging technologies. By doing so the IEEE fostered the development of local area networking equipment from different vendors that can work together. In addition,

IEEE LAN standards provided a common design goal for vendors to access a relatively larger market than if proprietary equipment were developed. This in turn enabled economies of scale to lower the cost of products developed for larger markets.

802 Committees

Table 2.1 lists the organization of IEEE 802 committees involved in local area networks. It is apparent that the IEEE early on noted that a number of different systems would be required to satisfy the requirements of a diverse end-user population. Accordingly, the IEEE adopted the CSMA/CD, Token Bus, and Token Ring as standards 802.3, 802.4, and 802.5, respectively.

The IEEE Committee 802 published draft standards for CSMA/CD and Token Bus local area networks in 1982. Standard 802.3, which describes a baseband CSMA/CD network similar to Ethernet, was published in 1983. Since then, several addenda to the 802.3 standard were adopted which govern the operation of CSMA/CD on different types of media. Those

Table 2.1   IEEE Series 802 Committees

802.1	High Level Interface
802.1d	Spanning Tree
802.1p	General Registration Protocol
802.1q	Virtual Bridged LANs
802.2	Logical Link Control
802.3	CSMA/CD
802.3μ	Fast Ethernet
802.4	Token-Passing Bus
802.5	Token-Passing Ring
802.6	Metropolitan Area Networks
802.7	Broadband Technical Advisory Group
802.8	Fiber Optic Technical Advisory Group
802.9a	IsoENET (proposed)
802.9	Integrated Voice and Data Networks
802.10	Network Security
802.11	Wireless LANs
802.12	100VG-AnyLAN

addenda include 10BASE-2, which defines a 10-Mbps baseband network operating on thin coaxial cable; 1BASE-5, which defines a 1-Mbps baseband network operating on twisted-pair; 10BASE-T, which defines a 10-Mbps baseband network operating on twisted-pair; and 10BROAD-36, which defines a broadband 10-Mbps network that operates on thick coaxial cable. Although Fast Ethernet, denoted as 802.3µ in Table 2.1, is an addendum to the 802.3 standard, it was not finalized until 1995.

The next standard published by the IEEE was 802.4, which describes a token-passing bus-oriented network for both baseband and broadband transmission. This standard is similar to the Manufacturing Automation Protocol (MAP) standard developed by General Motors.

The third LAN standard published by the IEEE was based upon IBM's specifications for its Token Ring network. Known as the 802.5 standard, it defines the operation of Token Ring networks on shielded twisted-pair cable at data rates of 1 and 4 Mbps. That standard was modified to acknowledge three IBM enhancements to Token Ring network operations. Those enhancements include the 16-Mbps operating rate, the ability to release a token early on a 16-Mbps network, and a bridge-routing protocol known as *source routing*.

Two relatively recent Ethernet standards are 802.3µ and 802.12, both of which have their foundation in IEEE efforts that occurred during 1992. In that year the IEEE requested proposals for *Fast Ethernet*, designed to raise the Ethernet operating rate from 10 Mbps to 100 Mbps. This request resulted in two initial proposals. One proposal, now referred to as a series of 100BASE proposals, was developed by a consortium which included Synoptics Communications, Inc., 3 Com Corporation, and Ungermann-Bass, Inc. This proposal retained the CSMA/CD access proposal which formed the basis for the operation of earlier versions of Ethernet. Now included in 802.3µ are 100BASE-TX, 100BASE-FX, and 100BASE-T4.

100BASE-TX defines the specifications for 100 Mbps CSMA/CD over two pairs of category 5 unshielded twisted-pair (UTP) cable. 100BASE-FX specifies 100 Mbps Ethernet over two pairs of optical fiber cable, while 100BASE-T4 defines the operation of

100 Mbps Ethernet over four pairs of category 3, 4, and 5 UTP or shielded twisted-pair (STP) cable.

The second 100-Mbps proposal, which is now referred to as 100VG-AnyLAN, was initially developed by AT&T Microelectronics and Hewlett-Packard Company. This proposal replaced the CSMA/CD access protocol by a demand priority scheme which enables the support of Ethernet, Token Ring, FDDI, and other types of local area networks. Since this proposal described operations on voice grade (VG) twisted pair, it received the mnemonic 100VG-AnyLAN.

At the time this book was prepared, the IEEE 802.9 working group completed a draft document that creates a 16.384-Mbps physical layer for operation on unshielded twisted-pair (UTP) category 3 or higher cable. Referred to as IsoENET, the draft document is technically referred to as 802.9a.

In the area of virtual LANs, a considerable effort was being performed by the IEEE 802.1 committee when this book was written. Although an official Project Authorization Request (PAR) entitled Standard for Virtual Bridged Local Area Networks denoted the development of an architecture and bridge protocol for the logical partitioning of a bridged local area network and was assigned the identifier 802.1Q, that project must work in conjunction with other IEEE projects and standards. The IEEE 802.1P project involves a general registration protocol that controls the span of domains across a bridged LAN configuration and uses a value of a field in the MAC header of its intradomain frames for domain identification. Thus, 802.1P is related to the efforts of the 802.1Q PAR. Similarly, the 802.1D standard, which defines the spanning tree protocol, governs the ability of spanning tree networks to be connected by compliant bridges. This means that the 802.1Q project must also consider the 802.1D standard in its work.

Data Link Subdivision

One of the more interesting facets of IEEE 802 standards was the initial subdivision of the ISO Open Systems Interconnection Reference Model's data link layer into two sublayers—logical link control and medium access control. Figure 2.5 illustrates

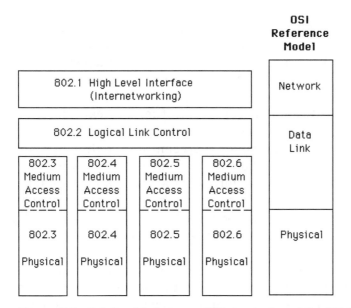

Figure 2.5 Relationship between IEEE standards and the OSI Reference Model.

the relationship between IEEE 802 local area network standards and the first three layers of the OSI Reference Model.

The separation of the data link layer into two entities provides a mechanism for regulating access to the medium independent of the method for establishing, maintaining, and terminating the logical link between workstations. Here the method of regulating access to the medium is defined by the medium access control portion of each local area network standard. This enables the logical link control standard to be applicable to each type of network.

Medium Access Control

The medium access control sublayer is responsible for controlling access to the network: It must ensure that a situation in which two or more stations attempt to simultaneously transmit data onto the network cannot occur. For Ethernet networks this is accomplished through the use of the CSMA/CD access protocol, while for Token Ring and FDDI networks a token access protocol governs when a station can access the network.

In addition to network access control, the MAC sublayer is responsible for the orderly movement of data onto and off the network. To accomplish this, the MAC sublayer is responsible for MAC addressing, frame type recognition, frame control, frame copying, and similar frame related functions.

The MAC address represents the physical address of each station or node connected to the network. That address can belong to a single station, or represent a predefined group of stations (group address) or all stations on the network (broadcast address). An address referencing a single station is referred to as a *unicast* address. In comparison, an address that references a group of stations is known as a *multicast* address. Through MAC addresses the physical source and destination of frames are identified.

Frame type recognition enables the type and format of a frame to be recognized. To ensure frames can be accurately processed, frame control prefixes each frame with a preamble which consists of a predefined sequence of bits. In addition, a frame check sequence (FCS) is computed based upon applying an algorithm to the contents of the frame, with the results of the operation placed into the frame. This enables a receiving station to perform a similar operation. Then, if the locally computed FCS matches the FCS carried in the frame, the frame is considered to have arrived without error.

Once a frame arrives at a station that has the same address as the destination address in the frame, the station must copy the frame. The copying operation moves the contents of the frame into a buffer area in a network adapter card. The adapter card removes certain fields from the frame, such as the preamble, and passes the information field into a predefined memory area in the station into which the adapter card is inserted.

Logical Link Control

Logical link control frames are used to provide a link between network layer protocols and media access control. This linkage is accomplished through the use of Service Access Points (SAPs), which operate as mailboxes. That is, both network layer protocols and logical link control have access to SAPs and can leave messages for each other in them.

As with mailboxes in a post office, each SAP has a distinct address. For the logical link control a SAP represents the location of a network layer process, such as the location of an application within a workstation as viewed from the network. From the network layer perspective, a SAP represents the place to leave messages concerning the network services requested by an application.

LLC frames contain two special address fields known as the Destination Services Access Point and the Source Services Access Point. The Destination Services Access Point (DSAP) is one byte in length and specifies the receiving network layer process. The Source Services Access Point (SSAP) is also one byte in length. The SSAP specifies the sending network layer process. Both DSAP and SSAP addresses are assigned by the IEEE.

Additional Sublayering

The standardization of high-speed 100-Mbps FDDI and Ethernet resulted in an additional sublayer at the data link layer and the subdivision of the physical layer. Figure 2.6 illustrates the relationship between the first two layers of the ISO Reference Model and the IEEE 802.3μ Fast Ethernet sublayers. The additional sublayering illustrated in Figure 2.6 became necessary as it was desired to support different media with one standard. This required the physical layer to be independent from the data link layer since there can be different coding schemes used to support transmission on different types of media.

Retaining the CSMA/CD access protocol while supporting the use of different media required the use of different connectors, resulting in the introduction of a physical medium dependent (PMD) sublayer. Since different data coding schemes are required to support 100 Mbps on different types of media, a physical coding sublayer was introduced. This sublayer defines the coding method used for transmission on different types of media. To map messages from the physical coding sublayer onto the transmission media resulted in those functions being performed by the physical medium attachment sublayer. Thus, the physical layer was subdivided into three sublayers.

At the data link layer an additional sublayer, known as the reconciliation sublayer, was introduced. This sublayer is responsible for reconciling the medium independent interface from the physical layer with the media access control signal.

Although Figure 2.6 illustrated IEEE 802.μ sublayering, it should be noted that the subdivision of the Physical Layer first occurred when ANSI standardized FDDI. At that time the Physical Layer was subdivided into the Physical Protocol sublayer and the Physical Medium Dependent (PMD) sublayer. The PMD layer specifies the type and size of optical fiber used by FDDI, the connectors, and the wavelength of the light used to transmit information. In comparison, the Physical Protocol Layer defines the signaling rate, method of data encoding, and clocking on the network. FDDI uses a technique in which data is transmitted as a series of four-bit symbols encoded within a five-bit pattern, a method known as 4B/5B encoding.

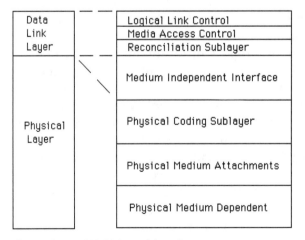

Figure 2.6 IEEE 802.μ sublayering.

LAN Frame Header

The construction of frame header information illustrated in Figure 2.4 requires a slight revision to illustrate LAN frame construction. Since the IEEE subdivided the Data Link Layer into Logical Link Control and Media Access Control sublayers, a protocol stack commonly adds separate headers instead of a single Data Link Layer header. Figure 2.7 illustrates the contribution of a typical LAN protocol stack to the creation of a frame. Note that although each layer of the stack contributes a protocol header to the frame, the MAC layer also adds a trailer in the form of the previously discussed frame check sequence (FCS). Also note that many, if not most, protocol stacks are not constructed using all seven layers of the ISO Reference Model. In fact, most protocol stacks operate at four or five distinct layers. It is also significant that LLC headers are placed within the information field of a data link frame, as we will discuss in the next chapter.

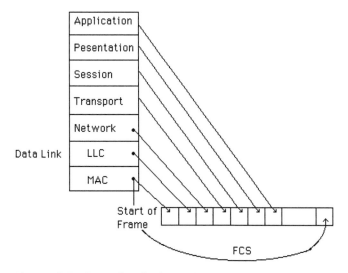

Figure 2.7 Frame header formation on a LAN.

Frame and Cell Operations

3

The ability to understand the basis for several vLAN construction techniques as well as interoperability problems and the state of virtual networking standards requires knowledge concerning how LANs operate, particularly in regard to their access methods, and the composition of frames used to transport information. In writing this book, space constraints, as well as the availability of my previously published books covering Ethernet and Token Ring networks, precluded a full review of Ethernet, Token Ring, and FDDI LAN characteristics. Instead, I decided to primarily concentrate on providing a review of the composition of Ethernet, Token Ring, and FDDI frames, and the use of ATM cells in network operations. I felt this would be more appropriate, as a majority of network vLAN construction techniques (both implicit and explicit tagging methods), as well as interoperability techniques and problems, are related to the use of various frame and cell fields. Readers requiring detailed information covering Ethernet and Token Ring access protocols and their cabling infrastructure are referred to my previously published books, *Ethernet Networks 2ED* and *Token Ring Networks*, both published by John Wiley & Sons (New York, 1996, 1994).

In this chapter, I will first focus on the composition of different types of Ethernet frames. In reality, there is only one Ethernet frame, while the CSMA/CD frame format standardized by the IEEE is technically referred to as an 802.3 frame. As I will note later in this chapter, the physical 802.3 frame can have several logical formats. For consistency and ease of reference, I will refer to Carrier Sense Multiple Access/Collision Detection (CSMA/CD) operations collectively as Ethernet, and when appropriate, indicate differences between Ethernet and the IEEE 802.3 Ethernet-based CSMA/CD standards. After describing the general composition of Ethernet and IEEE 802.3 frames, I will examine the function of the fields within each frame as well as the manner by which the placement of frames on the media is controlled—a process known as media access control. This will be followed by a similar examination oriented toward the Token Ring and FDDI frame formats and the function of each frame field within a Token Ring and FDDI frame. I will cover the three types of Token Ring frames defined by the IEEE 802.5 standard. Once the preceding is accomplished, I will focus on the 53-byte ATM cell as well as describe how "legacy" LANs, such as Ethernet and Token Ring, can be transported via the use of ATM. Thus, information in this chapter provides the foundation for understanding how vLANs and virtual networking techniques interact with the data link transport mechanism provided by different types of frames and cells.

ETHERNET FRAME COMPOSITION

Figure 3.1 illustrates the general frame composition of Ethernet and IEEE 802.3 frames. You will note that they differ slightly. An Ethernet frame contains an eight-byte preamble, while the IEEE 802.3 frame contains a seven-byte preamble followed by a one-byte start of frame delimiter field. A second difference between the composition of Ethernet and IEEE 802.3 frames concerns the two-byte Ethernet type field. That field is used by Ethernet to specify the protocol carried in the frame, enabling several protocols to be carried independently of one another. Under the IEEE 802.3 frame format, the type field was replaced

Ethernet

Preamble	Destination Address	Source Address	Type	Data	Frame Check Sequence
8 bytes	6 bytes	6 bytes	2 bytes	46–1500 bytes	4 bytes

IEEE 802.3

Preamble	Start of Frame Delimiter	Destination Address	Source Address	Length	Data	Frame Check Sequence
7 bytes	1 byte	2/6 bytes	2/6 bytes	2 bytes	46–1500 bytes	4 bytes

Figure 3.1   Ethernet and IEEE 802.4 frame formats.

by a two-byte length field which specifies the number of bytes that follow that field as data. In addition, to enable different types of protocols to be carried in a frame and correctly identified, the 802.3 frame format subdivides the data field into subfields. Those subfields include a Destination Service Access Point (DSAP), Source Service Access Point (SSAP), and a Control field that prefixes a reduced data field. The use of those fields defines a Logical Link Control (LLC) layer residing within an 802.3 frame, which will be discussed later in this chapter along with some common framing variations.

The differences between Ethernet and IEEE 802.3 frames, while minor, make the two incompatible with one another. This means that your network must contain all Ethernet-compatible network interface cards (NICs), all IEEE 802.3-compatible NICs, or adapter cards that can examine the frame and automatically determine its type, a process described later in this chapter. Fortunately, the fact that the IEEE 802.3 frame format represents a standard means that most vendors now market 802.3-compliant hardware and software. Although a few vendors continue to manufacture Ethernet or dual-functioning Ethernet/IEEE 802.3 hardware, such products are primarily used to provide organizations with the ability to expand previously developed networks without requiring the wholesale replacement of NICs. Although the IEEE 802.3 standard has essentially replaced

Ethernet, because of their similarities and the fact that 802.3 was based upon Ethernet, we will consider both to be Ethernet.

Now that we have an overview of the structure of Ethernet and 802.3 frames, let's probe deeper and examine the composition of each frame field. We will take advantage of the similarity between Ethernet and IEEE 802.3 frames to examine the fields of each frame on a composite basis, noting the differences between the two when appropriate.

Preamble Field

The preamble field consists of eight (Ethernet) or seven (IEEE 802.3) bytes of alternating 1 and 0 bits. The Ethernet chip set contained on the network interface adapter places the preamble and following start-of-frame delimiter on the front of each frame transmitted on the network.

The purpose of the preamble field is to announce the frame and to enable all receivers on the network to synchronize themselves to the incoming frame. In addition, this field by itself (under Ethernet) or in conjunction with the start-of-frame delimiter field (under the IEEE 802.3 standard) ensures there is a minimum spacing period of 9.6 ms between frames at 10-Mbps operations for error detection and recovery operations.

Start-of-Frame Delimiter Field

This field is applicable only to the IEEE 802.3 standard, and can be viewed as a continuation of the preamble. In fact, the composition of this field continues in the same manner as the format of the preamble, with alternating 1 and 0 bits used for the first six-bit positions of this one-byte field. The last two-bit positions of this field are 11—this breaks the synchronization pattern and alerts the receiver that frame data follows.

Both the preamble field and the start-of-frame delimiter field are removed by the Ethernet chip set or controller when it places a received frame in its buffer. Similarly, when a controller transmits a frame, it prefixes the frame with those two fields (if it is transmitting an IEEE 802.3 frame) or a preamble field (if it is transmitting a true Ethernet frame).

Destination Address Field

The destination address identifies the recipient of the frame. Although this may appear to be a simple field, in reality its length can vary between IEEE 802.3 and Ethernet frames. In addition, each field can consist of two or more subfields, whose settings govern such network operations as the type of addressing used on the LAN, and whether the frame is addressed to a specific station or more than one station. To obtain an appreciation for the use of this field, let's examine how this field is used under the IEEE 802.3 standard as one of the two field formats applicable to Ethernet.

Figure 3.2 illustrates the composition of the source and destination address fields. As indicated, the two-byte source and destination address fields are applicable only to IEEE 802.3 networks, while the six-byte source and destination address fields are applicable to both Ethernet and IEEE 802.3 networks. A

A. 2 byte field (IEEE 802.3)

B. 6 byte field (Ethernet and IEEE 802.3)

I/G bit subfield '0' = individual address '1' = group address
U/L bit subfield '0' = universally administrated addressing
                  '1' = locally administrated addressing

* Set to '0' in source address field

Figure 3.2 Source and destination address field formats.

user can select either a two- or six-byte destination address field; however, with IEEE 802.3 equipment, all stations on the LAN must use the same addressing structure. Today, almost all 802.3 networks use six-byte addressing, since the inclusion of a two-byte field option was designed primarily to accommodate early LANs that use 16-bit address fields.

I/G Subfield

The one-bit I/G subfield is set to a 0 to indicate that the frame is destined to an individual station, or 1 to indicate that the frame is addressed to more than one station—a group address. One special example of a group address is the assignment of all 1's to the address field. Hex FF-FF-FF-FF-FF-FF is recognized as a broadcast address, and each station on the network will receive and accept frames with that destination address. An example of the use of a broadcast address is the Service Advertising Protocol (SAP) transmitted every 60 seconds by NetWare servers. The SAP is used to inform other servers and workstations on the network of the presence of that server. Since the SAP uses a destination address of FF-FF-FF-FF-FF-FF, it is recognized by every device on the network.

When a destination address specifies a single station, the address is referred to as a *unicast address*. A group address that defines multiple stations is known as a *multicast address*, while a group address that specifies all stations on the network is, as previously mentioned, referred to as a *broadcast address*.

U/L Subfield

The U/L subfield is applicable only to the six-byte destination address field. The setting of this field's bit position indicates whether the destination address was assigned by the IEEE (universally administered) or assigned by the organization via software (locally administered).

Universally versus Locally Administered Addressing

Each Ethernet network interface card (NIC) contains a unique address burned into its read-only memory (ROM) at the time of manufacture. To ensure this universally administered address is not duplicated, the IEEE assigns blocks of addresses to each manufacturer. These addresses normally include a three-byte prefix, which identifies the manufacturer and is assigned by the IEEE, and a three-byte suffix, which is assigned by the adapter manufacturer to its NIC. For example, the prefix hex 02-60-8C identifies an NIC manufactured by 3Com.

Table 3.1 lists the three-byte identifiers associated with ten manufacturers of Ethernet network interface cards. Though it is theoretically possible to construct vLANs based upon the manufacturer of network adapter cards, doing so is normally not a practical method to form the basis for the construction of a vLAN. Instead, many vLAN-compatible switches provide a virtual LAN creation capability based upon the use of the entire six-byte MAC address, either burned into the adapter or generated by locally administered addressing.

Although the use of universally administered addressing eliminates the potential for duplicate network addresses, it does not provide the flexibility obtainable from locally administered addressing. For example, under locally administered addressing, you can configure mainframe software to work with a predefined group of addresses via a gateway PC. Then, as you add new stations to your LAN, you simply use your installation program to assign a locally administered address to the NIC instead of using its universally administered address. As long as

Table 3.1 Representative Ethernet Manufacturer IDs

Manufacturer	*Three-Byte Identifiers*
3Com	02-60-8C
Cabletron	00-00-1D
Excelan	08-00-14
NEC	00-00-4C
NeXT	00-00-0F
Novell	00-00-1B
Synoptics (Bay Networks)	00-00-81
Western Digital	00-00-C0
Xerox	00-00-AA
Xircom	00-80-C7

your mainframe computer has a pool of locally administered addresses that includes your recent assignment, you do not have to modify your mainframe communications software configuration. Since the modification of mainframe communications software typically requires recompiling and reloading, the attached network must become inoperative for a short period of time. Because a large mainframe may service hundreds to thousands of users, such changes are normally performed late in the evening or on a weekend. Thus, the changes required for locally administered addressing are more responsive to users than those required for universally administered addressing.

Source Address Field

The source address field identifies the station that transmitted the frame. Like the destination address field, the source address can be either two or six bytes in length.

The two-byte source address is supported only under the IEEE 802.3 standard and requires the use of a two-byte destination address; all stations on the network must use two-byte addressing fields. The six-byte source address field is supported by both Ethernet and the IEEE 802.3 standard. When a six-byte address is used, the first three bytes represent the address assigned by the IEEE to the manufacturer for incorporation into each NIC's ROM. The vendor then normally assigns the last three bytes for each of its NICs.

Type Field

The two-byte type field is applicable only to the Ethernet frame. This field identifies the higher-level protocol contained in the data field. Thus, this field tells the receiving device how to interpret the data field.

Under Ethernet, multiple protocols can exist on the LAN at the same time. Xerox served as the custodian of Ethernet address ranges licensed to NIC manufacturers and defined the protocols supported by the assignment of type field values. Table 3.2 lists ten common Ethernet type field identifiers, including their hex values. Note that the value of the type field al-

Table 3.2 Ethernet Type Field Identifiers

Protocol Specified	Hex Value
Address Resolution Protocol (ARP)	08-06
AppleTalk	80-9B
Apple Talk ARM	80-F3
DEC LAT	60-04
IBM SNA Service	80-DC
Internet Protocol (IP)	08-00
Netware IPX/SPX	81-37
SNMP	81-4C
X.25 Level 3	08-05
X.75 Internet	08-01

ways exceeds decimal 1500 (hex 05-DC) and provides a mechanism for a receiving station to determine the type of frame on the network since a length field (described next) cannot exceed decimal 1500. Under the IEEE 802.3 standard, the type field was replaced by a length field, which precludes compatibility between pure Ethernet and 802.3 frames.

Length Field

The two-byte length field, applicable to the IEEE 802.3 standard, defines the number of bytes contained in the data field. Under both Ethernet and IEEE 802.3 standards, the minimum size frame must be 64 bytes in length from preamble through FCS fields. This minimum size frame ensures that there is sufficient transmission time to enable Ethernet NICs to detect collisions accurately, based on the maximum Ethernet cable length specified for a network and the time required for a frame to propagate the length of the cable. Based on the minimum frame length of 64 bytes and the possibility of using two-byte addressing fields, this means that each data field must be a minimum of 46 bytes in length.

Because the data field cannot exceed 1500 bytes, the length field's maximum value cannot exceed 1500 decimals. Concerning its minimum value, when the data field contains less than

46 bytes, the data field is padded to reach 46 bytes in length. However, the length field does not include padding and reflects the actual number of characters in the data field.

Data Field

As previously discussed, the data field must be a minimum of 46 bytes in length to ensure that the frame is at least 64 bytes in length. This means that the transmission of one byte of information must be carried within a 46-byte data field; if the information to be placed in the field is less than 46 bytes, the remainder of the field must be padded. Although some publications subdivide the data field to include a PAD subfield, the latter actually represents optional fill characters that are added to the information in the data field to ensure a length of 46 bytes. The maximum length of the data field is 1500 bytes.

Frame Check Sequence Field

The frame check sequence (FCS) field, applicable to both Ethernet and the IEEE 802.3 standard, provides a mechanism for error detection. Each chip set transmitter computes a cyclic redundancy check (CRC) that covers both address fields, the type/length field, and the data field. The transmitter then places the computed CRC in the four-byte FCS field.

The CRC treats the previously mentioned fields as one long binary number. The n bits to be covered by the CRC are considered to represent the coefficients of a polynomial $M(X)$ of degree $n-1$. Here, the first bit in the destination address field corresponds to the X^{n-1} term, while the last bit in the data field corresponds to the X^0 term. Next, $M(X)$ is multiplied by X^{32} and the result of that multiplication process is divided by the following polynomial:

$$G(X) = X^{32} + X^{26} + X^{23} + X^{22} + X^{16} + X^{12} + X^{11} + X^{10} + X^8 + X^7 + X^5 + X^4 + X^2 + X + 1$$

Note that the term X^n represents the setting of a bit to a 1 in position n. Thus, part of the generating polynomial $X^5 + X^4 + X^2 + X^1$ represents the binary value 11011.

This division produces a quotient and remainder. The quotient is discarded, and the remainder becomes the CRC value placed in the four-byte FCS field. This 32-bit CRC reduces the probability of an undetected error to 1 bit in every 4.3 billion, or approximately 1 bit in 2^{32-1} bits.

Once a frame reaches its destination, the chip set's receiver uses the same polynomial to perform the same operation upon the received data. If the CRC computed by the receiver matches the CRC in the FCS field, the frame is accepted. Otherwise, the receiver discards the received frame, as it is considered to have one or more bits in error. The receiver will also consider a received frame to be invalid and discard it under two additional conditions. Those conditions occur when the frame does not contain an integral number of bytes, or when the length of the data field does not match the value contained in the length field. The latter condition obviously is only applicable to the 802.3 standard, since an Ethernet frame uses a type field instead of a length field.

ETHERNET MEDIA ACCESS CONTROL

Under the IEEE 802 series of standards, the data link layer of the OSI Reference Model was subdivided into two sublayers— logical link control (LLC) and medium access control (MAC). The frame formats previously examined represent the manner in which LLC information is transported. Directly under the LLC sublayer is the MAC sublayer.

Functions

The MAC sublayer, which is the focus of this section, is responsible for checking the channel and transmitting data if the channel is idle, checking for the occurrence of a collision, and taking a series of predefined steps if a collision is detected. Thus, this layer provides the required logic to control the network.

Figure 3.3 illustrates the relationship between the physical and LLC layers with respect to the MAC layer. The MAC layer is an interface between user data and the physical placement and retrieval of data on the network. To better understand the

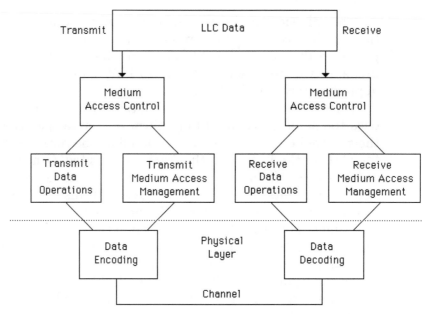

Figure 3.3 Medium access control. The medium access control (MAC) layer can be considered an interface between user data and the physical placement and retrieval of data on the network.

functions performed by the MAC layer, let us examine the four major functions performed by that layer—transmitting data operations, transmitting medium access management, receiving data operations, and receiving medium access management. Each of those four functions can be viewed as a functional area, since a group of activities is associated with each area.

Table 3.3 lists the four MAC functional areas and the activities associated with each area. Although the transmission and reception of data operations activities are self-explanatory, the transmission and reception of media access management require some elaboration. Therefore, let's focus our attention on the activities associated with each of those functional areas.

Transmit Media Access Management

CSMA/CD can be described as a *listen-before-acting* access method. Thus, the first function associated with transmit media access management is to find out whether any data is already

Table 3.3 MAC Functional Areas

Transmit Data Operations	• Accept data from the LLC sublayer and construct a frame by appending preamble and start-of-frame delimiter; insert destination and source address, length count; if frame is less than 64 bytes, insert sufficient PAD characters in the data field. • Calculate the CRC and place in the FCS field.
Transmit Media Access Management	• Defer transmission if the medium is busy. • Delay transmission for a specified interframe gap period. • Present a serial bit stream to the physical layer for transmission. • Half transmission when a collision is detected. • Transmit a jam signal to ensure that news of a collision propagates throughout the network. • Reschedule retransmissions after a collision until successful, or a specified retry limit is reached.
Receive Data Operations	• Discard all frames not addressed to the receiving station. • Recognize all broadcast frames and frames specifically addressed to station. • Performs a CRC check. • Remove preamble, start-of-frame delimiter, destination and source addresses, length count, FCS; if necessary, remove PAD fill characters. • Pass data to LLC sublayer.
Receive Media Access Management	• Receive a serial bit stream from the physical layer. • Verify byte boundary and length of frame. • Discard frames not an even eight bits in length or less than the minimum frame length.

being transmitted on the network and, if so, to defer transmission. During the listening process, each station attempts to sense the carrier signal of another station, hence the prefix *carrier sense* (CS) for this access method. Although broadband networks use RF modems that generate a carrier signal, a baseband network has no carrier signal in the conventional sense of a carrier as a periodic waveform altered to convey information. Thus, a logical question you may have is how the MAC sublayer on a baseband network can sense a carrier signal if there is no carrier. The answer to this question lies in the use of a digital signaling method known as *Manchester encoding*, which a station can monitor to detect whether another station is transmitting.

To understand the Manchester encoding signaling method used by baseband Ethernet LANs, let us first review the method of digital signaling used by computers and terminal devices. In that signaling method, a positive voltage is used to represent a binary 1, while the absence of voltage (0 volts) is used to represent a binary 0. If two successive 1 bits occur, two successive bit positions then have a similar positive voltage level or a similar zero voltage level. Since the signal goes from 0 to some positive voltage and does not return to 0 between successive binary 1's, it is referred to as a *unipolar non-return-to-zero signal* (NRZ). This signaling technique is illustrated at the top of Figure 3.4.

Although unipolar non-return-to-zero signaling is easy to implement, its use for transmission has several disadvantages. One of the major disadvantages associated with this signaling method involves determining where one bit ends and another begins. Overcoming this problem requires synchronization between a transmitter and receiver by the use of clocking circuitry, which can be relatively expensive.

To overcome the need for clocking, baseband LANs use *Manchester* or *Differential Manchester* encoding. In Manchester encoding, a timing transition always occurs in the middle of each bit, while an equal amount of positive and negative voltage is used to represent each bit. This coding technique provides a good timing signal for clock recovery from received data, due to its timing transitions. In addition, since the Manchester code always maintains an equal amount of positive and negative voltage, it prevents direct current (DC) voltage buildup, enabling repeaters to be spaced farther apart from one another.

The lower portion of Figure 3.4 illustrates an example of Manchester coding. Note that a low-to-high voltage transition represents a binary 1, while a high-to-low voltage transition represents a binary 0. Although NRZI encoding is used on broadband networks, the actual data is modulated after it is encoded. Thus, the presence or absence of a carrier is directly indicated by the presence or absence of a carrier signal on a broadband network.

Unipolar non-return to zero

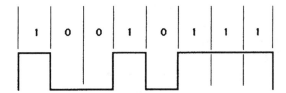

Manchester coding

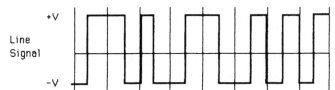

Figure 3.4 Unipolar non-return-to-zero signaling and Manchester coding. In Manchester coding, a timing transition occurs in the middle of each bit and the line code maintains an equal amount of positive and negative voltage.

Collision Detection As previously discussed, under Manchester coding a binary 1 is represented by a high-to-low transition, while a binary 0 is represented by a low-to-high voltage transition. Thus, an examination of the voltage on the medium of a baseband network enables a station to determine whether a carrier signal is present.

If a carrier signal is found, the station with data to transmit will continue to monitor the channel. When the current transmission ends, the station will then transmit its data, while checking the channel for collisions. Since Ethernet and IEEE 802.3 Manchester encoded signals have a 1-volt average DC voltage level, a collision results in an average DC level of 2 volts. Thus, a transceiver or network interface card can detect collisions by monitoring the voltage level of the Manchester line signal.

Jam Pattern If a collision is detected during transmission, the transmitting station will cease transmission of data and initiate transmission of a jam pattern. The jam pattern consists of 32 to

48 bits. These bits can have any value other than the CRC value that corresponds to the partial frame transmitted before the jam. The transmission of the jam pattern ensures that the collision lasts long enough to be detected by all stations on the network.

When a repeater is used to connect multiple segments, it must recognize a collision occurring on one port and place a jam signal on all other ports. Doing so results in a collision with signals from stations that may have been in the process of beginning to transmit on one segment when the collision occurred on the other segment. In addition, the jam signal serves as a mechanism to cause nontransmitting stations to wait until the jam signal ends prior to attempting to transmit, preventing additional potential collisions from occurring.

Wait Time   Once a collision is detected, the transmitting station waits a random number of slot times before attempting to retransmit. Here the term *slot* represents 512 bits on a 10-Mbps network, or a minimum frame length of 64 bytes. The actual number of slot times the station waits is selected by a randomization process, formerly known as a *truncated binary exponential backoff*. Under this randomization process, a random integer r defines the number of slot times the station waits before listening to determine whether the channel is clear. If it is, the station begins to retransmit the frame, while listening for another collision.

If the station transmits the complete frame successfully and has additional data to transmit, it will again listen to the channel as it prepares another frame for transmission. If a collision occurs on a retransmission attempt, a slightly different procedure is followed. After a jam signal is transmitted, the station simply doubles the previously generated random number and then waits the prescribed number of slot intervals prior to attempting a retransmission. Up to 16 retransmission attempts can occur before the station aborts the transmission and declares the occurrence of a multiple collision error condition.

Figure 3.5 illustrates the collision detection process by which a station can determine that a frame was not successfully transmitted. At time t_0 both stations A and B are listening and fail to detect the occurrence of a collision, and at time t_1 station

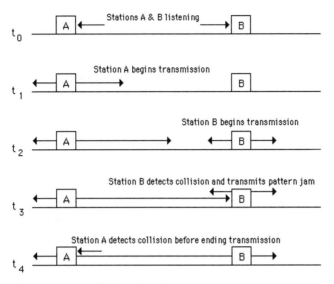

Figure. 3.5 Collision detection.

A commences the transmission of a frame. As station A's frame begins to propagate down the bus in both directions, station B begins the transmission of a frame, since at time t_2 it appears to station B that there is no activity on the network.

Shortly after time t_2 the frames transmitted by stations A and B collide, resulting in a doubling of the Manchester-encoded signal level for a very short period of time. This doubling of the Manchester-encoded signal's voltage level is detected by station B at time t_3, since station B is closer to the collision than station A. Station B then generates a jam pattern that is detected by station A.

Late Collisions   *Late collision* is a term used to reference the detection of a collision only after a station places a complete frame on the network. A late collision is normally caused by an excessive network cable segment length, resulting in the time for a signal to propagate from one end of a segment to another part of the segment being longer than the time required to place a full frame on the network. This results in two devices communicating at the same time, never seeing each other's transmission until their signals collide.

A late collision is detected by a transmitter after the first slot time of 64 bytes, and is only applicable for frames whose length exceeds 65 bytes. The detection of a late collision occurs in exactly the same manner as a normal collision; however, it happens later than normal. Although the primary cause of late collisions is excessive cable segment lengths, an excessive number of repeaters, faulty connectors, and defective Ethernet transceivers or controllers can also result in late collisions.

Service Primitives

As previously mentioned, the MAC sublayer isolates the physical layer from the LLC sublayer. Thus, one of the functions of the MAC sublayer is to provide services to the LLC. To accomplish this task, a series of service primitives was defined to govern the exchange of LLC data between a local MAC sublayer and its peer LLC sublayer.

The basic MAC service primitives used in all IEEE MAC standards include the medium access data request (MA_DATA. request), medium access data confirm (MA_DATA.confirm), medium access data indicate (MA_DATA.indicate), and medium access data response (MA_DATA.response).

MA_DATA.request   The medium access data request is generated whenever the LLC sublayer has data to be transmitted. This primitive is passed from layer n to layer $n-1$ to request the initiation of service, and results in the MAC sublayer formatting the request in a MAC frame and passing it to the physical layer for transmission.

MA_DATA.confirm   The medium access data confirm primitive is generated by the MAC sublayer in response to a MA_DATA.request generated by the local LLC sublayer. The confirm primitive is passed from layer $n-1$ to layer n, and includes a status parameter that indicates the outcome of the request primitive.

MA_DATA.indicate   The medium access data indicate primitive is passed from layer $n-1$ to layer n to indicate that a valid frame has arrived at the local MAC sublayer. Thus, this service primitive denotes that the frame was received without CRC, length, or frame alignment error.

MA_DATA.response   The medium access data response primitive is passed from layer *n* to layer *n*–1. This primitive acknowledges the MA_DATA.indicate service primitive.

Primitive Operations

To illustrate the use of MAC service primitives, let us assume that station A on a network wants to communicate with station B. As illustrated in Figure 3.6, the LLC sublayer of station A requests transmission of a frame to the MAC sublayer service interface via the issuance of a MA_DATA.request service primitive. In response to the MA_DATA.request, a frame is transmitted to station B. Upon receipt of that frame, the MAC sublayer at that station generates a MA_DATA.indicate to inform the LLC sublayer of the arrival of the frame. The LLC sublayer accepts the frame and generates a MA_DATA.response to inform the MAC sublayer that it has the frame. That response flows across the network to station A, where the MAC sublayer generates a MA_DATA.confirm to inform the LLC sublayer that the frame was received without error.

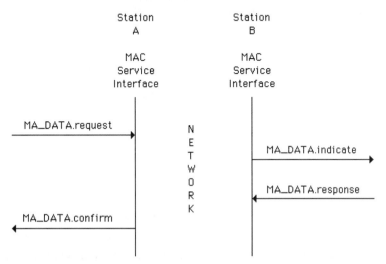

Figure 3.6 Relationship of medium access control service primitives.

ETHERNET LOGICAL LINK CONTROL

The logical link control (LLC) sublayer was defined under the IEEE 802.2 standard to make the method of link control independent of a specific access method. Thus, the 802.2 method of link control spans Ethernet (IEEE 802.3), Token Bus (IEEE 802.4), Token Ring (IEEE 802.5), and FDDI local area networks. Functions performed by the LLC include generating and interpreting commands to control the flow of data, and recovery operations for when a transmission error is detected.

Link control information is carried within the data field of an IEEE 802.3 frame as an LLC *protocol data unit* (PDU). Figure 3.7 illustrates the relationship between the IEEE 802.3 frame and the LLC protocol data unit.

The LLC Protocol Data Unit

Service Access Points (SAPs) function much like a mailbox. Since the LLC layer is bounded below the MAC sublayer and bounded above by the network layer, SAPs provide a mechanism for exchanging information between the LLC layer and the MAC and network layers. For example, from the network layer perspective, a SAP represents the place to leave messages about the services requested by an application.

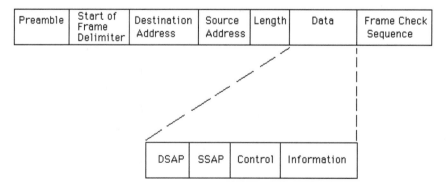

Figure 3.7 Formation of LLC protocol data unit. Control information is carried within a MAC frame.

In a multiprotocol networking environment the same LLC sublayer will be used to provide services to more than one network layer protocol. To do so each protocol uses a different SAP address value, enabling a SAP to uniquely identify an upper-layer protocol. One common example is the use of IP and IPX on a network for which dual software stacks use two unique SAP values to communicate with the LLC sublayer.

The *destination services access point* (DSAP) is one byte in length, and is used to specify the receiving network layer process, which is an IEEE term to denote the destination upper-layer protocol. The *source service access point* (SSAP) is also one byte in length. The SSAP specifies the sending network layer process which is in effect the source upper-layer protocol. Both DSAP and SSAP addresses are assigned by the IEEE and are always the same since destination and source protocols must always be the same. For example, hex address FF represents a DSAP broadcast address.

The control field provides information that can indicate the type of service and protocol format. For example, if the frame is transporting NetWare data, the control field will contain the hex value 03, which indicates that the frame uses the unnumbered format for connectionless services. The actual composition of the LLC control field depends upon whether the PDU is an information (I), supervisory (S), or unnumbered (U) frame. If the PDU is an I or S frame, the field is two bytes in length, as illustrated in Figure 3.8a and 3.8b. If the PDU is a U frame, then the control field is one byte in length, as illustrated in Figure 3.8c.

I frames are used for transmitting data and the method of control including the N(S), P/F, and N(R) fields functions, as with to the HDLC protocol. S frames guide the transfer of I frames and are applicable to a connection-oriented, Type 2 data transfer operation (described later in this section). An S frame is restricted to conveying supervisory information within its control field and does not include a data field. The third type of PDU is a U frame which corresponds to the use of an eight-bit or one-byte control field. U frames are employed to set up and break down the logical link between network nodes for a Type 1 or Type 2 service. U frames are also used to transmit data in connectionless Type 1 or Type 3 services. Both the types and

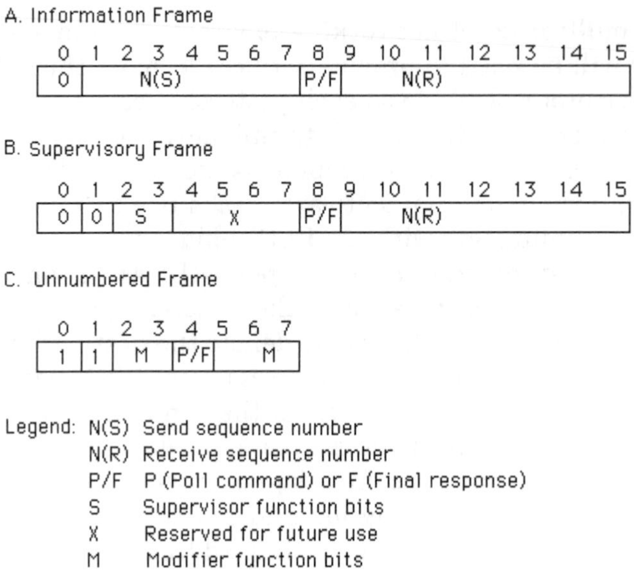

A. Information Frame

```
 0  1  2  3  4  5  6  7  8  9  10 11  12  13  14  15
┌──┬────────────────┬────┬──────────────────────────┐
│ 0│      N(S)      │P/F │          N(R)            │
└──┴────────────────┴────┴──────────────────────────┘
```

B. Supervisory Frame

```
 0  1  2  3  4  5  6  7  8  9  10 11  12  13  14  15
┌──┬──┬─────┬───────┬────┬──────────────────────────┐
│ 0│ 0│  S  │   X   │P/F │          N(R)            │
└──┴──┴─────┴───────┴────┴──────────────────────────┘
```

C. Unnumbered Frame

```
 0  1  2  3  4  5  6  7
┌──┬──┬───┬────┬───────┐
│ 1│ 1│ M │P/F │   M   │
└──┴──┴───┴────┴───────┘
```

Legend: N(S) Send sequence number
         N(R) Receive sequence number
         P/F   P (Poll command) or F (Final response)
         S   Supervisor function bits
         X   Reserved for future use
         M   Modifier function bits

Figure 3.8 LLC control field.

classes of service applicable to Ethernet's LLC are described in detail at the end of this section. Prior to discussing the types and classes of service defined by the 802.2 standard, let us examine two additional IEEE 802.3 logical frame formats.

Ethernet_SNAP Frame

The Ethernet_SNAP (Subnetwork Access Protocol) frame provides a mechanism for obtaining a type field identifier associated with a pure Ethernet frame in an IEEE 802.3 frame. To accomplish this, the data field is subdivided similarly to the previously illustrated LLC protocol data unit shown in Figure 3.7; however, two additional subfields are added after the control field. Those fields are an organization code of three bytes and an Ethernet type field of two bytes. Figure 3.9 illustrates the format of an Ethernet_SNAP frame.

Unlike the Ethernet_802.3 frame described next, an Ethernet_SNAP frame can be used to transport several protocols. AppleTalk Phase II, NetWare, and TCP/IP protocols can be

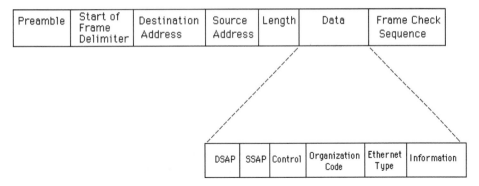

Figure 3.9   Ethernet_SNAP frame format.

transported by an Ethernet_SNAP frame due to the inclusion of the previously mentioned Ethernet type field in the frame. Thus, SNAP can be considered as an extension which permits vendors to create their own Ethernet protocol transports.

A value of hex AA is placed in the DSAP and SSAP fields to indicate that the frame is an Ethernet_SNAP frame. The control field functions similarly to the previously described LLC protocol data unit, indicating the type and class of service where hex 03 would indicate a connectionless service unnumbered format.

The organization code field references the assigner of the value in the following Ethernet type field. For most situations, a hex value of 00-00-00 is used to indicate that the Ethernet type field value was assigned by Xerox. When the organization code is hex 00-00-00, the Ethernet type field will contain one of the entries listed in Table 3.2.

NetWare Ethernet_802.3 Frame

One additional logical variation of the IEEE 802.3 frame format that warrants an elaboration is known as the NetWare Ethernet_802.3 frame. The Ethernet_802.3 frame represents a proprietary subdivision of the IEEE 802.3 data field to transport NetWare and is one of several types of frames that can be used to transport the IPX/SPX protocol. The actual frame type used is defined at system setup time by binding NetWare to a specific type of frame.

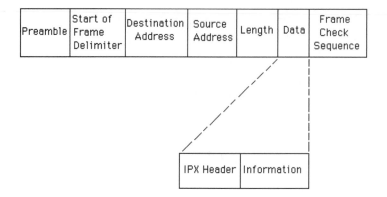

An Ethernet_802.3 field subdivides the data field into an IPX header field and an information field.

Figure 3.10   NetWare Ethernet_802.3 frame.

Instead of using the IEEE 802.2 subfields to form a LLC protocol data unit, Novell places the IPX header immediately after the length field, reducing the maximum data field length by 30 bytes. Figure 3.10 illustrates the format of a NetWare Ethernet_802.3 frame to indicate the position of the IPX header in the frame. The NetWare Ethernet_802.3 frame can be used only to transport NetWare IPX traffic and represents a common level of frustration when an administrator attempts to use this frame format to transport a different protocol.

Receiver Frame Determination

A receiving station can distinguish between different types of Ethernet frames and correctly interpret data transported in those frames. To do so, it must examine the value of the field following the source address field, which is either a type or length field. If the field value exceeds 1500 decimals, the field must be a type subfield. Thus, the frame is a "raw" Ethernet frame. If the value is less than 1500, the field is a length field and the two bytes following that field, which represent the first two bytes of an IEEE 802.3 frame's data field, must be examined. If those two bytes have the value hex FF-FF, the frame is a NetWare

Table 3.4 Protocols versus Frame Type

Frame Type	Protocols that Can Be Bound
Ethernet	NetWare, AppleTalk, Phase I, TCP/IP
IEEE 802.3	NetWare, FTAM
NetWare Ethernet_802.3	NetWare only
Ethernet-SNAP	NetWare, AppleTalk, Phase II, TCP/IP

Ethernet_802.3 frame used to transport IPX. If the value of the two bytes is hex AA-AA, the frame is an Ethernet_SNAP frame. Any other value in those bytes means that the frame is an IEEE_802.3 frame.

It is important during the LAN installation process to bind the appropriate protocol to the frame type capable of transporting the protocol. Table 3.4 lists several examples of protocols that can be bonded to different types of Ethernet frames.

Types of Service

Under the 802.2 standard, there are three types of service available for sending and receiving LLC data. These types are discussed in the next three subsections. Figure 3.11 provides a visual summary of the operation of each LLC service type.

Type 1

Type 1 is an unacknowledged connectionless service. The term *connectionless* refers to the fact that transmission does not occur between two devices as if a logical connection were established. Instead, transmission flows on the channel to all stations; however, only the destination address acts upon the data. As the name of this service implies, there is no provision for the acknowledgment of frames. Neither are there provisions for flow control or for error recovery. Therefore, this is an unreliable service.

Despite those shortcomings, Type 1 is the most commonly used service, since most protocol suites use a reliable transport mechanism at the transport layer, thus eliminating the need for reliability at the link layer. In addition, by eliminating the time

Type 1 Unacknowledged connectionless service

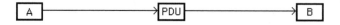

Type 2 Connection-oriented service

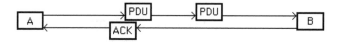

Type 3 Acknowledged connectionless source

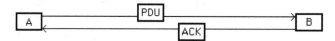

Legend:
PDU = protocol data unit
ACK = acknowledgement
A,B = stations on the network

Figure 3.11 Local link control service types.

needed to establish a virtual link and the overhead of acknowl-edgments, a Type 1 service can provide a greater throughput than other LLC types of services.

Type 2

The Type 2 connection-oriented service requires that a logical link be established between the sender and the receiver prior to information transfer. Once the logical connection is established, data will flow between the sender and receiver until either party terminates the connection. During data transfer, a Type 2 LLC service provides all of the functions lacking in a Type 1 service, using a sliding window for flow control. When IBM's SNA data is transported on a LAN, it uses connection-oriented services. Type 2 LLC is also commonly referred to as LLC2.

Type 3

The Type 3 acknowledged connectionless service contains provision for the setup and disconnection of transmission; it acknowledges individual frames using the stop-and-wait flow control method. Type 3 service is primarily used in an automated factory process-control environment, where one central computer communicates with many remote devices that typically have a limited storage capacity.

Classes of Service

All logical link control stations support Type 1 operations. This level of support is known as Class I service. The classes of service supported by LLC indicate the combinations of the three LLC service types supported by a station. Class I supports Type 1 service, Class II supports both Type 1 and Type 2, Class III supports Type 1 and Type 3 service, while Class IV supports all three service types. Since service Type 1 is supported by all classes, it can be considered a least common denominator, enabling all stations to communicate using a common form of service.

Service Primitives

The LLC sublayer uses service primitives similar to those that govern the exchange of data between the MAC sublayer and its peer LLC sublayer. In doing so, the LLC sublayer supports the Request, Confirm, Indicate, and Response primitives described in the section on Ethernet media access control, earlier in this chapter. The major difference between the LLC and MAC service primitives is that the LLC sublayer supports three types of services. As previously discussed, the available LLC services are unacknowledged connectionless, connection-oriented, and acknowledged connectionless. Thus, the use of LLC service primitives varies in conjunction with the type of LLC service initiated. For example, a connection-oriented service uses service primitives in the same manner as that illustrated in Figure 3.6. If the service is unacknowledged connectionless, the only service primitives used are the Request and Indicate, since there is no Response or Confirmation.

FAST ETHERNET

The term *Fast Ethernet* collectively references 100BASE-TX, 100BASE-FX, and 100BASE-T4. Although each standard is designed for operation on a different type of media, they use a common frame composition and retain the use of the CSMA/CD access protocol.

Each Fast Ethernet frame retains the core format of the Ethernet frame illustrated in Figure 3.1. The key difference between a Fast Ethernet frame and Ethernet frame concerns the manner by which the Ethernet interpacket gap of 9.6 μsec between frames is handled. For example, a 100BASE-TX frame adds a byte at the beginning and end of the Ethernet frame as a marker to note the beginning and end of the stream. Those bytes are appropriately known as the start-of-stream delimiter and end-of-stream delimiter. The 100BASE-TX Fast Ethernet frame is illustrated in Figure 3.12.

Encoding

In place of the use of Manchester coding and an interpacket gap of 9.6 μsec between Ethernet frames, Fast Ethernet 100BASE-TX is transmitted using 4B5B encoding and IDLE codes repre-

SSD 1 byte	Preamble 7 bytes	SFD 1 byte	Destination Address 6 bytes	Source Address 6 bytes	L/T 2 bytes	Data 46 to 1500 bytes	FCS 1 byte	ESD 1 byte

The 100BASE-TX frame differs from the IEEE 802.3 MAC frame through the addition of a byte at each end to mark the beginning and end of the stream delimiter.

SSD   Start of stream delimiter
SFD   Start of frame delimiter
L/T   Length (IEEE 802.3/Type(Ethernet))
ESD   End of stream delimiter

Figure 3.12   Fast Ethernet frame.

senting sequences of I (binary 11111) symbols to mark the gap between packets. Thus, the composition of the Fast Ethernet 100BASE-TX as well as the 100BASE-FX and 100BASE-T4 frames are identical to the Ethernet frame format without the stream delimiters.

Start-of-Stream Delimiter

The start-of-stream delimiter (SSD) is used to align a received frame for subsequent decoding. The SSD field consists of a sequence of J and K symbols from the 4B5B code, which represent the unique codes 11000 and 10001, respectively.

End-of-Stream Delimiter

The end-of-stream delimiter (ESD) is used as an indicator that data transmission terminated normally and a properly formed stream was transmitted. This one-byte field is created by the use of T and R codes from the 4B5B encoding table and have the bit composition 01101 and 00111, respectively. The ESD field lies outside of the Ethernet/IEEE 802.3 frame only for comparison purposes and can be considered to fall within the interframe gap of those frames.

TOKEN RING FRAME OPERATIONS

In this section we will examine Token Ring frame operations, in order to understand the manner in which different frame fields are used for access control, error checking, routing of data between interconnected networks, and other Token Ring network functions. By studying the composition of Token Ring frames we will be able to understand vLAN creation using explicit tagging as well as interoperability problems when multiple types of LANs in a common network require a vLAN capability.

A Token Ring network consists of ring stations representing devices that attach to a ring and an attaching medium. Concerning the latter, the attaching medium can be shielded or unshielded, twisted-pair, or fiber optic cable, each having constraints concerning transmission distance and number of stations allowed on the network.

A *ring station*, also referred to as a station or workstation, transfers data to the ring in a transmission unit referred to as a *frame*. Frames are transmitted sequentially from one station to another physically active station in a clockwise direction. The next active station is referred to as *downstream neighbor*, which regenerates the frame and performs MAC address checking and other functions. In performing a media access control (MAC) address check, the station compares its address to the destination address contained in the frame. If the two match or if the station has a functional address that matches the frame destination's address, the station copies the data contained in the frame. While performing the previously described operations, the station performs a number of error checks based upon the composition of data in the frame and reports errors via the generation of different types of error-reporting frames. Thus, it is important to understand the composition of the fields within the Token Ring frames as they govern the operation of a Token Ring network.

Transmission Formats

Three types of transmission formats are supported on a Token Ring network—token, abort, and frame. The token format as illustrated in Figure 3.13a is the mechanism by which access to the ring is passed from one computer attached to the network to another device connected to the network. Here the token format consists of three bytes, of which the starting and ending delimiters are used to indicate the beginning and end of a token frame. The middle byte of a token frame is an access control byte. Three bits are used as a priority indicator and three bits are used as a reservation indicator, while one bit is used for the token bit and another bit position functions as the monitor bit.

When the token bit is set to a binary 0 it indicates that the transmission is a token. When it is set to a binary 1 it indicates that data in the form of a frame is being transmitted.

The second Token Ring frame format signifies an abort token. In actuality there is no token, since this format is indicated by a starting delimiter followed by an ending delimiter.

The transmission of an abort token is used to abort a previous transmission. The format of an abort token is illustrated in Figure 3.13b.

The third type of Token Ring frame format occurs when a station seizes a free token. At that time the token format is converted into a frame that includes the addition of frame control, addressing data, an error-detection field, and a frame status field. The format of a Token Ring frame is illustrated in Figure 3.13c. At any given point in time, only one token can reside on a ring, represented either as a token format, abort token format, or frame. By examining each of the fields in the frame we will

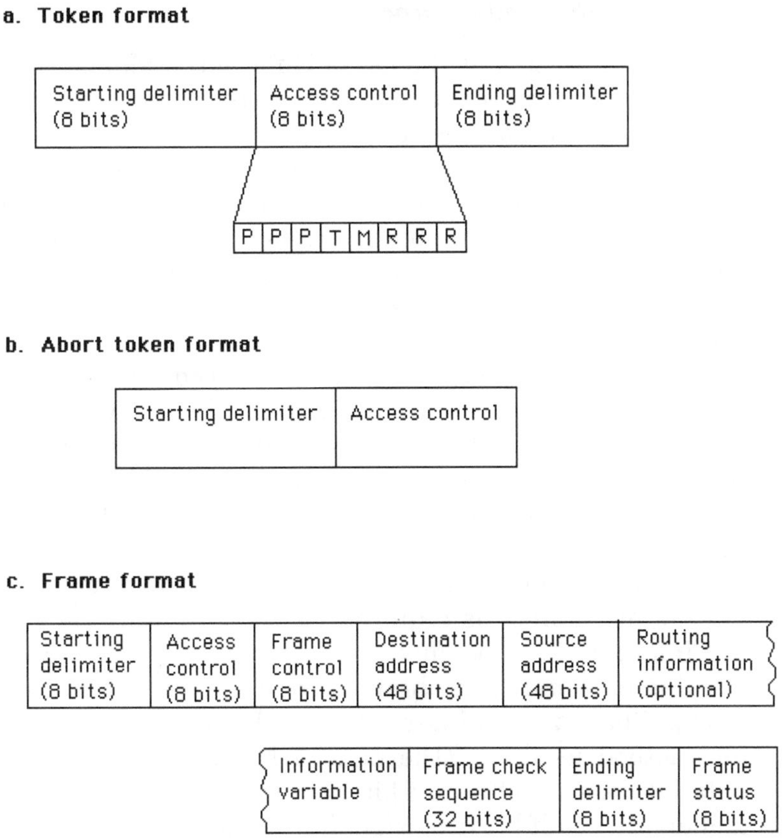

a. Token format

Starting delimiter (8 bits)	Access control (8 bits)	Ending delimiter (8 bits)

| P | P | P | T | M | R | R | R |

b. Abort token format

Starting delimiter	Access control

c. Frame format

Starting delimiter (8 bits)	Access control (8 bits)	Frame control (8 bits)	Destination address (48 bits)	Source address (48 bits)	Routing information (optional)

Information variable	Frame check sequence (32 bits)	Ending delimiter (8 bits)	Frame status (8 bits)

Figure 3.13 Token Ring token, abort, and frame formats (P: priority bits, T: token bit, M: monitor bit, R: reservation bits).

also examine the token and token abort frames, due to the commonality of fields between each frame.

Starting/Ending Delimiters

The starting and ending delimiters mark the beginning and ending of a token or frame. Each delimiter consists of a unique code pattern which identifies it to the network. Understanding the composition of the starting and ending delimiter fields requires us to review the method by which data is represented on a Token Ring network using Differential Manchester encoding.

Differential Manchester Encoding

Figure 3.14 illustrates the use of Differential Manchester encoding, comparing its operation to non-return-to-zero (NRZ) and conventional Manchester encoding.

In Figure 3.14a, NRZ coding illustrates the representation of data by holding a voltage low (–V) to represent a binary 0 and high (+V) to represent a binary 1. As previously noted in our review of Ethernet signaling, this method of signaling is called *non-return to zero* since there is no return to a 0 V position after each data bit is coded.

One problem associated with NRZ encoding is the fact that a long string of 0 or 1 bits does not result in a voltage change. Thus, to determine that bit m in a string of n bits of 0's or 1's is set to a 0 or 1 requires sampling at predefined bit times. This in turn requires each device on a network using NRZ encoding to have its own clocking circuitry.

To avoid the necessity of building clocking circuitry into devices, a mechanism is required for encoded data to carry clocking information. One method by which encoded data carries clocking information is obtained from the use of Manchester encoding, illustrated in Figure 3.14b, which represents the signaling method used by Ethernet. In Manchester encoding, each data bit consists of a half-bit time signal at a low voltage (–V) and another half-bit time signal at the opposite positive voltage (+V). Every binary 0 is represented by a half-bit time at a low voltage and the remaining bit time at a high voltage. Every bi-

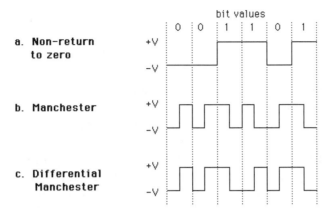

Figure 3.14 Differential Manchester encoding. In Differential Manchester encoding, the direction of the signal's voltage transition changes whenever a binary 1 is transmitted but remains the same for a binary 0.

nary 1 is represented by a half-bit time at a high voltage followed by a half-bit time at a low voltage. By changing the voltage for every binary digit, Manchester encoding ensures that the signal carries self-clocking information.

In Figure 3.14c, Differential Manchester encoding is illustrated. The difference between Manchester encoding and Differential Manchester encoding occurs in the method by which binary 1's are encoded. In Differential Manchester encoding, the direction of the signal's voltage transition changes whenever a binary 1 is transmitted, but remains the same for a binary 0. The IEEE 802.5 standard specifies the use of Differential Manchester encoding and this encoding technique is used on Token Ring networks at the physical layer to transmit and detect four distinct symbols—a binary 0, a binary 1, and two nondata symbols.

Nondata Symbols

Under Manchester and Differential Manchester encoding there are two possible code violations that can occur. Each code violation produces what is known as a nondata symbol and is used in the Token Ring frame to denote starting and ending delimiters, similar to the use of the flag in an HDLC frame. However, unlike the flag whose bit composition 01111110 is uniquely maintained by inserting a 0 bit after every sequence of five set bits and removing a 0 following every sequence of five set bits, Differential Manchester encoding maintains the uniqueness of frames by the use of nondata J and nondata K symbols. This eliminates the bit-stuffing operations required by HDLC.

The two nondata symbols each consist of two half-bit times without a voltage change. The J symbol occurs when the voltage is the same as that of the last signal, while the K symbol occurs when the voltage becomes opposite of that of the last signal. Figure 3.15 illustrates the occurrence of the J and K nondata symbols based upon different last bit voltages. Readers will note in comparing Figure 3.15 to Figure 3.14c that the J and K nondata symbols are distinct code violations that cannot be mistaken for either a binary 0 or a binary 1.

Now that we have an understanding of the operation of Differential Manchester encoding and the composition of the J and K nondata symbols, we can focus our attention upon the actual format of each frame delimiter.

The start delimiter field marks the beginning of a frame. The composition of this field is the bits and nondata symbols JK0JK000. The end delimiter field marks the end of a frame as well as denotes whether the frame is the last frame of a multiple frame sequence using a single token or whether there are additional frames following this frame.

The format of the end delimiter field is JK1JK1IE, where I is

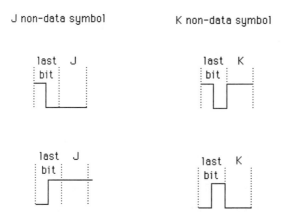

Figure 3.15 J and K nondata symbol composition. J and K nondata symbols are distinct code violations that cannot be mistaken for data.

the intermediate frame bit. If I is set to 0, this indicates it is the last frame transmitted by a station. If I is set to 1, this indicates that additional frames follow this frame.

E is an error-detected bit. The E bit is initially set to 0 by the station transmitting a frame, token, or abort sequence. As the frame circulates the ring, each station checks the transmission for errors. Upon detection of a frame check sequence (FCS) error, inappropriate nondata symbol, illegal framing, or another type of error, the first station detecting the error will set the E bit to a value of 1. Since stations keep track of the number of times they set the E bit to a value of 1, it becomes possible to use this information as a guide to locating possible cable errors. For example, if one workstation accounted for a very large percentage of E bit settings in a network, there is a high degree of probability that there is a problem with the lobe cable to that workstation. The problem could be a crimped cable or a loose connector and represents a logical place to commence an investigation in an attempt to reduce E bit errors.

Access Control Field

The second field in both token and frame formats is the access control byte. As illustrated at the top of Figure 3.13, this byte consists of four subfields and serves as the controlling mechanism for gaining access to the network. When a free token circulates the network, the access control field represents one-third of the length of the frame since it is prefixed by the start delimiter and suffixed by the end delimiter.

The lowest priority that can be specified by the priority bits in the access control byte is 0 (000), while the highest is seven (111), providing eight levels of priority. Table 3.5 lists the normal use of the priority bits in the access control field. Workstations have a default priority of three, while bridges have a default priority of four.

To reserve a token, a workstation will attempt to insert its priority level in the priority reservation subfield. Unless another station with a higher priority bumps the requesting station, the reservation will be honored and the requesting station will obtain the token. If the token bit is set to 1, this serves as an indication that a frame follows instead of the ending delimiter.

Table 3.5 Priority Bit Settings

Priority Bits	Priority
000	Normal user priority, MAC frames that do not require a token and response type MAC frames
001	Normal user priority
010	Normal user priority
011	Normal user priority and MAC frames that require tokens
100	Bridge
101	Reserved
110	Reserved
111	Specialized station management

A station that needs to transmit a frame at a given priority can use any available token that has a priority level equal to or less than the priority level of the frame to be transmitted. When a token of equal or lower priority is not available, the ring station can reserve a token of the required priority through the use of the reservation bits. In doing so the station must follow two rules. First, if a passing token has a higher priority reservation than the reservation level desired by the workstation, the station will not alter the reservation field contents. Second, if the reservation bits have not been set or indicate a lower priority than that desired by the station, the station can now set the reservation bits to the required priority level.

Once a frame is removed by its originating station, the reservation bits in the header will be checked. If those bits have a nonzero value, the station must release a nonzero priority token, with the actual priority assigned based upon the priority used by the station for the recently transmitted frame, the reservation bit settings received upon the return of the frame, and any stored priority.

On occasion, the Token Ring protocol will result in the transmission of a new token by a station prior to that station having the ability to verify the settings of the access control field in a returned frame. When this situation arises, the token will be issued according to the priority and reservation bit settings in the access control field of the transmitted frame.

Figure 3.16 illustrates the operation of the priority (P) and reservation (R) bit fields in the access control field. In this example, the prevention of a high-priority station from monopolizing the network is illustrated by station A entering a priority-hold state. This occurs when a station originates a token at a higher priority than the last token it generated. Once in a priority-hold state, the station will issue tokens that will bring the priority

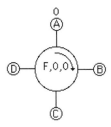

a. Station A generates a frame using a non-priority token P,R=0,0.

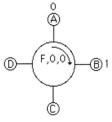

b. Station B reserves a priority 1 in the reservation bits in the frame P,R=0,1; Station A enters a priority-hold state.

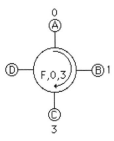

c. Station C reserves a priority of 3, overriding B's reservation of 1; P,R=0,3.

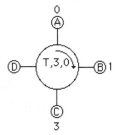

d. Station A removes its frame and generates a token at reserved priority level 3; P,R=3,0.

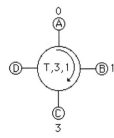

e. Station B repeats priority token and makes a new reservation of priority level 1; P,R=3,1

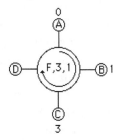

f. Station C grabs token and transmits a frame with a priority of 3; P,R=3,1.

Figure 3.16 Priority and reservation field utilization.

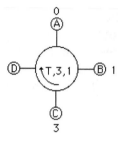

g. Upon return of frame to Station C
it's removed. Station C generates a
token at the priority just used; P,R=3,1

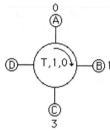

h. Station A in a priority-hold state
grabs token and changes its
priority to 1; P,R=1,0. Station A
stays in priority-hold state until
priority reduced to 0.

Legend:

ⓐ, ⓑ, ⓒ, ⓓ = stations

Numeric outside station identifier
indicates priority level.

Figure 3.16 (Continued)

level eventually down to zero as a mechanism to prevent a high-priority station from monopolizing the network.

The Monitor Bit

The monitor bit is used to prevent a token with a priority exceeding zero or a frame from continuously circulating on the Token Ring. This bit is transmitted as a 0 in all tokens and frames, except for a device on the network which functions as an active monitor and thus obtains the capability to inspect and modify that bit.

When a token or frame is examined by the active monitor it will set the monitor bit to a 1 if it was previously found to be set to 0. If a token or frame is found to have the monitor bit already set to 1 this indicates that the token or frame has already made at least one revolution around the ring and an error condition has occurred, usually caused by the failure of a station to remove its transmission from the ring or the failure of a high-priority station to seize a token. When the active monitor finds a monitor bit set to 1 it assumes an error condition has occurred. The active monitor then purges the token or frame and releases a new token onto the ring. Now that we have an understanding of the role of the monitor bit in the access control field and the operation of the active monitor on that bit, let's focus our attention upon the active monitor.

The Active Monitor

The active monitor is the device that has the highest address on the network. All other stations on the network are considered as standby monitors and watch the active monitor.

The function of the active monitor is to determine if a token or frame is continuously circulating the ring in error. To accomplish this the active monitor sets the monitor count bit as a token or frame goes by. If a destination workstation fails or has its power turned off the frame will circulate back to the active monitor, where it is then removed from the network. In the event the active monitor should fail or be turned off, the standby monitors watch the active monitor by looking for an active monitor frame. If one does not appear within seven seconds, the standby monitor that has the highest network address then takes over as the active monitor.

In addition to detecting and removing frames that might otherwise continue to circulate the ring, the active monitor performs several other ring management functions. Those functions include the detection and recovery of multiple tokens and the loss of a token or frame on the ring, as well as initiation of a token when a ring is started. The loss of a token or frame is detected by the expiration of a timer whose timeout value exceeds the time required for the longest possible frame to circulate the ring. The active monitor restarts this time and each time it transmits a starting delimiter which precedes every frame and token. Thus, if the timer expires without the appearance of a frame or token, the active monitor will assume the frame or token was lost and initiate a purge operation, which is described later in this section.

Frame Control Field

The frame control field informs a receiving device on the network of the type of frame that was transmitted and how it should be interpreted. Frames can be either logical link control (LLC) or reference physical link functions according to the IEEE 802.5 media access control (MAC) standard. A media access control frame carries network control information and responses, while a logical link control frame carries data.

The eight-bit frame control field has the format FFZZZZZZ, where FF are frame definition bits. The top of Table 3.6 indicates the possible settings of the frame bits and the assignment of those settings. The ZZZZZZ bits convey media access control (MAC) buffering information when the FF bits are set to 00. When the FF bits are set to 01 to indicate an LLC frame, the ZZZZZZ bits are split into two fields, designated rrrYYY. Currently, the rrr bits are reserved for future use and are set to 000. The YYY bits indicate the priority of the logical link control (LLC) data. The lower portion of Table 3.6 indicates the value of

Table 3.6 Frame Control Field Subfields

Frame Type Field	
F bit settings	Assignment
00	MAC frame
01	LLC frame
10	Undefined (reserved for future use)
11	Undefined (reserved for future use)
Z bit settings	Assignment*
000	Normal buffering
001	Remove ring station
010	Beacon
011	Claim token
100	Ring purge
101	Active monitor present
110	Standby monitor present

*When F bits set to 00, Z bits are used to notify an adapter that the frame is to be express buffered.

the Z bits when used in MAC frames to notify a Token-Ring adapter that the frame is to be express buffered.

Destination Address Field

Although the IEEE 802.5 standard supports both 16-bit and 48-bit address fields, IBM's implementation requires the use of 48-bit address fields. IBM's Token Ring destination address field is made up of five subfields, as illustrated in Figure 3.17. The first bit in the destination address identifies the destination as an individual station (bit set to 0) or as a group (bit set to 1) of one or more stations. The latter provides the capability for a message to be broadcast to a group of stations.

Universally Administered Address

Similar to an Ethernet universally administered address, a Token Ring universally administered address represents a unique address permanently encoded into an adapter's ROM. Because it is placed into ROM, it is also known as a burned-in address. The IEEE assigns blocks of addresses to each vendor manufacturing Token Ring equipment, which ensures that Token Ring adapter cards manufactured by different vendors are uniquely defined. Token Ring adapter manufacturers are assigned universal addresses that contain an organizationally unique identifier. This identifier consists of the first six hex digits of the adapter card address and is also referred to as the manufacturer identification. For example, cards manufactured by IBM will begin with the hex address 08-00-5A or 10-00-5A, whereas adapter cards manufactured by Texas Instruments will begin with the address 40-00-14. Table 3.7 lists over 50 vendor universal address prefixes assigned by the IEEE.

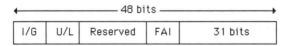

Figure 3.17 Destination address subfields (I/G: individual or group bit address identifier, U/L: universally or locally administered bit identifier, FAI: functional address indicator). The reserved field contains the manufacturer's identification in 22 bits represented by 6 hex digits.

Table 3.7 Vendors Assigned Universal Address Prefix

6-Digit Address Prefix	Vendor	6-Digit Address Prefix	Vendor
00-00-0D	RND	48-00-09	HP
00-00-A6	NwkGnl	48-00-0A	Nestar
00-00-C9	Prteon	48-00-10	AT&T
00-01-3A	Agilis	48-00-14	Exceln
00-01-C8	TmsCrd	48-00-17	NSC
00-DD-00	UB	48-00-1E	Apollo
00-DD-01	UB	48-00-20	Sun
08-00-5A	IBM	48-00-25	CDC
10-00-58	DG	48-00-28	TI
10-00-5A	IBM	48-00-2B	DEC
10-00-D8	DG	48-00-36	Intrgr
48-00-0C	Cisco	48-00-39	Spider
40-00-14	TI	48-00-45	Xylogx
40-00-22	VisTec	48-00-47	Sequnt
40-00-2A	TRW	48-00-49	Univtn
40-00-65	NwkGnl	48-00-4C	Encore
40-00-9F	Amrstr	48-00-4E	BICC
40-00-A9	NSC	48-00-67	ComDes
40-00-AA	Xerox	48-00-68	Ridge
40-00-B3	Cimlin	48-00-69	SilGrf
40-00-C0	WstDig	48-00-6A	AT&T
40-00-C9	Prteon	48-00-6E	Exceln
40-00-DD	Gould	48-00-7C	Vtalnk
42-07-01	Intrln	48-00-89	Kinetx
42-60-8C	3Com	48-00-8B	Pyramd
42-CF-1F	CMC	48-00-8D	Xyvisn
48-00-02	Bridge	48-00-90	Retix
48-00-03	ACC	50-00-14	TI
48-00-05	Symblx	EA-00-03	DEC
48-00-08	BBN	EA-00-04	DECnet

Locally Administered Address

A key problem with the use of universally administered addresses is the requirement to change software coding in a mainframe computer whenever a workstation connected to the mainframe via a gateway is added or removed from the network. To avoid constant software changes, locally administered addressing can be used. This type of addressing functions similarly to its operation on an Ethernet LAN, temporarily overriding universally administered addressing; however, the user is now responsible for ensuring the uniqueness of each address. To accomplish locally administered addressing, a statement is inserted into a configuration file which sets the adapter's address at adapter-open time, normally when a station is powered on or a system reset operation is performed.

Functional Address Indicator

The functional address indicator subfield in the destination address identifies the function associated with the destination address, such as a bridge, active monitor, or configuration report server.

The functional address indicator indicates a functional address when set to 0 and the I/G bit position is set to a 1—the latter indicating a group address. This condition can occur only when the U/L bit position is also set to a 1 and results in the ability to generate locally administered group addresses that are called functional addresses. Table 3.8 lists the functional addresses defined by the IEEE. Currently, 21 functional addresses have been defined out of a total of 31 that are available for use, with the remaining addresses available for user definitions or reserved for future use.

Address Values

The range of addresses that can be used on a Token Ring primarily depends upon the settings of the I/G, U/L, and FAI bit positions. When the I/G and U/L bit positions are set to 00 the manufacturer's universal address is used. When the I/G and U/L bits are set to 01, individual locally administered addresses are used in the defined range listed in Table 3.8. When all three bit positions are set, this situation indicates a group address within the range contained in Table 3.9. If the I/G and U/L bits are set to 11 but the FAI bit is set to 0, this indicates that the address is a functional address. In this situation the range of addresses is bit sensitive, permitting only those functional addresses listed in Table 3.8.

A number of destination ring stations can be identified

Table 3.8   IEEE Functional Addresses

Function	Address
Active Monitor	C0-00-00-00-00-01
Ring Parameter Server	C0-00-00-00-00-02
Network Server Heartbeat	C0-00-00-00-00-04
Ring Error Monitor	C0-00-00-00-00-08
Configuration Report Server	C0-00-00-00-00-10
Synchronous Bandwidth Manager	C0-00-00-00-00-20
Locate-Directory Server	C0-00-00-00-00-40
NETBIOS	C0-00-00-00-00-80
Bridge	C0-00-00-00-01-00
IMPL Server	C0-00-00-00-02-00
Ring Authorization Server	C0-00-00-00-04-00
LAN Gateway	C0-00-00-00-08-00
Ring Wiring Concentrator	C0-00-00-00-10-00
LAN Manager	C0-00-00-00-20-00
User-defined	C0-00-00-00-80-00
	through
	C0-00-40-00-00-00
ISO OSI ALL ES	C0-00-00-00-40-00
ISO OSI ALL IS	C0-00-00-00-80-00
IBM Discovery Nonserver	C0-00-00-01-00-00
IBM Resource Manager	C0-00-00-02-00-00
TCP/IP	C0-00-00-04-00-00
6611 DECnet	C0-00-20-00-00-00
LAN Network Manager	C0-00-40-00-00-00

through the use of a group address. Table 3.10 lists a few of the standard group addresses that have been defined when the I/G, U/L and FAI bits are set to one.

In addition to the previously mentioned addresses, there are two special destination address values that are defined. An address of all 1's (FF-FF-FF-FF-FF-FF) identifies all stations as destination stations. If a null address is used in which all bits are set to 0 (00-00-00-00-00), the frame is not addressed to any workstation. In this situation it can only be transmitted but not received, enabling you to test the ability of the active monitor to purge this type of frame from the network.

Table 3.9 Token Ring Addresses

	Bit Settings			
	I/G	*U/L*	*FAI*	*Address/Address Range*
Individual, universally administered	0	0	0/1	Manufacturer's serial no.
Individual, locally administered	0	1	0	40-00-00-00-00-00 - 40-00-7F-FF-FF-FF
Group address	1	1	1	40-00-80-00-00-00 - 40-00-FF-FF-FF-FF
Functional address	1	1	0	C0-00-00-00-00-01 - C0-00-FF-FF-FF-FF (bit-sensitive)
All stations broadcast	1	1	1	FF-FF-FF-FF-FF-FF
Null address	0	0	0	00-00-00-00-00-00

Table 3.10 Representative Standardized Group Addresses

Bridge	80-02-43-00-00-00
Bridge management	80-01-43-00-00-08
Novell IPX	90-00-72-00-00-40
Hewlett-Packard probe	90-00-90-00-00-80
Vitalink gateway	90-00-3C-A0-00-80
Customer use	D5-00-20-00-XX-XX
DECnet phase IV station addresses	55-00-20-00-XX-XX

Source Address Field

The source address field always represents an individual address which specifies the adapter card responsible for the transmission. The source address field consists of three major subfields, as illustrated in Figure 3.18. When locally administered addressing occurs, only 24 bits in the address field are used since the 22 manufacturer identification bit positions are not used.

The routing information bit identifier indicates the fact that routing information is contained in an optional routing information field. This bit is set when a frame is routed across a bridge using IBM's source routing technique.

Figure 3.18 Source address field (RI: routing information bit identifier, U/L: universally or locally administered bit identifier). The 46 address bits consist of 22 manufacturer identification bits and 24 universally administered bits when the U/L bit is set to 0. If set to 1, a 31-bit locally administered address is used with the manufacturer's identification bit set to 0.

Routing Information Field

The routing information field is optional and is included in a frame when the RI bit of the source address field is set. Figure 3.19 illustrates the format of the optional routing information field. If this field is omitted, the frame cannot leave the ring it was originated on under IBM's source routing bridging method. Under transparent bridging, the frame can be transmitted onto another ring. The routing information field is of variable length and contains a control subfield and one or more two-byte route designator fields when included in a frame as the latter are required to control the flow of frames across one or more bridges.

The maximum length of the routing information field (RIF) is 18 bytes. Since each RIF field must contain a two-byte routing control field, this leaves a maximum of 16 bytes available for use by up to eight route designators. As illustrated in Figure 3.19, each two-byte route designator consists of a 12-bit ring number and a four-bit bridge number. Thus, a maximum total of 16 bridges can be used to join any two rings in an Enterprise Token Ring network. Readers are referred to Chapter 5 for detailed information concerning source routing.

Information Field

The information field is used to contain Token Ring commands and responses as well as carry user data. The type of data carried by the information field depends upon the F bit settings in the frame type field. If the F bits are set to 00 the information field carries media access control (MAC) commands and responses that are used for network management operations. If the F bits are set to 01 the information field carries logical link

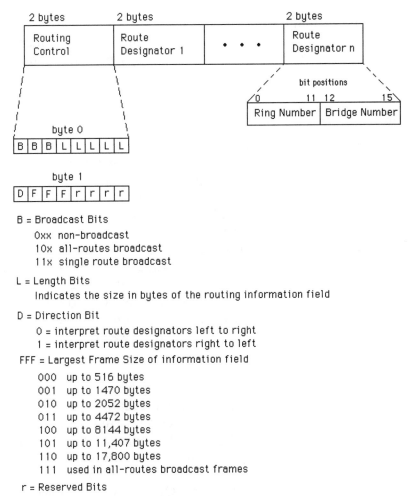

Figure 3.19   Routing information field.

control (LLC) or user data. Such data can be in the form of portions of a file being transferred on the network or an electronic mail message being routed to another workstation on the network. The information field is of variable length and represents the higher-level protocol enveloped or encapsulated in a Token Ring frame.

In the IBM implementation of the IEEE 802.5 Token Ring standard the maximum length of the information field depends upon the Token Ring adapter used and the operating rate of the network. Token Ring adapters with 64 Kbytes of memory can handle up to 4.5 Kbytes on a 4-Mbps network and up to 18 Kbytes on a 16-Mbps network.

Frame Check Sequence

The frame check sequence field contains four bytes which provide the mechanism for checking the accuracy of frames flowing on the network. The cyclic redundancy check data included in the frame check sequence field covers the frame control, destination address, source address, routing information, and information fields. If an adapter computes a cyclic redundancy check that does not match the data contained in the frame check sequence field of a frame, the destination adapter discards the frame information and sets an error bit (E bit) indicator. This error bit indicator, as previously discussed, actually represents a ninth bit position of the ending delimiter and serves to inform the transmitting station that the data was received in error.

Frame Status Field

The frame status field serves as a mechanism to indicate the results of a frame's circulation around a ring to the station that initiated the frame. Figure 3.20 indicates the format of the frame status field. The frame status field contains three subfields that are duplicated for accuracy purposes since they reside outside of CRC checking. One field (A) is used to denote whether an address was recognized, while a second field (C)

```
A C r r A C r r
```

A = Address-Recognized Bits
B = Frame-Copied Bits
r = Reserved Bits

Figure 3.20 Frame status field. The frame status field denotes whether the destination address was recognized and whether the frame was copied. Since this field is outside of CRC checking, its subfields are duplicated for accuracy.

indicates whether the frame was copied at its destination. Each of these fields is one bit in length. The third field, which is two bit positions in length (rr), is reserved for future use.

TOKEN RING MEDIUM ACCESS CONTROL

As previously discussed, a MAC frame is used to transport network commands and responses. As such, the MAC layer controls the routing of information between the LLC and the physical network. Examples of MAC protocol functions include the recognition of adapter addresses, physical medium access management, and message verification and status generation. A MAC frame is indicated by the setting of the first two bits in the frame control field to 00. When this situation occurs, the contents of the information field which carries MAC data is known as a *vector*.

Vectors and Subvectors

Only one vector is permitted per MAC frame. That vector consists of a major vector length (VL), a major vector identifier (VI), and zero or more subvectors.

As indicated in Figure 3.21, there can be multiple subvectors within a vector. The vector length (VL) is a 16-bit number that gives the length of the vector, including the VL subfield in bytes. VL can vary between decimal 4 and 65 535 in value. The minimum value that can be assigned to VL results from the fact that the smallest information field must contain both VL and VI subfields. Since each subfield is two bytes in length, the minimum value of VL is 4.

When one or more subvectors is contained in a MAC information field, each subvector contains three fields. The subvector length (SVL) is an eight-bit number which indicates the length of the subvector. Since an eight-bit number has a maximum value of 255 and cannot indicate a length exceeding 256 bytes (0-255), a method was required to accommodate subvector values (SVV) longer than 254 bytes. The method used is the placement of hex FF in the SVL field to indicate that SVV exceeds

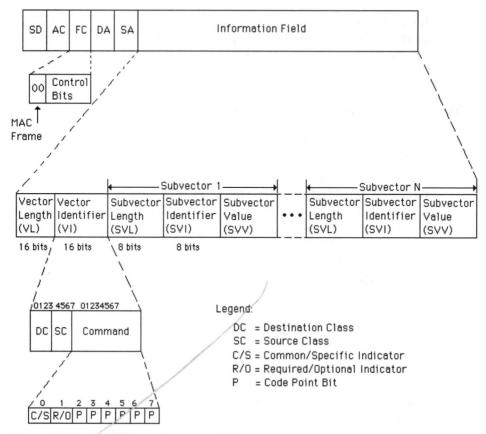

Figure 3.21 MAC frame information field format.

254 bytes. Then, the actual length is placed in the first two bytes following SVL. Finally, each SVV contains the data to be transmitted. The command field within the major vector identifier contains bit values referred to as code points which uniquely identify the type of MAC frame. Figure 3.21 illustrates the format of the MAC frame information field, while Table 3.11 lists currently defined vector identifier codes for six MAC control frames defined under the IEEE 802.5 standard.

MAC Control

As previously discussed, each ring has a station known as the active monitor which is responsible for monitoring tokens and taking action to prevent the endless circulation of a token on a ring.

Table 3.11 Vector Identifier Codes

Code Value	MAC Frame Meaning
010	Beacon (BCN)
011	Claim token (CL_TK)
100	Purge MAC frame (PRG)
101	Active monitor present (AMP)
110	Standby monitor present (SMP)
111	Duplicate address test (DAT)

Other stations function as standby monitors and one such station will assume the functions of the active monitor if that device should fail or be removed from the ring. For the standby monitor with the highest network address to take over the functions of the active monitor, the standby monitor needs to know there is a problem with the active monitor. If no frames are circulating on the ring but the active monitor is operating, the standby monitor might falsely presume the active monitor has failed. Thus, the active monitor will periodically issue an active monitor present (AMP) MAC frame. This frame must be issued every 7 seconds to inform the standby monitors that the active monitor is operational. Similarly, standby monitors periodically issue a standby monitor present (SMP) MAC frame to denote they are operational.

If an active monitor fails to send an AMP frame within the required time interval, the standby monitor with the highest network address will continuously transmit claim token (CL_TK) MAC frames in an attempt to become the active monitor. The standby monitor will continue to transmit CL_TK MAC frames until one of three conditions occurs:

■ A MAC CL_TK frame is received and the sender's address exceeds the standby monitor's station address.
■ A MAC beacon (BCN) frame is received.
■ A MAC purge (PRG) frame is received.

If one of the preceding conditions occurs, the standby monitor will cease its transmission of CL_TK frames and resume its standby function.

Purge Frame

If a CL_TK frame issued by a standby monitor is received back without modification and neither a beacon nor a purge frame is received in response to the CL_TK frame, the standby monitor becomes the active monitor and transmits a purge MAC frame. The purge frame is also transmitted by the active monitor each time a ring is initialized or if a token is lost. Once a purge frame is transmitted, the transmitting device will place a token back on the ring.

Beacon Frame

In the event of a major ring failure, such as a cable break or the continuous transmission by one station (known as jabbering), a beacon frame will be transmitted. The transmission of BCN frames can be used to isolate ring faults. For an example of the use of a beacon frame consider Figure 3.22, in which a cable fault results in a ring break. When a station detects a serious problem with the ring, such as the failure to receive a frame or token, it transmits a beacon frame. That frame defines a failure domain which consists of the station reporting the failure via the transmission of a beacon and its *nearest active upstream neighbor* (NAUN), as well as everything between the two.

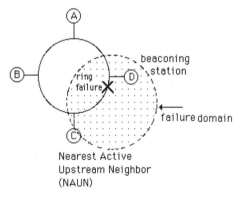

Figure 3.22 Beaconing. A beaconing frame indicates a failure occurring between the beaconing station and its nearest active upstream neighbor—an area referred to as a failure domain.

If a beacon frame makes its way back to the issuing station, that station will remove itself from the ring and perform a series of diagnostic tests to determine if it should attempt to reinsert itself into the ring. This procedure ensures that a ring error caused by a beaconing station can be compensated for by having that station remove itself from the ring. Since beacon frames indicate a general area where a failure occurred, they also initiate a process known as autoreconfiguration. The first step in the autoreconfiguration process is the diagnostic testing of the beaconing station's adapter. Other steps in the autoreconfiguration process include diagnostic tests performed by other nodes located in the failure domain in an attempt to reconfigure a ring around a failed area.

Duplicate Address Test Frame

The last type of MAC command frame is the duplicate address test (DAT) frame. This frame is transmitted during a station initialization process when a station joins a ring. The station joining the ring transmits a MAC DAT frame with its own address in the frame's destination address field. If the frame returns to the originating station with its address-recognized (A) bit in the frame control field set to 1, this means that another station on the ring is assigned that address. The station attempting to join the ring will send a message to the ring network manager concerning this situation and will not join the network.

Station Insertion

Depending upon the type of LAN adapter installed in your workstation, you may observe a series of messages at the format "Phase X" followed by the message "Completed" or "Passed" when you power on your computer. Those messages reference a five-phase ring insertion process during which your workstation's Token Ring adapter attempts to become a participant on the ring. Table 3.12 lists the steps in the ring insertion process.

During the lobe testing phase, the adapter transmits a series of Lobe Media Test MAC frames to the multistation access unit (MAU). Those frames should be wrapped at the MAU, re-

Table 3.12 Ring Station Insertion Process

Phase 0: Lobe testing
Phase 1: Monitor check
Phase 2: Duplicate address check
Phase 3: Participation in neighbor notification
Phase 4: Request initialization

sulting in their return to the adapter. Assuming the returned frames are received correctly, the adapter sends a five-volt DC current, which opens a relay at the MAU port and results in an attachment to the ring.

After the station attaches to the ring, it sets a value in a timer known as the Insert-timer and watches for an AMP, SMP, or Purge MAC frame prior to the timer expiring. If the timer expires, a token-claiming process is initiated. If the station is the first station on the ring, it then becomes the active monitor.

Once the Monitor Check Phase is completed, the station transmits a Duplicate Address Test frame during which the destination and source address fields are set to the station's universal address. If a duplicate address is found when the A bit is set to 1, the station cannot become a participant on the ring and detaches itself from the ring.

Assuming the station has a unique address, it next begins the neighbor notification process. During this ring insertion phase, the station learns the address of its nearest active upstream neighbor (NAUN) and reports its address to its nearest active downstream neighbor.

The address learning process begins when the active monitor transmits an AMP frame. The first station that receives the frame and is able to copy it sets the address-recognized (A) and frame-copied (C) bits to "1." The station then saves the source address from the copied frame as the NAUN address and initiates a Notification-Response timer. As the frame circulates the ring, other active stations only repeat it as its A and C bits were set.

When the Notification-Response timer of the first station downstream from the active monitor expires, it broadcasts an SMP frame. The next station downstream copies its NAUN address from the source address field of the SMP frame and sets the A and C bits in the frame to "1." Then, it starts its own Noti-fication-Response time which, upon expiration, results in that station transmitting its SMP frame. As the SMP frames origi-nate from different stations, the notification process proceeds around the ring until the active monitor copies its NAUN ad-dress from an SMP frame. At this point, the active monitor sets its Neighbor-Notification Complete flag to 1, which indicates that the neighbor notification process was successfully com-pleted.

The final phase in the ring insertion process occurs after the neighbor notification process is completed. During this phase, the station's adapter transmits a Request Initialization frame to the ring parameter server. The server responds with an Initial-ize-Ring-Station frame which contains values that enable all stations on the ring to use the same ring number and soft error report time value, thereby completing the insertion process.

TOKEN RING LOGICAL LINK CONTROL

Similar to Ethernet, the Token Ring LLC sublayer is responsible for performing routing, error control, and flow control. In addi-tion, this sublayer is responsible for providing a consistent view of a LAN to upper OSI layers, regardless of the type of media and protocols used on the network.

Figure 3.23 illustrates the format of an LLC frame which is carried within the information field of the Token Ring frame. The setting of the first two bits in the frame control field of a Token Ring frame to 01 indicates that the information field should be interpreted as an LLC frame. The portion of the Token Ring frame which carries LLC information is known as a proto-col data unit and consists of either three or four fields, depend-ing upon the inclusion or omission of an optional information field. The control field is similar to the control field used in the HDLC protocol and defines three types of frames—information (I-frames) are used for sequenced messages, supervisory (S-frames) are used for status and flow control, while unnumbered (U-frames) are used for unsequenced, unacknowledged mes-sages.

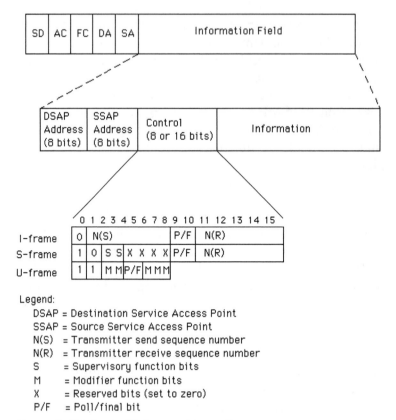

Figure 3.23 Logical link control frame format.

Service Access Points

Similar to our discussion concerning Ethernet, service access points (SAPs) can be considered interfaces to the upper layers of the OSI Reference Model, such as the network layer protocols. A station can have one or more SAPs associated with it for a specific layer and can have one or more active sessions initiated through a single SAP. Thus, a SAP functions much like a mailbox, containing an address which enables many types of mailings to reach the box. However, instead of mail, SAP addresses identify different network layer processes or protocols and function as locations where messages can be left concerning desired network services.

The first field in the LLC protocol data unit is the destination services access point (DSAP). The DSAP address field identifies one or more service access points for which information is to be delivered.

The second field in the LLC protocol data unit is the source services access point (SSAP). The SSAP address field identifies the service access point which transmitted the frame. Both DSAP and SSAP addresses are assigned to vendors by the IEEE to ensure that each is unique.

Both DSAPs and SSAPs are eight-bit fields; however, only seven bits are used for addressing, which results in a maximum of 128 distinct addresses available for each service access point. The eighth DSAP bit indicates whether the destination is an individual or a group address, while the eighth SSAP bit indicates whether the PDU contains a request or a response.

The control field contains information which defines how the LLC frame will be handled. U-frames are used for what is known as connectionless service in which frames are not acknowledged, while I-frames are used for connection-oriented services in which frames are acknowledged.

Types and Classes of Service

The types and classes of service supported by Token Ring is the same as those supported by Ethernet which was described in the section on Ethernet logical link control. Thus, readers are referred there for information concerning the types and classes of service supported by a Token Ring LAN.

FDDI

Fiber Distributed Data Interface (FDDI) represents an evolving local area networking standard which provides a 100-Mbps operating rate. In addition, due to the design of FDDI networks which incorporate counter-rotating rings, reliability is increased, since one ring functions as a backup to the other.

Work on FDDI dates to 1982, during which both vendors and standards bodies recognized the need for higher-speed LAN products and standards to govern the operation of those products. The FDDI standard was developed by the American National Standards Institute (ANSI) X3T9.5 Task Group. In addition, this standard is also being incorporated by the ISO as part of its OSI protocol suite.

The original intention of FDDI standards organizations was for the development of specifications for fiber optic media, optical transmitters and receivers, frame formats, protocols, and media access. However, recent developments in the use of twisted-pair has expanded the operation of FDDI to operate over that transmission medium. Known as CDDI with the C referencing copper, this technique has generated a considerable amount of interest. Several vendors had introduced FDDI over twisted-pair products and standards bodies were developing specifications that are expected to result in a new standard that will define 100-Mbps operations on twisted-pair cable.

Network Advantages

The major advantages of FDDI relate to its operating rate, reliability, and immunity to electromagnetic interference.

Operating Rate

FDDI provides an approximate five- to twentyfold increase in operating rates over previously developed Token Ring local area networks. This makes an FDDI network into an attractive mechanism to provide an interconnection capability to link lower-speed networks as well as to interconnect minicomputers and mainframes via an attachment to their high-speed channels. When functioning as a mechanism to interconnect lower-speed local area networks, an FDDI network serves as a backbone net. One example of its use would be the situation where each floor in a building has its own local area network. An FDDI network might then be routed vertically within the building, providing a high-speed link between individual networks on each floor.

Reliability

As previously mentioned, the FDDI standard specified dual fiber optic counter-rotating rings. The dual rings provide an architecture that permits redundancy that can negate the effect of a network failure. In fact, the FDDI standard defines a ring self-heading mechanism that enables stations to identify a failure and take corrective action. In doing so a station that identifies a cable fault would wrap an incoming signal on its healthy side onto an outgoing fiber. Its neighbor on the other side of the fault would also wrap away from the failure, resulting in a dual ring being converted into a single ring, which maintains network connectivity. This mechanism will be illustrated later in this section once we review the basic components of an FDDI network.

Use of Optical Media

Other advantages of FDDI primarily relate to its use of optical media. Those advantages include the ability to install optical cable without the use of a conduit, the extended transmission distance of an optical system, its immunity to electrical interference, and a high degree of security since an optical cable is almost impossible to tap.

Hardware Components, Network Topology, and Access

There is a range of hardware components used to construct an FDDI network. Those components include optical transmitters and receivers, the optical fiber used to carry information, single and dual attachment stations, and a concentrator.

The physical medium dependent (PMD) layer discussed in Chapter 2 defines the fiber type and size used in an FDDI network. In addition, this layer defines the connectors used on the fiber cable and the wavelength of the light beam transmitted. Thus, to comply with the PMD layer, optical transmitters and receivers must be compatible with the PMD layer's specifications.

Optical Transmitters

The function of the optical transmitter is to convert electrical signals into light signals that can be carried by the optical fiber used with FDDI networks. FDDI standards specify the use of a light-emitting diode (LED) in the optical transmitter that generates a light signal at a wavelength of 1300 nanometers (nm). This wavelength is shorter than the 1550 nm wavelength produced by lasers and permits less expensive LEDs to be used as the driving light source.

Currently, LEDs are used with multimode optical fiber cables. Although not standardized for use, laser diodes (LDs) are commonly used as the optical transmitter when single-mode optical fiber cables are used in an FDDI network. Both single-mode and multimode optical fiber cables are described later in this section.

Optical Receiver

An optical receiver recognizes an optical signal and converts that signal into an electrical signal. To accomplish this task, an optical receiver includes a photodetector which recognizes an optical signal as well as circuitry to generate an electrical signal.

Fiber Optic Cable

Under the PMD standard the type of cable, the wavelength of the optical signal, and the amount of power loss in the cable, which is known as *signal attenuation*, are specified.

The standard fiber specified by FDDI is a multimode fiber of 62.5/125 micron (10^{-6} meters). Multimode fiber references the fact that multiple modes or rays of light can flow over the fiber at the same time. The first number (62.5) references the core of the fiber, while the second number (125) references the fiber's cladding diameter. Figure 3.24 illustrates the components of a fiber optic cable and their relationship to one another.

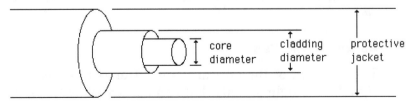

Figure 3.24 Fiber optic cable. The FDDI Physical Medium Dependent (PMD) standard specifies the use of multimode 62.5 (core diameter)/125 (cladding diameter) µm cable.

Although the PMD standard specifies the use of multimode 62.5/125 micron fiber, fiber sizes of 50/125, 82.5/125, and 100/40 microns are listed as alternatives. Smaller diameters provide a higher bandwidth capability, however, they are more expensive to manufacture. Conversely, larger diameters provide a lower bandwidth capability and are less expensive to produce.

Single-mode fiber, known as *monomode* in Europe, permits only one ray to be transmitted and has a much smaller core than multimode fiber—typically between 8 and 10 microns. Such fibers are designed to operate at a wavelength of 1300 nm, similar to FDDI multimode fiber. Due to the small core size of single-mode fiber, its use requires an optical transmitter containing a laser which is capable of concentrating more power into a smaller area than that obtainable through the use of an LED. The use of single-mode fiber and laser-based optical transmitters can significantly extend the transmission distance in comparison to the use of multimode fiber and LED-based optical transmitters.

Power Loss

In addition to specifying the type of cable and wavelength that flows on the cable, the PMD standard also specifies the permitted power loss of the cable. That loss, which is 1.5 dB per km at a wavelength of 1300 nm, results in a maximum fiber drive distance of 2 km between stations. Theoretically, this means that support of 500 stations representing the maximum number of stations on an FDDI network could result in a ring which extends over a 1000-km area. In reality, a total fiber length of 200 km is specified for FDDI networks, which means that many stations must be closer than 2 km from one another.

Connectors

A considerable amount of planning resulted in the specifications for connectors used for attaching physical stations to an FDDI ring. Physical connections between stations occur through the use of duplex connectors that are polarized to prevent transmitting and receiving fibers from being inadvertently interchanged. To both simplify cable assembly as well as prevent miswiring, cables are normally fabricated with different types of connectors. For example, the FDDI dual ring is implemented by a cable assembly which contains a type A connector on one end and a type B connector on the opposite end of the cable. Similarly, another type of cable assembly used to connect a single attached station to a concentrator has two different connectors. An M connector plugs into the M (master) port on a concentrator, while the S connector (slave) plugs into the S port on the single attached station. Although the use of different connectors precludes miswiring, it should be noted that you can obtain a cable with S type connectors on each cable end. The S connector can be considered a universal FDDI connector and a cable with dual S connectors can be used to interconnect any two FDDI ports. However, this type of cable should be used with care since it does not provide the cabling protection afforded by the use of cables with different connectors on each end.

Network Topology

To obtain an appreciation for the use of different devices used to connect stations to an FDDI network requires a short discussion of the topology and flow of tokens on that network.

Counter-Rotating Rings

FDDI uses two rings which are formed in a ring-star topology. One ring is known as the primary, while the other ring is known as the secondary ring. The primary ring is similar to the main ring path in a Token Ring network, while the secondary ring acts like the Token Ring backup ring path. However, the FDDI backup ring, unlike the Token-Ring backup path, can automatically be placed into operation as a "self-healing" mechanism. When this occurs, data flow is counter to the flow of data that occurred on the primary ring; this is the reason FDDI is known as a *counter-rotating ring topology*.

Token Use

Similar to the IEEE 802.5 token ring standard, a rotating token is used to provide stations with permission to transmit data. When an FDDI station wants to transmit information, it waits until it detects the token and captures or absorbs it. Once the station controls the token, it can transmit information until it either has no more data to send or until a token-holding timer expires. When either situation occurs, the station then releases the token onto the ring so it can be used by the next station that has data to transmit. This token-passing technique is more formally known as a timed-token-passing technique and uses bandwidth more efficiently than the 802.5 token-passing method. This is because only one token and one frame can be present on a Token Ring network. In comparison, although only one token is present on an FDDI network at any time, multiple frames from one or more stations can be traversing an FDDI network. Readers will find detailed information concerning the use of the token-holding timer and other timers used by FDDI stations to allocate bandwidth later in this section.

Network Access

Access to an FDDI network is accomplished through the use of three types of stations—a single attached station (SAS) and two types of dual attached stations (DAS).

Dual Attached Station

A dual attached station connects to both counter-rotating rings used to form an FDDI ring. Each DAS contains two defined optical connection pairs. One pair, called the A interface or port, contains one primary ring input and the secondary ring output. The second pair, called the B interface or port, contains the primary ring output and the secondary ring input. Through the use of two optical transceivers each DAS can transmit and receive data on each ring.

A second type of DAS is known as a concentrator. In addition to the previously described A and B interfaces, a DAS concentrator contains a series of extra ports that are called M, or master ports. The M ports on a DAS concentrator provide connectivity to single attached stations (SASs), a DAS, or another concentrator. Thus, the concentrator provides additional ports, which extends the ability to access the primary ring to other stations.

The connection between DAS nodes occurs through the use of two cable sheaths, each containing two fiber optic cables. One pair of cables functions as the primary ring, while the second pair of cables functions as a counter-rotating secondary ring used for backup operations. As previously noted, to insure the correct cabling to form a dual ring, a main ring cable used to interconnect two dual attached stations or a DAS to a concentrator contains a type A connector on one end and a type B connector on the other end of the cable.

Single Attached Station

In comparison to dual attached stations that provide a connection to the dual FDDI rings, a single attached station can only be connected to a single ring. The connection of single attached stations to a DAS concentrator can resemble a star topology, even though the interconnection of DAS and DAS concentrators forms a ring. The connection between SAS nodes is accomplished through the use of a single cable sheath containing two fiber optic cables. Since a single attached station contains only a single optical transceiver, its cost is less than a dual attached station. However, its inability to connect to the dual ring lowers its reliability in comparison to the connection of workstations to an FDDI network through a dual attached station.

One of the functions performed by the concentrator includes sensing when an attached SAS is not powered on. When this situation occurs, the concentrator electronically reroutes data to the next sequentially located station. This permits cable faults or a malfunctioning SAS to be electronically bypassed.

Figure 3.25 illustrates the major components of an FDDI network as well as how a ring can be reconfigured in the event of a cable fault or DAS failure. In this example, it was assumed that a cable fault occurred between the upper-right and extreme-right dual attached stations. Each of those stations has the capability to monitor light levels and recognize a cable failure. By two adjacent stations wrapping away from the failure, the dual ring becomes converted into a single ring and connectivity is restored. When the failure condition is corrected the restoration of an appropriate light level causes each DAS to remove the previously implemented wrap and restores the network to its dual ring operation.

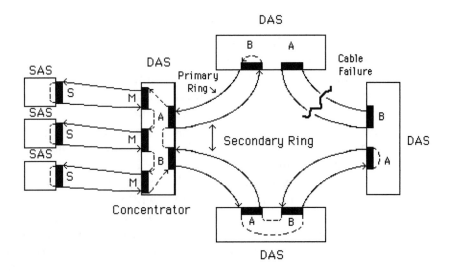

Legend:

A   – A interface contains primary ring input and secondary
        ring input
B   – B interface contains primary ring output and secondary
        ring input
M   – master port
S   – slave port
DAS – dual attached station
SAS – single attached station

Figure 3.25 FDDI ring operation during cable fault failure. Two dual-attached stations can perform a wrap operation to convert a dual ring into a single ring which bypasses a cable or device failure.

Data Encoding

The transmission of data on fiber optic cable is accomplished through the use of intensity modulation. That is, a binary 1 is represented by a pulse of light, while a binary 0 is represented by the absence of an optical signal.

One of the key problems associated with any signaling technique that uses the presence or absence of voltage, current, or light to denote binary digits is the potential lack of synchronization from the coding method. Intensity modulation is no exception to this problem, since long strings of 1s or 0s produced by simply turning a light signal on and off will result in a situation where a receiver must either have clocking circuitry or it will lose synchronization with the transmitter. Since clocking circuitry can be costly, a more economical alternative to obtain synchronization between transmitters and receivers is to encode binary data in such a manner that it guarantees the presence of signal transitions even when there are few transitions in the data being transmitted.

As previously explained in this chapter, 10 Mbps Ethernet networks use Manchester encoding while Token Ring networks use Differential Manchester encoding to obtain signal transitions that enable clocking to be derived from an incoming data stream. Although intensity modulation could be performed to encode data according to Manchester or Differential Manchester encoding, doing so would result in a baud rate of 200 M signals per second to obtain a 100-Mbps operating rate. This high signaling rate would be expensive to implement, thus, designers looked for another method to encode data and obtain the required level of signal transitions for receivers to derive clocking from a transmitted signal. That encoding and signaling method is first obtained by placing each group of four bits into a five-bit code (4B/5B encoding). Then, the five-bit group is transmitted using a non-return-to-zero inverted (NRZI) signaling method.

NRZI Signaling

NRZI signaling results in a change of state used to represent a 0 bit, while no change of state represents a binary 1. NRZI is a form of differential signaling in that the polarity of different signal elements can change when their state changes. This enables the signal to be decoded by comparing the polarity of adjacent signal elements instead of the absolute value of the signal element. However, by itself NRZI signaling will not insure a level of transitions necessary to keep a receiver in synchronization with a transmitter. This is because a long string of 0s or 1s will not have transitions. Thus, data must be encoded using the 4B/5B encoding technique, which enables NRZI signaling to produce the required signal transitions.

4B/5B Encoding

Under 4B/5B encoding, each group of four bits is encoded into a five-bit symbol. In addition to permitting signaling to be achieved at a 125-Mbps signal rate in comparison to a 200-M baud rate that would be required under Differential Manchester encoding, the use of 4B/5B encoding permits the design of the resulting 5B codes to insure that a transition occurs at least twice for each five-bit code.

Table 3.13 lists the FDDI 4B/5B codes. The use of the 5B code permits patterns beyond the 16 combinations available from a four-bit code to be used to represent special network-related functions. For example, the J and K bits used in Differential Manchester encoding for the Token Ring starting delimiter are developed as special 5B codes in FDDI to prefix tokens and frames. When we examine the FDDI frame formats later in this section, we will also examine the use of certain 5B code functions.

In examining Table 3.13, you will note that only twenty-four 5B codes are defined, even though 32 could be defined. The remaining eight 5B code combinations are either invalid, since under NRZI signaling no more than three zeros in a row are allowed, or represent a "Halt" if received code.

Frame Formats

Similar to Token Ring networks, there are distinct frames and frame formats that are used on FDDI networks for information transfer. Figure 3.26 illustrates two FDDI frame formats used to transfer information. Like Token Ring networks, the basic FDDI frame can convey MAC control data and LLC information. In addition, a station management frame permits management information to be transported between stations and higher-level processes. As defined by ANSI, the station management (SMT) standard is used to control the FDDI PMD, PHY, and MAC layers. Services provided by SMT include fault detection, fault isolation, and ring reconfiguration. Data carried by SMT frames can be used by such higher-level processes as Simple Network Management Protocol (SNMP) services to

Table 3.13 FDDI 4B/5B Codes

Function/4-Bit Group	5B Code	Symbol
Starting delimiter		
First symbol of sequential SD pair	11000	J
Second symbol of sequential SD pair	10001	K
Ending delimiter	01101	T
Data symbols		
0000	11110	0
0001	01001	1
0010	10100	2
0011	10101	3
0100	01010	4
0101	01011	5
0110	01110	6
0111	01111	7
1000	10010	8
1001	10011	9
1010	10110	10
1011	10111	11
1100	11010	12
1101	11011	13
1110	11100	14
1111	11101	15
Control indicators		
Logical ZERO (reset)	00111	R
Logical ONE (set)	11001	S
Line status symbols		
Quiet	00000	Q
Idle	11111	I
Halt	00100	H

permit network administrators to monitor and control each FDDI network node from a central console. In addition to collecting data, SMT provides network administrators with the ability to dynamically alter the network by adding or removing predefined stations. Thus, SMT frames carry both monitoring and control information.

FDDI Token

As illustrated in the top portion of Figure 3.26, the FDDI token consists of five fields. The preamble field is variable in length and is formed by 16 or more 5B I symbols. The starting delimiter field consists of the 5B J symbol followed by the 5B K symbol. That field is followed by the frame control field, which identifies the type of frame.

The frame control field is eight bits in length, with the class and length of address fields bit positions used to indicate one of

a. FDDI Token

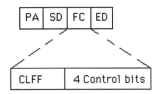

b. FDDI Frame

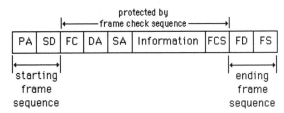

PA – Preamble
SD – Starting delimiter
FC – Frame control
ED – Ending delimiter
DA – Destination address
SA – Source address
FCS – Frame check sequence
FS – Frame status
C – Class bit
L – Length of address fields
FF – Format
Control bits – depend upon frame type

Figure 3.26 FDDI frame formats.

two possible settings per bit position. When the class bit is set to 0, this indicates an asynchronous class of transmission, while setting the class bit to 1 indicates a synchronous class of transmission. The length of address fields bit indicates the use of 48 bit addressing fields when set to 0 and the use of 16 bit addressing fields when set to 1. The two format bits are used to indicate a MAC or SMT frame when set to 00 or an LLC frame when set to 01. A setting of 10 is implementation dependent, while a setting of 11 is reserved for future use. The second half of the frame control field consists of four control bits whose values are dependent upon the type of frame defined by the format bits.

There are two special values that can be assigned to the frame control field—hex 80 and hex C0. If the frame control field is set to hex 80 it indicates an unrestricted token, while a value of hex C0 in this eight-bit field indicates a restricted token. The restricted token is generated by a station on an FDDI network that wishes to communicate with another station using all of the asynchronous bandwidth available on the network. Later in this section we will discuss the allocation of bandwidth on an FDDI network and the two classes of traffic on that network—*asynchronous* and *synchronous*.

When the frame control field is directly followed by the ending delimiter an FDDI token is formed. Here the ending delimiter is the 5B T symbol.

FDDI Frame

As indicated in Figure 3.26, the first three fields of the FDDI token and frame are the same. Thereafter, the frame contains destination and source address fields which identify the frame recipient and frame originator, respectively. Each address field can be either 16 or 48 bits in length but must be of similar length.

The source address field is followed by a variable information field that can range in length from 0 to 4472 bytes. That field is followed by a frame check sequence (FCS) field 32 bits in length which protects all data from the frame control field through the information field. The ending delimiter and frame status fields function as the ending FDDI frame sequence, with the ending delimiter formed by the use of the 5B T symbol which consists of the bit pattern 01101.

There are two versions of the FDDI frame format that warrant a degree of elaboration. Those frame formats are FDDI_ 802.2 and FDDI_SNAP, both created through the modification of the FDDI's information field.

FDDI_802.2

Similar to the manner by which Token Ring's information field can convey MAC and LLC information, an FDDI frame's I field provides the same capability. When doing so the Frame control field value indicates the occurrence of a MAC/SMT or LLC field within the information field. Figure 3.27 illustrates what is referred to as an FDDI_802.2 FDDI MAC frame containing 802.3 LLC information.

In examining Figure 3.27, the DSAP and SSAP again identify the protocol or application above the data link layer which will receive the frame. The control field specifies the type of LLC

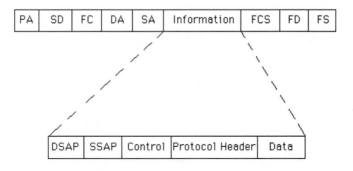

Legend: PA – Preamble
SD – Starting delimiter
FC – Frame control
DA – Destination address
SA – Source address
FCS – Frame check sequence
FS – Frame status
DSAP – Destination service access point
SSAP – Source service access point

Figure 3.27 FDDI_802.2 MAC with 802.3 LLC.

service and can be either one or two bytes in length. The most common service is Type 1, which uses a one-byte control field, while a reliable delivery service (Type 2) uses an extra byte.

The FDDI_802.2 frame does not include a mechanism for equipment vendors and other organizations to define proprietary protocols in a manner which eliminates the possibility that such protocols can be confused with other proprietary protocols operating on the same LAN. Recognizing that problem as well as the small range of DSAP and SSAP values resulted in the definition of an FDDI SubNetwork Access Protocol (SNAP) frame.

FDDI_SNAP

The FDDI_SNAP protocol frame extends the DSAP and SSAP fields through the use of a five-byte *protocol identification field*. By convention, an FDDI_SNAP frame uses the Type 1 LLC service with DSAP and SSAP values of hex AA and a control field value of 03.

Figure 3.28 illustrates the format of the FDDI_SNAP frame. Note that the five-byte protocol identifier consists of a three-byte *organizationally unique identifier* (OUI) and a two-byte extension. The OUI represents the unique three-byte prefix assigned by the IEEE for the creation of vendor six-byte MAC addresses. Thus, a vendor that is assigned an OUI can use it to generate up to 65,000 private proprietary protocol identifiers for SubNetwork Access protocols.

One common use of the FDDI_SNAP frame format is the encoding of Ethernet in the 802.2 SNAP frame. To do so, DSAP and SSAP values of hex AA, a control value of 03, and an OUI value of 00-00-00 are used. This method of encoding is defined by the Internet Engineering Task Force (IETF) in Request For Comment (RFC) 1042. Under RFC 1042, the two-byte protocol type field contains the Ethernet type field value.

Bandwidth Allocation

In a Token Ring network, access is obtained by the setting of priority and reservation bits which enables a station to acquire a token. Once a token is acquired, it is converted into a single

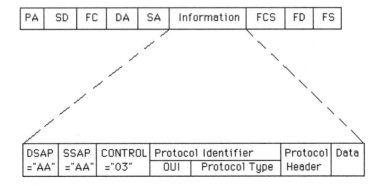

Legend: PA – Preamble
SD – Starting delimiter
FC – Frame control
DA – Destination address
SA – Source address
FCS – Frame check sequence
FS – Frame status
DSAP – Destination service access point
SSAP – Source service access point
OUI – Organizationally unique identifier

Figure 3.28 FDDI_SSNAP frame format.

frame to transport a unit of information. In comparison, a token flowing on an FDDI network is removed from the network by a station that has data to transmit—a process referred to as *absorption*. Once a token is absorbed, the absorbing station can transmit one or more frames prior to returning the token onto the network, with the number of frames that can be transmitted based upon the frame size and the setting of timers within the station. Thus, any discussion of FDDI bandwidth allocation must consider the timers supported by each station in an FDDI network. Since those timers, as well as the frame control field of an FDDI token, govern the two classes of traffic that can be carried by an FDDI network, a logical place to initiate an explanation of FDDI bandwidth allocation is by explaining the two classes of traffic supported by this network. Once we do this we will then examine the timers supported by each FDDI station and then use the preceding to discuss how an FDDI network allocates bandwidth capacity.

Classes of Traffic

FDDI defines two classes of traffic—asynchronous and synchronous. These classes of transmission should not be confused with an asynchronous and synchronous mode of transmission. The asynchronous class of transmission is transmission that occurs when the token-holding rules of an FDDI network permit transmission. In comparison, the synchronous class of transmission results in a guaranteed percentage of the ring's bandwidth allocated for a particular transmission. Once synchronous bandwidth is allocated, the remaining bandwidth becomes available for asynchronously transmitted frames. That bandwidth is shared by all stations in a fair and equitable manner based upon the use of timers.

Timers

The control of the amount of asynchronous and synchronous traffic that can be transmitted by a station is governed by FDDI's timed token access protocol. This protocol is based upon the use of timers used by each station to regulate their operation. These timers include a token rotation timer (TRT), token-holding timer (THT), and valid transmission timer (TVX).

Token Rotation Timer The TRT is used to time the period between the receipt of tokens. Under the timed token access protocol, stations expect to see a token within a specified period of time, referred to as the *target token rotation time* (TTRT). The value for the TTRT is set when a station initializes itself on the ring and is the same for all stations on the ring.

When a token passes a station, the station sets its TRT to the value of the TTRT and then decrements its TRT timer. If the TRT timer expires prior to the token returning to the station, a counter known as the late counter is incremented. The decision on whether a station can transmit a synchronous or asynchronous class of traffic depends upon the value of the TRT and the value of a counter known as the late counter.

When a token arrives at a station three events occur which govern the allocation of bandwidth. First, upon receiving a token a station can initiate the transmission of synchronous frames. Whether it does so and the number of frames it can transmit depend upon several factors that will be discussed shortly.

Token-Holding Timer   If the token was received earlier than expected, the token rotation time (TRT) timer will be positive and the station will store that value in its token-holding timer (THT). Thus, the value of the THT timer represents the amount of time by which the token was received earlier than expected. Finally, the station resets the TRT timer to the value assigned to the target token rotation timer (TTRT) and begins to decrement that timer.

Synchronous Transmission

As previously mentioned, the receipt of a token enables a station to initiate the transmission of synchronous frames. The ability of a station to transmit synchronous frames depends upon whether the station was enabled by an application for synchronous transmission. If enabled, the number of synchronous frames the station can transmit is based upon the size of each frame to be transmitted and the time allocated for synchronous transmission. The frame size governs the amount of time required to place a frame on the ring, while the total time the station can transmit synchronously is based upon the value of the station's synchronous allocation timer. That timer is set to zero when a station is not enabled by an application for synchronous transmission. When enabled for synchronous transmission, the value of the synchronous allocation timer can be different for each station on the ring; however, the sum of all synchronous allocation timers on the active stations on the ring must always be less than the target token rotation time.

  If enabled for synchronous transmission, a station will either transmit all the frames it has synchronously or only those frames that can be transmitted within the allocated synchronous allocation timer value. When that timer expires or all synchronous frames are transmitted and the timer has not expired, the station may then be able to transmit asynchronous frames.

Asynchronous Transmission

The decision of whether a station can transmit asynchronous frames is based upon the value of the late counter. If the value of the late counter is zero, which means that the TRT timer did not expire, asynchronous frames can be transmitted for the length of time stored in the token-holding timer (THT). When the value of that timer reaches zero the token must then be placed back onto the ring.

During both synchronous and asynchronous transmission, the token rotation timer (TRT) continues to decrement. If both synchronous and asynchronous transmissions were stopped due to the expiration of the synchronous allocation timer and the token-holding timer and other stations have data to send, the TRT can be expected to expire prior to the token reappearing at the station. When this occurs, the token will be late, the TRT will be zero, and the THT will also be set to zero. With a value of zero in the token-holding timer, the station cannot transmit any asynchronous frames the next time it receives a token. Thus, the timed token access protocol penalizes a station that transmitted its fully allocated amount of traffic; however, the penalty only applies to asynchronous traffic and a station can always transmit synchronous traffic when it receives a token.

If the station is penalized, the next token will arrive early and the station's late counter will be decremented. Once the value of the late counter reaches zero, the station can again begin to transmit asynchronous traffic.

The preceding bandwidth allocation method guarantees an amount of ring capacity to synchronous traffic. Asynchronous traffic is only transmitted when there is spare capacity on the ring and the use of the previously described counters and timers provides a level of fairness for asynchronous transmission.

In discussing the composition of the frame control field, we mentioned that a setting of hex 80 indicates a restricted token. The use of this type of token provides another mechanism for allocating asynchronous transmission by permitting two stations to use all of the asynchronous bandwidth available on the ring. When one station wishes to communicate with another station using all of the available asynchronous bandwidth, it transmits its asynchronous frames and then releases a restricted token. Due to

FDDI rules, only the last station that receives an asynchronous frame can use a restricted token for asynchronous transmission; this enables two stations to continue transmitting to one another. Since the restricted token is applicable only to asynchronous transmission, any station that has synchronous traffic can use that token, insuring that the guaranteed level of synchronous bandwidth remains available to all stations on the ring.

Transmission Example

To illustrate the FDDI capacity-allocation algorithm, let us assume that the target token rotation timer was set to 100 milliseconds for all stations, while the synchronous allocation timer was set to 10 milliseconds for our station. Table 3.14 lists the settings of the different station timers and the occurrence of different events during the capacity allocation process for a station on an FDDI network based upon several predefined events occurring on the ring. By examining the entries in Table 3.14, readers will obtain an appreciation for the method by which timers and the late counter govern the ability of stations to transmit asynchronous and synchronous traffic.

ATM

In concluding this section we will focus our attention upon an emerging technology which represents a mechanism for the integration of LANs and WANs as well as the ability to transport voice, data, and video between private and public networks. This emerging technology is known as *asynchronous transfer mode* (ATM) and offers the ability to remove the barriers between local and wide area networks, providing a seamless interconnection for LAN internetworking between geographically separated areas.

Benefits

ATM has several significant benefits over such legacy LANs as Ethernet and Token Ring. First, unlike Ethernet and Token Ring, which are shared media access networks, ATM is a point-to-point switched based network. This means that unlike Ether-

Table 3.14 FDDI Capacity Allocation Process Example

1. Token arrives at stations.
2. TRT is set to value of TTRT (100 ms).
3. Token absorbed by station.
4. Synchronous traffic transmitted for 10 ms (synchronous allocation timer value).
5. Token released onto ring.
6. Token reappears 50 ms later.
7. Token absorbed.
8. TRT now 40 ms due to 10 ms transmission of synchronous traffic and 50 ms on ring.
9. Token holding timer set to TRT value (40 ms).
10. TRT reset to 100 and begins to decrement.
11. Synchronous traffic again sent for 10 ms.
12. Asynchronous traffic sent for 40 ms (THT value).
13. TRT now has a value of 50 (100-10-40).
14. Token released.
15. Assume other stations transmit data and token reappears after 70 ms.
16. TRT expires and late counter incremented to a value of 1.
17. THT set to a value of 0.
18. Assume no synchronous traffic to be sent. Asynchronous traffic cannot be sent since TRT expired and THT now has a value of 0.
19. TRT reset to 100.
20. Assume token reappears in 30 ms.
21. TRT now set to 70 ms. Although token is early the late count has a value of 1. Thus, token considered to be late and the station can only transmit synchronous traffic.
22. Token absorbed.
23. Station transmits synchronous traffic for 10 ms (synchronous allocation timer value).
24. Late count value decremented to 0.
25. Token placed back on ring.
26. Assume token reappears 40 ms later.
27. TRT now set to 70-40, or 30 ms. Since late count is 0, station can transmit asynchronous traffic for up to 30 ms.

net and Token Ring, where the bandwidth is shared by all users, an ATM user receives the full bandwidth of the connection. Second, ATM transmits data in fixed-sized cells suitable for transporting voice, data, and video. In actuality, ATM can be considered to represent a special type of packet switching in which the packet size is fixed. In comparison, most other types of packet-switching technologies, such as X.25 and frame relay, are based upon variable-length packets.

The ATM packet is relatively short, containing a 48-byte information field and a five-byte header. This fixed-length packet, which is illustrated in Figure 3.29, is called a *cell*, and the umbrella technology for the movement of cells is referred to as *cell relay*. ATM represents a specific type of cell relay service which is defined under broadband ISDN (BISDN) standards.

The selection of a relatively short 53-byte ATM cell was based upon the necessity to minimize the effect of data transportation upon voice.

In addition to its relatively short cell length facilitating the integration of voice and data, ATM provides three additional benefits. Those benefits are in the areas of scalability, transparency, and traffic classification.

Scalability

ATM cells can be transported on LANs and WANs at a variety of operating rates. This enables different hardware, such as LAN and WAN switches to support a common cell format, a feature lacking with other communications technologies. Within a few years, an ATM cell generated on a 25-Mbps LAN will be able to be transported from the LAN via a T1 line at 1.544 Mbps to a central office where it might be switched onto a 2.4 Gbps SONET network for transmission on the communications carrier infrastructure, with the message maintained in the same series of 53-byte cells, with only the operating rate scaled for a particular transport mechanism.

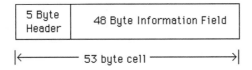

The ATM cell is of fixed length, consisting of a 48-byte information field and five-byte header.

Figure 3.29 The ATM cell.

Transparency

The ATM cell is application transparent, enabling it to transport voice, data, images, and video. Due to its application transparency, ATM enables networks to be constructed to support any type of application or application mix instead of requiring organizations to establish separate networks for different applications.

Traffic Classification

Five classes of traffic are supported by ATM to include one constant bit rate, three types of variable bit rates, and a user-definable class. By associating such metrics as cell transit delay, cell loss ratio, and cell delay variation to a traffic class, it becomes possible to provide a guaranteed quality of service on a demand basis. This enables a traffic management mechanism to adjust network performance during periods of unexpected congestion to favor traffic classes based upon the metrics associated with each class.

The ATM Protocol Stack

Similar to other networking architectures, ATM is a layered protocol. The ATM protocol stack is illustrated in Figure 3.30 and consists of three layers—the ATM adaptation layer (AAL), the ATM layer, and the physical layer. Both the AAL and physical layers are subdivided into two sublayers. Although the ATM protocol stack consists of three layers, as we will shortly note, those layers are essentially equivalent to the first two layers of the ISO Reference Model.

ATM Adaptation Layer

As illustrated in Figure 3.30, the ATM adaptation layer consists of two sublayers—a convergence sublayer and a segmentation and reassembly sublayer. The function of the AAL is to adapt higher-level data into formats compatible with ATM layer requirements. To accomplish this task the ATM adaptation layer subdivides user information into segments suitable for encapsulation into the 48-byte information fields of cells. The actual

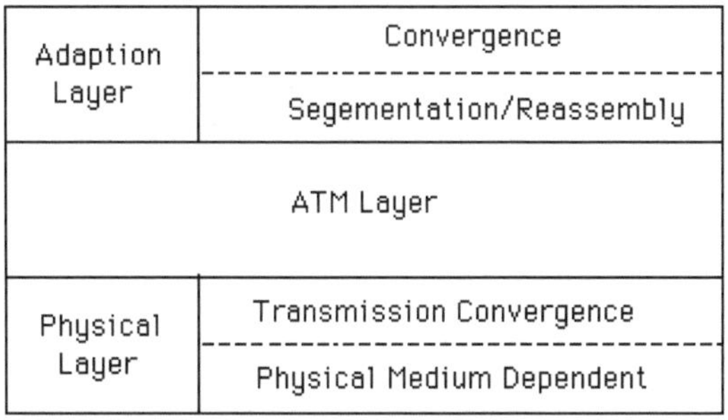

Adaption Layer	Convergence
	Segementation/Reassembly
ATM Layer	
Physical Layer	Transmission Convergence
	Physical Medium Dependent

Figure 3.30   The ATM protocol stack.

adaptation process depends upon the type of traffic to be transmitted, although all traffic winds up in similar cells. Currently there are five different AALs defined, referred to as AAL classes, which are described later in this section.

When receiving information, the ATM adaptation layer performs a reverse process. That is, it takes cells received from the network and reassembles them into a format that the higher layers in the protocol stack understand. This process is known as *reassembly*. Thus, the segmentation and reassembly processes result in the name of the sublayer that performs those processes.

ATM Layer

As illustrated in Figure 3.30, the ATM layer provides the interface between the AAL and the physical layer. The ATM layer is responsible for relaying cells both from the AAL to the physical layer and to the AAL from the physical layer. The actual method by which the ATM layer performs this function depends upon its location within an ATM network. Since an ATM network consists of endpoints and switches, the ATM layer can reside at either location. Similarly, a physical layer is required at both ATM endpoints and ATM switches.

Since a switch examines the information within an ATM cell to make switching decisions, it does not perform any adaptation functions. Thus, the ATM switch operates at layers 1 and 2, while ATM endpoints operate at layers 1 through 3 of the ATM protocol stack, as shown in Figure 3.31.

When the ATM layer resides at an endpoint, it will generate idle or "empty" cells whenever there is no data to send, a func-

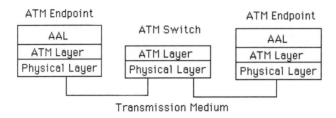

The ATM Adaption Layer is only required at endpoints within an ATM network.

Figure 3.31 The ATM protocol stack within a network.

tion not performed by a switch. Instead, in the switch the ATM layer is concerned with facilitating switching functions, examining cell header information which enables the switch to determine where each cell should be forwarded to. For both endpoints and switches, the ATM layer performs a variety of traffic management functions to include buffering incoming and outgoing cells as well as monitoring the transmission rate and conformance of transmission to service parameters that define a quality of service. At endpoints the ATM layer also indicates to the AAL whether or not there was congestion during transmission, permitting higher layers to initiate congestion control.

Physical Layer

Although Figures 3.30 and 3.31 illustrate an ATM physical layer, a specific physical layer is not defined within the protocol stack. Instead, ATM uses the interfaces to existing physical layers defined in other protocols which enables organizations to construct ATM networks on different types of physical interfaces which in turn connect to different types of media. Thus, the omission of a formal physical layer specification results in a significant degree of flexibility which enhances the capability of ATM to operate on LANs and WANs.

ATM Operation

ATM networks are constructed upon the use of five main hardware components. Those components include ATM network interface cards, LAN switches, ATM routers, ATM WAN switches, and ATM service processors.

ATM Network Interface Cards

An ATM network interface card (NIC) is used to connect a LAN-based workstation to an ATM LAN switch. The NIC converts data generated by the workstation into cells that are transmitted to the ATM LAN switch and converts cells received from the switch into a data format recognizable by the workstation.

LAN Switch

A LAN switch is a device used to provide interoperability between older LANs, such as Ethernet, Token Ring or FDDI, and ATM. To do so the LAN switch supports a minimum of two types of interfaces, with one being an ATM interface which enables the switch to be connected to an ATM switch that forms the backbone of the ATM infrastructure. The other interface or interfaces represent connections to older types of LANs.

The LAN switch functions as both a switch and protocol converter. Data received on one port destined to the ATM network is converted from frames to cells and transferred to the switch port providing a connection to the ATM switch. Since one LAN switch port can be capable of servicing a LAN segment, the use of a switch can minimize an organization's investment in ATM NICs. This is illustrated in Figure 3.32, which shows the use of a LAN switch with a single ATM port to provide access to an ATM network for individual workstations connected directly to individual switch ports as well as a group of workstations on a LAN segment. Through the use of the LAN switch, an organization can selectively upgrade existing LANs to ATM while obtaining a connection to the ATM network, however, to do so, a process known as LAN emulation, which is described both later in this chapter and in Chapter 7, must be performed.

ATM Router

An ATM router is a router containing one or more ATM NICs. As such, it can provide a direct or indirect capability for LAN workstations to access an ATM network or for two ATM networks to be interconnected. For example, a network segment or individual workstations could be connected to a router which in turn is connected to a LAN switch or directly to an ATM switch.

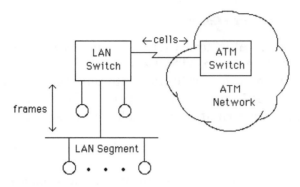

A LAN switch provides both a switching and protocol conversion function, allowing non-ATM devices to access an ATM
network.

legend
○ workstations

Figure 3.32 Using a LAN switch.

ATM Switch

An ATM switch is a multiport device which forms the basic infrastructure for an ATM network. Unlike a LAN switch, an
ATM switch permits only a single end station to be connected to
each switch port. By interconnecting ATM switches an ATM
network can be constructed to span a building, city, country, or
the globe.

The basic operation of an ATM switch is to route cells from
an input port onto an appropriate output port. To accomplish
this, the switch examines fields within each cell header and uses
that information in conjunction with table information maintained in the switch to route cells. Later in this section we will
examine the composition of the ATM cell header in detail.

One of the key features of ATM switches reaching the market during the mid 1990s is their rate adaptation capability
which in general is a function of the transmission media used to
connect endpoints and to connect switches to other switches.
Table 3.15 lists some of the communications rates associated
with different transmission media.

Table 3.15 ATM Communications Operating Rates

Operating Rate (Mbps)	Transmission Media
25-51	Unshielded twisted pair category 3
100	Multimode fiber
155	Shielded twisted pair
622	Single-mode fiber

ATM Service Processor

An ATM service processor is a computer operating software which performs services required for ATM network operations. For example, an ATM network address can have one of three formats, with one format similar to a telephone number. In comparison, the NIC in a LAN has a hardware address burned into the adapter. Stations on a LAN can register their addresses using the facilities of an Address Resolution Protocol (ARP) server. That server would then act as a translator between the burned-in LAN-specific hardware addresses and ATM public or private network addresses that could considerably differ from the LAN addressing scheme.

Network Interfaces

ATM supports two types of basic interfaces—user-to-network interface (UNI) and network-to-node interface (NNI).

User-to-Network Interface

The UNI represents the interface between an ATM switch and an ATM endpoint. Since the connection of a private network to a public network is also known as a UNI, the terms *public* and *private UNI* were used to differentiate between the two types of user-to-network interfaces. That is, a private UNI references the connection between an endpoint and switch on an internal, private ATM network, such as an organization's ATM-based LAN. In comparison, a public UNI would reference the interface between either a customer's endpoint or switch and a public ATM network.

Network-to-Node Interface

The connection between an endpoint and switch is simpler than the connect between two switches. This results from the fact that switches communicate information concerning the utilization of their facilities as well as pass setup information required to support endpoint network requests.

The interface between switches is known as a network-to-node or network-to-network interface (NNI). Similar to the UNI, there are two types of NNIs. A *private NNI* describes the switch-to-switch interface on an internal network such as an organization's LAN. In comparison, a *public NNI* describes the interface between public ATM switches, such as those used by communications carriers. Figure 3.33 illustrates the four previously described ATM network interfaces.

ATM Cell Header

The structure of the ATM cell is identical in both public and private ATM networks, with Figure 3.34 illustrating the fields within the five-byte cell header. As we will soon note, although

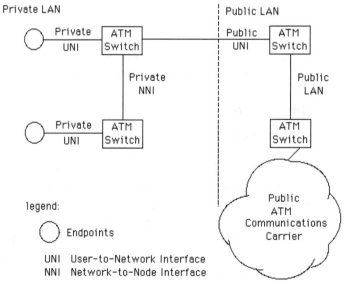

Figure 3.33 ATM network interfaces.

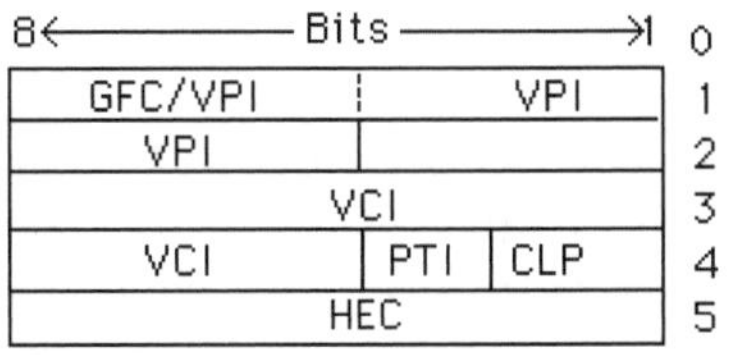

```
8←——————— Bits ———————→| 0
  ┌─────────────┬──────────────┐
  │  GFC/VPI    ┊    VPI       │ 1
  ├─────────────┴──────────────┤
  │  VPI        │              │ 2
  ├─────────────┴──────────────┤
  │        VCI                 │ 3
  ├──────────────┬─────┬───────┤
  │  VCI         │ PTI │ CLP   │ 4
  ├──────────────┴─────┴───────┤
  │        HEC                 │ 5
  └────────────────────────────┘
```

```
GFC   Generic Flow Control
VPI   Virtual Path Identifier
VCI   Virtual Circuit Identifier
PTI   Payload Type Identifier
CLP   Cell Loss Priority
HEC   Header Error Check
```

Figure 3.34   The ATM cell header.

the cell header fields are identical throughout an ATM network, the use of certain fields depends upon the interface or the presence or absence of data being transmitted by an endpoint.

Generic Flow Control Field

The Generic Flow Control (GFC) field consists of the first four bits of the first byte of the ATM cell header. This field is used to control the flow of traffic across the user-to-network interface (UNI) and is used only at the UNI. When cells are transmitted between switches, the four bits become an extension of the VPI field, permitting a larger VPI value to be carried in the cell header.

Virtual Path Identifier Field

The Virtual Path Identifier (VPI) identifies a path between two locations in an ATM network that provides transportation for a group of virtual channels, where a virtual channel represents a connection between two communicating ATM devices. When an endpoint has no data to transmit, the VPI field is set to all zeros to indicate an idle condition. As previously explained, when transmission occurs between switches, the GFC field is used to support an extended VPI value.

Virtual Circuit Identifier Field

The Virtual Cell Identifier (VCI) can be considered to represent the second part of the two-level routing hierarchy used by ATM, where a group of virtual channels are used to form a virtual path.

Figure 3.35 illustrates the relationship between virtual paths and virtual channels. Here the virtual channel represents a connection between two communicating ATM entities, such as an endpoint to a central office switch, or between two switches. The virtual channel can represent a single ATM link or a concatenation of two or more links, with communications on the channel occurring in cell sequence order at a predefined quality of service. In comparison, each virtual path (VP) represents a group of VCs transported between two points that can flow over one or more ATM links. Although VCs are associated with a VP, they are not unbundled or processed. Thus, the purpose of a virtual path is to provide a mechanism for bundling traffic routed toward the same destination. This technique enables switches to examine the VPI field within the cell header to make a decision concerning the relaying of the cell instead of having to examine the entire three-byte address formed by the VPI and the VCI. When an endpoint is in an idle condition, the VPI field is set to all zeros. Although the VCI field will also be set to all zeros to indicate the idle condition, other nonzero VCI values are reserved for use with a VPI zero value to indicate certain predefined conditions, for example, the VPI field value of zero when a VCI field value of 5 is used to transmit a signaling/connection request.

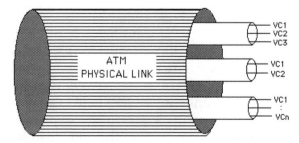

Figure 3.35 Relationship between virtual paths and virtual channels.

Payload Type Identifier Field

The payload type identifier (PTI) field consists of three bits in the fourth byte of the cell header. This field is used to identify the type of information carried by the cell. Values 0–3 are reserved to identify various types of user data, 4 and 5 denote management information, while 6 and 7 are reserved for future use.

Cell Loss Priority Field

The last bit in the fourth byte of the cell header represents the cell loss priority (CLP) field. This bit is set by the AAL layer and used by the ATM layer throughout an ATM network as an indicator of the importance of the cell. If the CLP is set to 1, it indicates the cell can be discarded by a switch experiencing congestion. If the cell should not be discarded due to the necessity to support a predefined quality of service, the AAL layer will set the CLP bit to 0. The CLP bit can also be set by the ATM layer if a connection exceeds the quality of service level agreed to during the initial communications handshaking process when setup information is exchanged.

Header Error Check Field

The last byte in the ATM cell header is the header error check (HEC). The purpose of the HEC is to provide protection for the first four bytes of the cell header against the misdelivery of cells due to errors affecting the addresses within the header. To accomplish this the HEC functions as an error detecting and correcting code. The HEC is capable of detecting all single and certain multiple bit errors as well as correcting single bit errors.

ATM Connections and Cell Switching

Now that we have a basic understanding of the ATM cell header and the virtual path and virtual channel identifiers, we can turn our attention to the methods used to establish connections between endpoints as well as how connection identifiers are used for cell switching to route cells to their destination.

Connections

In comparison to most LANs that are connectionless, ATM is a connection-oriented communications technology. This means that a connection has to be established between two ATM endpoints prior to actual data being transmitted between the endpoints. The actual ATM connection can be established as a permanent virtual circuit (PVC) or as a switched virtual circuit (SVC).

A PVC is similar to a leased line, with routing established for long-term use. Once a PVC is established, no further network intervention is required any time a user wishes to transfer data between endpoints connected via a PVC. In comparison, a SVC is similar to a telephone call made on the switched telephone network. That is, the SVC requires network intervention to establish the path linking endpoints each time a SVC occurs.

Both PVCs and SVCs represent *virtual* rather than permanent or dedicated connections. This means that through statistical multiplexing, an endpoint can receive calls from one or more distant endpoints.

Cell Switching

The VPI and VCI fields within a cell header can be used individually or collectively by a switch to determine the output port for relaying or transferring a cell. To determine the output port, the ATM switch first reads the incoming VPI, VCI, or both fields with the field read dependent upon the location of the switch in the network. Next, the switch will use the connection identifier information to perform a table lookup operation. That operation uses the current connection identifier as a match criteria to determine the output port the cell will be routed onto as well as a new connection identifier to be placed into the cell header. The new connection identifier is then used for routing between the next pair of switches or from a switch to an endpoint.

Types of Switches

There are two types of ATM switches, with the differences between each related to the type of header fields read for establishing cross-connections through the switch. A switch limited to reading and substituting VPI values is commonly referred to as a VP switch. This switch operates relatively fast. A switch that reads and substitutes both VPI and VCI values is commonly referred to as a virtual channel switch (VC switch). A VC switch generally has a lower cell operating rate than a VP switch as it must examine additional information in each cell header. A VP switch is similar to a central office switch, while a VC switch is similar to end office switches.

Using Connection Identifiers

To illustrate the use of connection identifiers in cell switching, consider Figure 3.36, which illustrates a three-switch ATM network with four endpoints. When switch 1 receives a cell on port 2 with VPI = 0, VCI = 10, it uses the VPI and VCI values to perform a table lookup, assigning VPI = 1, VCI = 12 for the cell header and then switches the cell onto port 1. Similarly, when switch 1 receives a cell on port 3 with VPI = 0, VCI = 18, its table lookup operation results in the assignment of VPI = 1, VCI = 15 to the cell's header and the forwarding of the cell onto port 1. If we assume switch 2 is a VP switch, it only reads and modifies the VP; thus, the VCIs are shown exiting the switch with the same values they had upon entering the switch. At switch 3, the

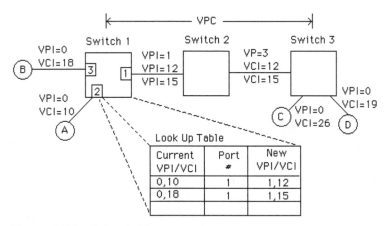

Figure 3.36 Cell switching example.

VPC is broken down, with virtual channels assigned to route cells to endpoints C and D that were carried in a common virtual path from switch 1 to switch 3.

The assignment of VPI and VCI values is an arbitrary process which considers those already in use, with the lookup tables being created when a connection is established through the network. Concerning that connection, it results from an ATM endpoint requesting a connection setup via the User-Network Interface through the use of a signaling protocol which contains an address within the cell. That address can be in one of three formats. One known as E.164 is the same used in public telephone networks, while the other two address formats include domain identifiers that allow address fields to be assigned by different organizations. The actual signaling method is based upon the signaling protocol used in ISDN and enables a quality of service to be negotiated and agreed to during the connection setup process. The quality of service is based upon metrics assigned to different traffic classes, permitting an endpoint to establish several virtual connections where each connection transports different types of data with different performance characteristics assigned to each connection. To obtain a better understanding of this important concept, let's first focus our attention upon the traffic classes supported by ATM which are listed in Table 3.16. By using different qualities of service for different traffic classes, an ATM endpoint could prioritize Class B so as to correctly receive time-sensitive frames for a videoconference while allowing relatively time-insensitive traffic, such as Class C, to be delayed or for cells to even be dropped during periods of congestion.

LAN Emulation

Although ATM provides a significant number of advantages over Ethernet and Token Ring networks, it is not realistic to expect those legacy networks to be ripped out and immediately replaced with ATM. Instead, many network managers and administrators will require their legacy LANs to coexist with ATM. To accomplish this requires a technique known as LAN emulation.

Table 3.16 ATM Traffic Classes

Class	Name	Description
A	Constant bit rate (CBR)	Connection-oriented voice or video, such as DS0s.
B	Variable bit rate (VBR)	Connection-oriented data services, such as packet video, requiring the transfer of timing information between endpoints.
C	Connection-oriented (VBR)	Used for bursty data transfer for connection oriented asynchronous traffic, such as IPX, X.25, frame relay.
D	Connectionless VBR	Used for transmitting VBR data without requiring a previously established connection (i.e., SMDS).
X	Simple and efficient adaptation layer (SEAL)	Similar to C but assumes higher-layer process provides error recovery.

LAN emulation is an evolving ATM standard which defines how classical LAN adapters, network drivers, and protocols at or above layer 2 of the OSI Reference Model coexist with ATM. Three types of connectivity are possible using LAN emulation: complete-ATM; classical LAN-to-ATM; and classical LAN–to–classical LAN using ATM as the backbone.

For the first type of connectivity, complete-ATM, both the workstation (client) and file server to be accessed are physically located on an ATM network. This situation is illustrated by the arrow labeled "complete-ATM" in Figure 3.37. Although all devices are connected to an ATM network, LAN emulation is required to support operating systems and applications that do not run natively on ATM. Thus, the use of LAN emulation on workstations (clients) and the file server would, for example, make it possible to run NetWare or Windows NT, which currently do not run natively on ATM.

The arrow labeled "classical LAN-to-ATM" indicates how workstations connected to legacy Ethernet or Token Ring networks can access file servers connected to an ATM network. To obtain this connectivity requires the use of a LAN switch or emulation bridge capable of translating Ethernet or Token Ring

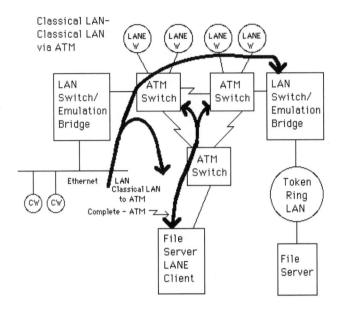

Legend:

LANE	LAN Emulation
LANEW	Emulation Workstation Client
CW	Classical Workstation

Figure 3.37 Connectivity methods using LAN emulation.

frames into ATM cells and performing a reverse translation when ATM cells are received from the ATM network.

The third type of connectivity supported by LAN emulation is based upon using an ATM backbone to connect legacy LANs. This type of emulation is indicated by the arrow labeled "classical LAN–classical LAN via ATM," which shows the routing of data from the Ethernet LAN to the LAN switch or emulation bridge connected to the Token Ring network.

The key to the ability to perform LAN emulation resides in the capability of LAN switches or emulation bridges. Since most classical LANs operate in a connectionless manner and use MAC addressing, the switch or bridge must perform several operations in addition to frame to cell mapping. Those functions include converting the connectionless protocol into a point-to-point connection for transmitting data and converting MAC addresses into ATM addresses. Concerning the latter, the switch or bridge must maintain a table of MAC and ATM addresses while each LAN-emulated client must map MAC addresses to ATM addresses. In addition, since classical LANs use broadcasting and multicasting transmission while ATM uses a connection-oriented transmission method, LAN emulation must support broadcast and multicast transmission. To provide this support requires the use of a *broadcast and unknown server* (BUS). Here the BUS is responsible for handling such broadcasts as NetWare SAPs as well as multicast transmissions and its actual functionality can be incorporated into a LAN switch or emulation bridge. Thus, the actual effort and functionality of the switch or bridge is considerably more complex than simple frame to cell mapping. In Chapter 7, we will examine how LAN emulation provides the ability to construct virtual LANs via an ATM backbone.

Network Layer Operations

The primary method used to obtain communications between vLANs is based upon network layer operations. Thus, a detailed examination of the use of vLANs and virtual networking requires knowledge of network layer operations, which is the focus of this chapter.

In this chapter we will turn our attention to two popular network layer protocol suites, NetWare and TCP/IP. Although the title of this chapter indicates that we will examine transmission at the third layer of the OSI Reference Model, since both protocol stacks extend beyond that layer we will also, when applicable, move up each protocol stack to obtain familiarity with how the higher levels of each stack interact with the third layer. In addition, since understanding IP addressing is important for an appreciation of the transportation of data under TCP/IP, we will also focus on a variety of addressing topics in this chapter, such as IP address classes, subnetting, and the Domain Name Service (DNS), which provides the translation between English mnemonics, or words used to reference a computer, and their dotted-decimal IP address.

NETWARE IPX/SPX AND RELATED PROTOCOLS

NetWare primarily provides communications services using two protocols that are variations of the Xerox Network Systems (XNS) Internet Transport Protocol–Internetwork Packet Exchange (IPX)

133

and Sequence Packet Exchange (SPX). IPX is a best effort connectionless protocol, operating at the network layer of the OSI Reference Model. In comparison, SPX is a connection-oriented protocol which supports reliable peer-to-peer communications and operates at the transport layer of the OSI Reference Model.

IPX

Although IPX is a connectionless protocol it can be used in an implied verification mode. That is, file servers use IPX for request and reply packets. Thus, if a server responds to a request it is implied that it received the request. Conversely, if a station times out waiting for a response you can logically assume that the server never received the request. Figure 4.1 illustrates the format or structure of an IPX packet header.

Checksum Field

The header contains a total of 30 bytes, of which the checksum field was included for compatibility with the XNS packet header and is always set to hex FF-FF. Since adapter cards perform a hardware checksum on the entire IPX packet, the checksum field is not used.

Length Field

The length field is set by IPX and denotes the length of the complete IPX packet inclusive of the header and data. The data field can vary from zero to a maximum of 576 bytes.

Transport Control Field

The transport control field is used by internetwork bridges and is initially set by IPX to zero prior to transmission. Thereafter, the transport control field contains the number of hops from source to destination.

Packet Type Field

The packet type field denotes the type of service either offered or requested by the packet. Under XNS, Xerox defined eight packet types. Those types and their values are listed in Table 4.1.

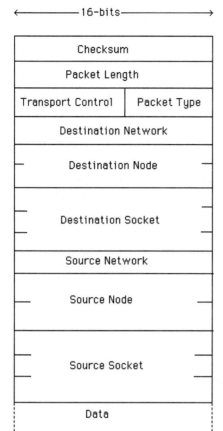

Figure 4.1   IPX packet header.

Table 4.1   Packet Type Field Values

Value	Meaning
0	Unknown Packet Type
1	Routing Information Packet
2	Echo Packet
3	Error Packet
4	Packet Exchange Packet
5	Sequenced Packed Protocol Packet
16-31	Experimental Protocols
17	NetWare Core Protocol

Under IPX the packet type field value is set to either 0 or 4, while SPX sets the value to 5.

Destination Network Field

The destination network field contains the network number on which the station address in the destination node field resides. This is the administration assigned network number. NetWare uses four-byte network numbers as identifiers for servers on the same network segment. If the value of the destination network field is 0, it is assumed that the destination node is on the same physical network as the source node and that the packet is not transmitted through an internetwork bridge. Together, the destination network field and the destination node field define a unique destination in a NetWare network, while a third field, known as the destination socket, identifies a process at the destination.

Destination Node Field

The six-byte destination node field contains the physical address of the destination station. A destination address of hex FF-FF-FF-FF-FF-FF represents a broadcast packet that is sent to all nodes on the destination network.

Destination Socket Field

The destination socket field contains the address of the packet's destination process, a term referred to as the destination socket address. Table 4.2 lists socket numbers used by Xerox under XNS as well as socket numbers Xerox assigned to Novell.

In examining the entries in Table 4.2, it's important to note that Novell also administers a list of sockets. Programmers can request Novell to register a socket number of their programs or can use the dynamic socket assignment of the NetWare shell. Dynamic socket numbers begin at hex 4000, while numbers assigned by Novell begin at hex 8000.

Source Network Field

The field of the IPX header that follows the destination socket field is the source network field. This field contains the network

Table 4.2 Destination Socket Addresses

hex Value	Meaning
Reserved by Xerox	
1	Routing Information Packet
2	Echo Protocol Packet
3	Error Handler Packet
20-3F	Experimental
1-BB8	Registered with Xerox
BB9-	Dynamically assignable
Assigned to Novell	
451	File Service Packet
452	Service Advertising Packet
455	Routing Information Packet
456	NetBIOS Packet
	Diagnostic Packet

number of the station transmitting the IPX packet. Similar to the destination network field, the source network field uses the four-byte network number given to servers on the same network segment. If this field has a value of zero, this indicates that the physical network is unknown. The combination of the source network field and the source node field results in a unique network address for the originator of network traffic.

Source Node and Source Socket Fields

The source node and source socket fields are set by IPX to indicate the physical address of the source node and the socket address of the process sending the packet, respectively. Similar to the destination socket, the source socket can be static or dynamic and the same numbering convention as described for destination socket numbers is followed.

IPX Data Field Composition

As we will soon note, the structure of the IPX header provides a common foundation for the extension of information which converts an IPX header into a different transport mechanism. This extension occurs through the use of the data field as its compo-

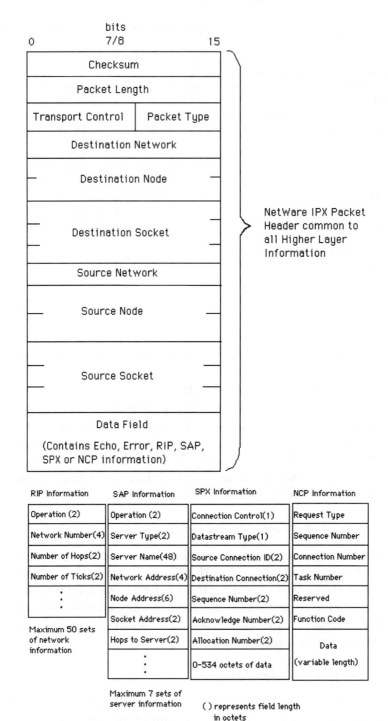

Figure 4.2 NetWare packet composition.

sition results in the development of several types of transport mechanisms which Novell references as different types of Net-Ware protocols.

The data field can contain Routing Information Protocol (RIP), Service Advertising Protocol (SAP), SPX, Echo, Error, or NetWare Core Protocol (NCP) information. In fact, via the extension of the previously described IPX header the packet can be converted into a different type of packet, such as an SPX packet.

Figure 4.2 illustrates the composition of the NetWare packet data field for RIP, SAP, SPX, AND NCP information. In the remainder of this section I will discuss the contents of the SPX packet header in terms of its 12-byte extension of an IPX header as well as the operation of SAP and RIP, since many problems as well as performance issues are attributable to those protocols.

SPX

In examining the composition of the data field which turns an IPX packet into an SPX packet you will note the addition of 12 bytes to the IPX header. I will focus on those bytes in discussing SPX.

Connection Control Field

The first new field, connection control, contains four-bit flags used by the protocol to control the bidirectional flow of data. Table 4.3 lists the connection control field single-bit flags and their meanings.

Datastream Type Field

The second field in the SPX extension is a one-byte flag which indicates the type of data contained in the packet. Known as the datastream type field, possible values include hex O-FD for client defined, hex FE for end-of-connection, and hex FF for end-of-connection acknowledgment. A client defined setting results from an application and is ignored by SPX. An end-of-connection is generated by SPX when a client requests the termination of an active connection and represents the last message delivered on the connection. The third type of data, end-of-connection ac-

Table 4.3 Connection Control Bit Flags

Bit Flag Value	Meaning
10h	(End-of-Message) A client sets this flag to signal its partner an end of connection. SPX passes it unaltered.
20h	(Attention) A client sets this flag if a packet is an attention packet. SPX passes it unaltered.
40h	(Acknowledgment Required) SPX sets this bit if an acknowledgment packet is required.
80h	(System Packet) SPX sets this bit if the packet is a system packet.

knowledgment, is generated by SPX and is not delivered to connected clients.

Source and Destination Connection ID Fields

Following the datastream type field is the source connection ID field. This field contains a number assigned by SPX at the packet's source. That field is followed by the destination connection ID field which contains a number assigned by SPX at the packet's destination. Since multiple connections active on a computer can use the same socket, the destination connect ID field provides a mechanism for demultiplexing incoming packets arriving on the same socket from different connections.

Sequence Number Field

The sequence number field varies from hex O to FF-FF and is used to count packets exchanged in one direction on a connection. SPX wraps to 0 when the maximum value is reached.

Acknowledgment Number Field

The acknowledgment number field contains the sequence number of the next packet SPX expects to receive.

Allocation Number Field

The last field, allocation number, contains the number of listen buffers outstanding in one direction on the connection. SPX can transmit packets only until the sequence number equals the remote allocation number.

SAP and RIP

The Service Advertising Protocol (SAP) and Routing Information Protocol (RIP) govern the ability to have multiple servers on a common network or on geographically separated networks that can be recognized and then become accessible to client workstations. SAP and RIP are used to provide a request/reply sequence which provides a mechanism for workstations being able to locate and access servers.

SAP Operation

When a NetWare workstation loads NETX or VLM, the station transmits a SAP request onto the network. That request is a request for the nearest server unless altered by the use of the NetWare ATTACH command to request attachment to a specific server. Servers receiving the SAP request respond with SAP replies, which include the server's network address. Since the first response is considered to represent the nearest server, the workstation responds to the first SAP reply it receives by broadcasting a RIP request. The RIP request and the RIP reply sent from a router to the workstation enables the workstation to construct a table, which associates the hardware address of the router with a network address for the requested service. This enables the workstation to correctly address its packets to the service it seeks.

In addition to supporting the connection of clients to servers when NETX or VLM is loaded, SAPs support the ability of routers and certain network commands (SLIST) to discern the presence of servers on a network. Every 60 seconds (default) servers broadcast a SAP to advertise their services as well as all known services. The SAP format which is shown in the third column in Figure 4.2 can contain up to seven sets of server descriptors whose contents specify information about the server.

SAP Fields

The server type field specifies the type of server, such as file server or print server. The server name field contains the name of the server and explains how you can use the SLIST command to obtain a list of server names. The network address field is the internal network address.

In a NetWare environment there are two network addresses you must consider—the network address assigned by the administrator and the internal network address. The first network address is assigned by the administrator when a file server is configured. The internal address is used to support file service requests as such requests are routed from a workstation's network address to a NetWare server's internal network address where the file service processes reside. The node address field is a six-byte address which represents the data link address of the server, normally the Ethernet or Token Ring adapter address. The two-byte socket address field is similar to other IPX sockets, representing the internal address of a service, such as a Print Server.

The information carried in SAPs is used by servers and routers to construct Server Information Tables (SITs). SITs contain the information required to associate network services with network locations; however, they do not provide information required to send packets to a destination network. The information necessary to transmit packets to a destination network is contained in the Routing Information Table (RIT), which is constructed via RIP broadcasts that also occur every 60 seconds.

RIP Operation

The RIP packet shown in column 2 of Figure 4.2 is used by routers to construct RIT tables. RIP packets received on one port are updated via the incrementation of the Hop and Tick fields and transmitted to all other attached networks. In examining the IPX extension to construct a RIP packet the Hop field contains the distance in routers that must be traversed to reach the destination network. In comparison, the Tick field contains the time in one-eighteenth-second increments required to reach the destination network.

Under RIP a network is considered to be unreachable if it is 16 hops away. This enables routers to gracefully exit a network and allow other routers to reconfigure themselves to provide a better route. Here the router exiting a route simply broadcasts that it is 16 hops away from the networks it no longer supports.

Performance Issues

Because SAP and RIP broadcasts occur every 60 seconds or whenever a change occurs in a network, they can cause performance problems due to the bandwidth they consume. This is especially true when an Internetwork consists of LANs connected by relatively slow 56-Kbps WAN links.

Through the establishment of appropriate virtual LANs, you can significantly reduce the effect of SAP and RIP broadcasts upon the bandwidth of a physical network. This reduction becomes possible since a vLAN represents a broadcast domain logically created from a physical network topology and restricts broadcasts to stations on the logical domain.

TCP/IP

TCP/IP represents a collection of network protocols that provide services at the network and transport layers of the ISO's OSI Reference Model. Originally developed based upon work performed by the U.S. Department of Defense Advanced Research Projects Agency Network (ARPANET), TCP/IP is also commonly referred to as the DOD protocols or the Internet protocol suite.

Figure 4.3 illustrates the relationship of the TCP/IP protocol suite and the services they provide with respect to the OSI Reference Model. In the remainder of this section I will review IP and TCP packet headers as well as discuss the use of several related network and transport layer protocols and higher-level protocols implemented over TCP and its related protocol suite.

ISO Layers

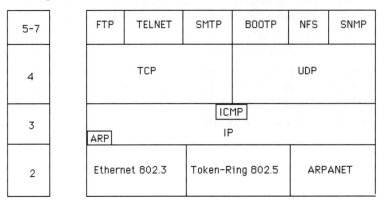

Legend

```
ARP    Address Resolution Protocol
BOOTP  Bootstrap Protocol
FTP    File Transfer Protocol
NSF    Network File System
SMTP   Simple Mail Transfer Protocol
SNMP   Simple Network Management Protocol
```

Figure 4.3 TCP/IP protocols and services.

Datagrams versus Virtual Circuits

In Figure 4.3, the Internet Protocol (IP) provides a common layer 3 transport for TCP and UDP. TCP is a connection-oriented protocol, which requires the acknowledgment of the existence of the connection as well as each packet transmitted once the connection is established. In comparison, UDP, an acronym for User Datagram Protocol, is a connectionless mode service that provides a parallel service to TCP. Here datagram represents a term used to identify the basic unit of information transported across a TCP/IP network. A datagram can be transported either via an acknowledged connection-oriented service or via an unacknowledged, connectionless service, where each information element is addressed to its destination and its transmission is at the mercy of network nodes. Datagrams are routed via the best path available to the destination as the datagram is placed onto the network. An alternative to datagram transmission is the use of a virtual circuit, where network nodes establish a fixed path when a connection is initiated and subsequent data exchanges occur on that path. TCP implements transmission via the use of a virtual circuit, while IP provides a datagram-oriented gateway transmission service between networks. Two additional network layer protocols in the TCP/IP suite are ICMP and ARP.

ICMP and ARP

The Internet Control Message Protocol (ICMP) provides a mechanism for communicating control message and error reports. Both gateways and hosts use ICMP to transmit problem reports about datagrams back to the datagram originator. In addition, ICMP includes an echo request/reply that can be used to determine if a destination is reachable and, if so, is responding. The Address Resolution Protocol (ARP) maps the high-level IP address configured via software to a low-level physical hardware address, typically the network interface card's (NIC) ROM address.

TCP

The Transmission Control Protocol (TCP) represents a layer-4 connection-oriented reliable protocol. TCP provides a virtual circuit connection mode service for applications that require connection setup and error detection and automatic retransmission.

Each unit of data carried by TCP is referred to as a *segment*. Segments are created by TCP subdividing the stream of data passed down by application layer protocols that use its services, with each segment identified by the use of a sequence number. This segment identification process enables a receiver, if required, to reassemble data segments into their correct order.

Figure 4.4 illustrates the format of the TCP protocol header. The source and destination ports are each 16 bits in length and identify a process or service at the host receiver. For example, port 23 is normally used for Telnet.

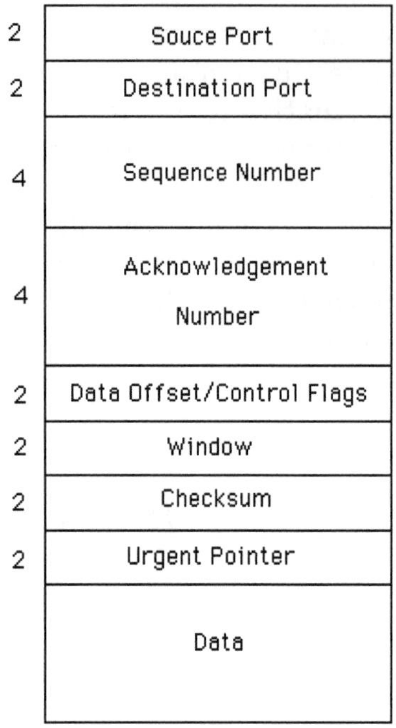

2	Souce Port
2	Destination Port
4	Sequence Number
4	Acknowledgement Number
2	Data Offset/Control Flags
2	Window
2	Checksum
2	Urgent Pointer
	Data

Figure 4.4   TCP protocol header.

The sequence number is used to identify the data segment transported. The acknowledgment number interpretation depends upon the setting of the ACK control flag (not directly shown in Figure 4.4). If the ACK control flag bit position is set, the acknowledgment field will contain the next sequence number the sender expects to receive. Otherwise the field is ignored.

There are six control field flags that are used to establish, maintain, and terminate connections. Those flags include URG (urgent), SYN, ACK, RST (reset), PSH (push), and FIN (finish).

Setting URG = 1 indicates to the receiver urgent data is arriving. The SYN flag is set to 1 as a connection request and thus serves to establish a connection. As previously discussed, the ACK flag when set indicates that the acknowledgment flag is relevant. When set, the RST flag means the connection should be reset, while the PSH flag tells the receiver to immediately deliver the data in the segment. Finally, the setting of the FIN flag indicates the sender is done and the connection should be terminated.

The window field is used to convey the number of bytes the sender can accept and functions as a flow control mechanism. The checksum provides error detection for the TCP header and data carried, while the urgent pointer field is used in conjunction with the URG flag. When the URG flag is set the value in the urgent pointer field represents the last byte of urgent data.

When an application uses TCP, TCP breaks the stream of data provided by the application into segments and adds an appropriate TCP header. Next, an IP header is prefixed to the TCP header to transport the segment via the network layer. As data arrives at its destination network it's converted into a data link layer transport mechanism. For example, on a Token Ring network, TCP data would be transported within Token Ring frames.

UDP

The User Datagram Protocol (UDP) is the second layer-4 transport service supported by the TCP/IP protocol suite. UDP is a connectionless service, which means that the higher-layer application is responsible for the reliable delivery of the transported message.

Figure 4.5 illustrates the composition of the UDP header. The source and destination port fields are each 16 bits in length and, as previously described for TCP, identify the port number of the sending and receiving process, respectively. Here each port number process identifies an application running at the corresponding IP address in the IP header prefixed for the UDP header. The use of a port number provides a mechanism for identifying network services as they denote communications points where particular services can be accessed. For example, a value of 161 in a port field is used in UDP to identify SNMP.

The length field indicates the length of the UDP packets in octets to include the header and user data. The checksum, which is a one's complement arithmetic sum, is computed over a

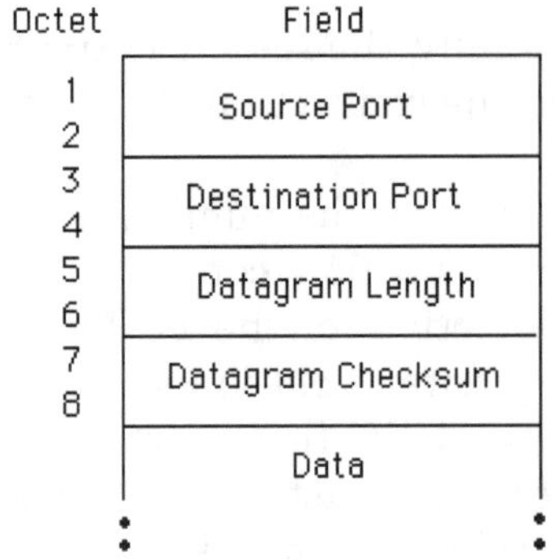

Octet   Field

```
 1    ┌─────────────────────┐
 2    │    Source Port      │
      ├─────────────────────┤
 3    │   Destination Port  │
 4    ├─────────────────────┤
 5    │   Datagram Length   │
 6    ├─────────────────────┤
 7    │  Datagram Checksum  │
 8    ├─────────────────────┤
      │        Data         │
      │                     │
         ⋮             ⋮
```

Figure 4.5 The UDP header.

pseudoheader and the entire UDP packet. The pseudoheader is created by the conceptual prefix of 12 octets to the header illustrated in Figure 4.5. The first 8 octets are used by source and destination IP addresses obtained from the IP packet. This is followed by a zero-filled octet and an octet which identifies the protocol. The last two octets in the pseudoheader denote the length of the UDP packet. By computing the UDP checksum over the pseudoheader and user data a degree of additional data integrity is obtained.

IP

As previously mentioned, IP provides a datagram-oriented gateway service for transmission between subnetworks. This provides a mechanism for hosts to access other hosts on a best-effort basis but does not enhance reliability as it relies on upper-layer protocols for error detection and correction. As a layer-3 protocol, IP is responsible for the routing and delivery of datagrams. To accomplish this task, IP performs a number of communications functions, such as addressing, status information, management, and the fragmentation and reassembly of datagrams when necessary.

IP Header Format Figure 4.6 illustrates the IP header format while Table 4.4 provides a brief description of the fields in the IP header. In examining the IP header a common network

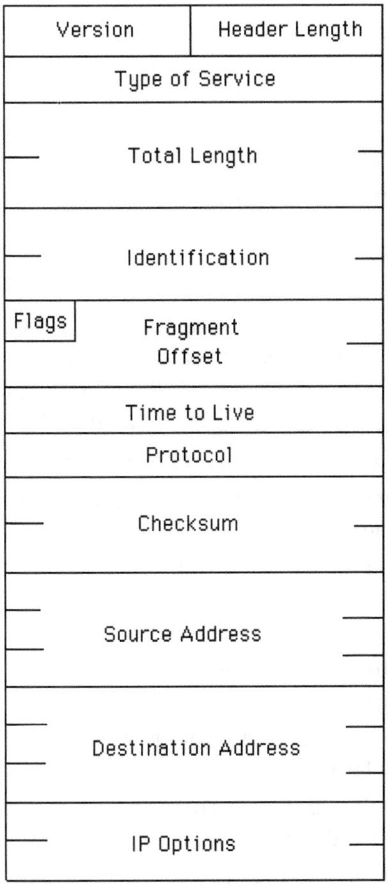

Figure 4.6 IP header format.

problem relates to the IP address carried in the source and destination address fields. Thus, a description of IP addressing is warranted, as it forms the basis for network addressing as well as the Domain Name Service translation of English-type mnemonics into what is known as dotted-decimal IP addresses.

IP Addressing The IP addressing scheme uses a 32-bit address which is divided into an assigned network number and a host number. The latter can be further segmented into a subnet number and a host number. Through subnetting you can con-

Table 4.4 IP Header Fields

Field	Description
Version	The version of the IP protocol used to create the datagram.
Header Length	Header length in 32-bit words.
Type of Service	Specifies how the datagram should be handled.

```
 0   1   2   3 4 5   6   7
┌─────────────┬─┬─┬─┬───────┐
│ PRECEDENCE  │D│T│R│ UNUSED│
└─────────────┴─┴─┴─┴───────┘
```

PRECEDENCE	Indicates importance of the datagram
D	When set requests low delay
T	When set requests high throughput
R	When set requests high reliability

Field	Description
Total Length	Specifies the total length to include header and data.
Identification	Used with source address to identify fragments belonging to specific datagrams.
Flags	Middle bit when set disables possible fragmentation. Low-order bit specifies whether the fragment contains data from the middle of the original datagram or the end.
Fragment Offset	Specifies the offset in the original datagram of data being carried in a fragment.
Time to Live	Specifies the time in seconds a datagram is allowed to remain in the Internet.
Protocol	Specifies the higher-level protocol used to create the message carried in the data field.
Header Checksum	Protects the integrity of the header.
Source IP Address	The 32-bit IP address of the datagram's sender.
Destination IP Address	The 32-bit IP address of the datagram's intended recipient.
IP Options	Primarily used for network testing or debugging.

```
 0    1    2    3    4    5   6   7
┌────┬────────────┬──────────────┐
│COPY│OPTION CLASS│ OPTION NUMBER│
└────┴────────────┴──────────────┘
```

When copy bit is set it tells gateways that the option should be copied into all fragments. When set to 0 the option is copied into the first fragment.

Option Class	Meaning
0	Datagram or network control
1	Reserved for future use
2	Debugging
3	Reserved for future use

The option number defines a specific option within a class.

struct multiple networks while localizing the traffic of hosts to specific subnets, a technique I will shortly illustrate.

IP addressing numbers are assigned by the InterNIC network information center and can fall into one of five unique network classes, referenced as Class A through Class E. Figure 4.6 illustrates the IP address formats for Class A, B, and C networks. Class D addresses are reserved for multicast groups, while Class E addresses are reserved for future use.

In Figure 4.7, by examining the first bit in the IP address you can distinguish a Class A address from Class B and C addresses. Thereafter, examining the composition of the second bit position enables a Class B address to be distinguished from a Class C address.

An IP 32-bit address is expressed as four decimal numbers, with each number ranging in value from 0 to 255 and separated from another number by a dot (decimal point). This explains why an IP address is commonly referred to as a dotted-decimal address.

In Figure 4.7, a Class A address has three octets available for identifying hosts on one network or on subnets, which provides support for more hosts than other address classes. Thus, Class A addresses are assigned only to large organizations or

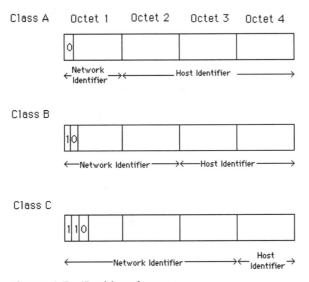

Figure 4.7 IP address formats.

countries. Since the first bit in a Class A address must be zero, the first octet ranges in value from 1 to 127 instead of to 255.

A Class B address uses two octets for the network identifier and two for the host or subnet identifier. This permits up to 65,636 hosts and/or subnets to be assigned. In a Class C address three octets are used to identify the network, leaving one octet to identify hosts and/or subnets. Since one octet permits only 256 hosts or subnets to be identified, many small organizations with a requirement to provide more than 256 hosts with access to the Internet must obtain multiple Class C addresses.

Subnetting Through the use of subnetting you can use a single IP address as a mechanism for connecting multiple physical networks. To accomplish subnetting, you logically divide the host portion of an IP address into a network address and a host address.

Figure 4.8 illustrates an example of the IP subnet addressing format for a Class B address. In this example, all traffic routed to the address XY where X and Y represent the value of the first two Class B address octets flow to a common location connected to the Internet, typically a router. The router in turn connects two or more Class B subnets, each with a distinct address formed by the third decimal digit, which represents the subnet identifier. Figure 4.9 illustrates a Class B network ad-

Class B Address Format

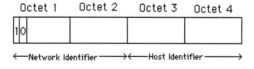

Class B Subnet Address Format

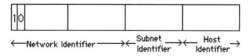

Figure 4.8 Class B subnetting.

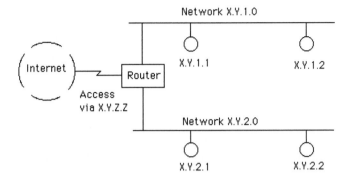

IP datagrams with the destination address X.Y.Z.Z where Z can be
any decimal value represent a Class B network address that can
consist of 256 subnets, with 256 hosts on each subnet.

Figure 4.9 A Class B network address location with two physical networks using subnet addressing.

dress location with two physical networks using subnet addressing.

Subnet Masks The implementation of a subnet addressing scheme is accomplished by the partitioning of the host identifier portion of an IP address. To accomplish this, a 32-bit subnet mask must be created for each network, with bits set to 1 in the subnet mask to indicate the network portion of the IP address, while bits are set to 0 to indicate the host identifier portion. Thus, the Class B subnet address format illustrated in the lower portion of Figure 4.8 would require the following 32-bit subnet mask:

```
11111111 11111111 00000000 00000000
```

The prior mask would then be entered as 255.255.0.0 in dotted-decimal representation into a router configuration screen as well as in software configuration screens on TCP/IP program stacks operating on each subnet. Concerning the latter, you must then configure each station to indicate its subnet and host identifier so that each station obtains a full four-digit dotted-decimal address.

Although the prior example used octet boundaries for creating the subnet mask, this is not an addressing requirement. For example, you could assign the following mask to a network:

```
11111111 11111111 00001110 00001100
```

The only submask restriction is to assign 1's to at least all the network identifier positions, resulting in the ability to extend masking into the host identifier field if you desire to arrange the specific assignment of addresses to computers. However, doing so can make it more difficult to verify the correct assignment of addresses in routers and workstations. Because of this, it is highly recommended that you should implement subnet masking on integral octet boundaries.

Domain Name Service

Addressing on a TCP/IP network occurs through the use of four decimal numbers ranging from 0 to 255, which are separated from one another by a dot. This dotted-decimal notation represents a 32-bit address which consists of an assigned network number and a host number as previously described during our examination of IP addressing. Since numeric addresses are difficult to work with, TCP/IP also supports a naming convention based upon English words or mnemonics that are both easier to work with and remember. The translation of English words or mnemonics to 32-bit IP addresses is performed by a Domain Name Server. Each network normally has at least one Domain Name Server and the communications established among such servers on TCP/IP networks connected to the Internet are referred to as a Domain Name Service (DNS).

The Domain Name Service (DNS) is the naming protocol used in the TCP/IP protocol suite which enables IP routing to occur indirectly through the use of names instead of IP addresses. To accomplish this, DNS provides a domain name to IP address translation service.

A domain is a subdivision of a wide area network. When applied to the Internet, where the capital I references the collection of networks interconnected to one another, there are six

Table 4.5 Internet Top-Level Domain Names

Domain Name	Assignment
.COM	Commercial Organization
.EDU	Educational Organization
.GOV	Government Agency
.MIL	Department of Defense
.NET	Networking Organization
.ORG	Not-for-Profit Organization

top-level domain names which were specified by the Internet Network Information Center (InterNIC) at the time this book was prepared. Those top-level domains are listed in Table 4.5.

Under each top-level domain, the InterNIC will register subdomains which are assigned an IP network address. An organization receiving an IP network address can further subdivide its domain into two or more subdomains. In addition, instead of using dotted-decimal notation to describe the location of each host, it can assign names to hosts as long as they follow certain rules and install a name server which provides IP address translation between named hosts and their IP addresses.

To illustrate the operation of a name server consider the network domain illustrated in Figure 4.10. In this example we will assume that a government agency has a local area network with

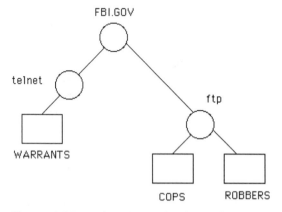

Figure 4.10 A domain-naming hierarchy.

several computers that will be connected to the Internet. Each host address will contain the specific name of the host plus the names of all of the subdomains and domains to which it belongs. Thus, the computer "warrants" would have the official address:

```
warrants.telnet.fbi.gov
```

Similarly, the computer "cops" would have the address:

```
cops.ftp.fbi.gov
```

In examining the domain-naming structure illustrated in Figure 4.10, note that computers were placed in subdomains using common Internet application names, such as Telnet and ftp. This is a common technique organizations use to make it easier for network users within and outside the organization to remember mnemonics that represent specific hosts on their network.

Although domain names provide a mechanism for identifying objects connected to wide area networks, hosts in a domain require network addresses to transfer information. Thus another host functioning as a name server is required to provide a name to address translation service.

Name Server

The name server plays an important role in TCP/IP networks. In addition to providing a name-to-IP address translation service it must recognize that an address is outside its administrative zone of authority. For example, assume a host located on the domain illustrated in Figure 4.10 will use the address fred .microwear.com to transmit a message. The name server must recognize that that address does not reside in the domain and must forward the address to another name server for translation into an appropriate IP address. Since most domains are connected to the Internet via an Internet service provider, the name server on the domain illustrated in Figure 4.10 would have a pointer to the name server of the Internet service provider and forward the query to that name server. The Internet service provider's name server will either have an entry in its table or forward the query to another name server. Eventually a name server will be reached that has administrative authority over the domain containing the host name to resolve and will return an IP address through a reversed hierarchy to provide the originating name server with a response to its query. Most name servers cache the results of previous name queries, which can considerably reduce off-domain or Internet DNS queries.

5

LAN Equipment Operations

Virtual networking depends upon the operation of three types of communications devices—bridges, switches, and routers. Thus, an understanding of the construction and operation of virtual LANs and virtual networking techniques requires detailed knowledge of the operation of those devices, which is the focus of this chapter.

BRIDGES

Bridges are intelligent devices that can connect similar and dissimilar local area networks. Bridges designed to connect similar LANs are referred to as *transparent bridges*, while those that are designed to connect dissimilar local area networks are referred to as *translating bridges*.

Operational Overview

Bridges operate at the data link layer of the OSI Reference Model, using MAC addresses to make forwarding decisions. Figure 5.1a illustrates the operation of a bridge with respect to the OSI Reference Model, while Figure 5.1b shows the use of a transparent bridge to connect two Ethernet segments.

A. OSI Reference Model

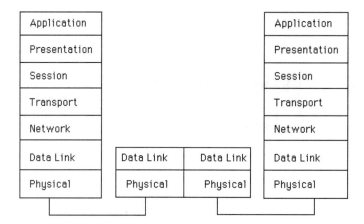

B. Application Example

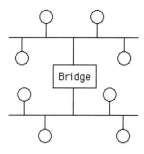

Legend: ◯ = workstations

Figure 5.1 Bridge operation.

Most bridges are self-learning. This means that when the bridge begins to operate, it examines each frame transmitted on each local area network it is connected to. By reading the source address included in each frame, the bridge assembles a table of local addresses for each network. In addition to reading each source address, the bridge also reads the destination address contained in the frame. If the destination address is not contained in the local address table that the bridge constructs, this fact indicates that the frame's destination is not on the current network or network segment, resulting in the bridge forwarding the frame onto all other ports other than the port from which it was read. We can summarize the operation of the bridge illustrated in the lower portion of Figure 5.2 as follows:

- Bridge reads all frames transmitted on network A.
- Frames with destination address on network A are not forwarded.
- Frames with destination address on network B are retransmitted onto that network.
- The reverse process is repeated for traffic on network B.

Filtering and Forwarding

The process of examining each frame is known as *filtering*. The filtering rate of a bridge is directly related to its level of performance. That is, the higher the filtering rate of a bridge, the lower the probability it will become a bottleneck to network performance.

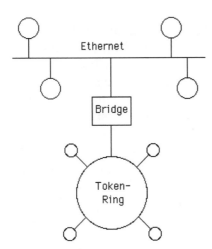

A translating bridge connects local area networks that employ different protocols at the data link layer.

Figure 5.2 Translating bridge operation.

A second performance measurement associated with bridges is their *forwarding* rate. The forwarding rate is expressed in frames per second and denotes the maximum capability of a bridge to transmit traffic from one network to another.

Types

As previously mentioned, there are two general types of bridges: transparent and translating. A transparent bridge provides a connection between two local area networks that employ the same data link protocol. At the physical layer, some transparent bridges have multiple ports that support different media. Thus, a transparent bridge does not have to be transparent at the physical layer.

A translating bridge provides a connection capability between two local area networks that employ different protocols at the data link layer. Since networks using different data link layer protocols normally use different media, a translating bridge also provides support for different physical layer connections.

Figure 5.2 illustrates the use of a translating bridge to interconnect a Token Ring and an Ethernet local area network. In this example, the bridge functions as an Ethernet node on the Ethernet LAN, and as a Token Ring node on the Token Ring LAN. When a frame on one network has a destination on the other network, the bridge will perform a series of operations, including frame and transmission rate conversion. For example, consider an Ethernet frame destined to the Token Ring network. The bridge will strip the frame's preamble and FCS, then it will convert the frame into a Token Ring frame format. Once the bridge receives a free token on its Token Ring connection, the new frame is transmitted onto the Token Ring network at the operating rate of the Token Ring LAN. For frames on the Token Ring network destined to a station on the Ethernet, the process is reversed.

One of the problems associated with the use of a translating bridge is the conversion of frames from their format on one network to the format required for use on another network. As indicated in Chapter 3, the information field of an Ethernet frame has a maximum length of 1500 bytes, while a Token Ring LAN has a maximum information field length of 4500 bytes when operating at 4 Mbps and 18000 bytes when the ring operates at 16 Mbps. If a station on the Token Ring network has a frame with an information field that exceeds 1500 bytes in a length, the bridging of that frame onto an Ethernet network cannot occur. This is because there is no provision at the data link layer for each protocol to inform a station that a frame flowing from one network to another was fragmented and requires reassembly. Using a bridge effectively in this situation requires that software on each workstation on each network be configured to use the smallest maximum frame size of any interconnected bridged network. In the previous example, the Token Ring workstations would not be allowed to transmit information fields greater than 1500 bytes.

Bridge Table Operations

To illustrate the operation of bridge routing tables, let's use the internet consisting of one Ethernet and two Token Ring local area networks illustrated in Figure 5.3. In this example, the three networks are assumed to be connected through the use of two self-learning bridges. For simplicity of illustration, only two workstations are shown and labeled on each local area network.

Frame Conversion

As previously noted, the frame formats used by Ethernet and Token Ring networks, while similar, are not equal to one another. For example, Ethernet frames are prefixed with a preamble field which is followed by a starting delimiter field. The Ethernet preamble field is not used in a Token Ring frame and the Ethernet starting delimiter field differs in composition from its Token Ring equivalent field. Similarly, each Token Ring frame is prefixed with a starting delimiter field which is quite different from the field with that name used on an Ethernet frame. Another significant difference between Ethernet and Token Ring networks concerns the methods used for bridging. Ethernet networks use transparent bridging employing a span-

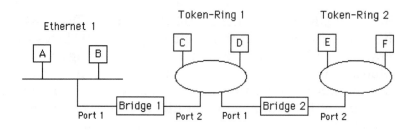

Figure 5.3 Transparent bridge operation. A transparent bridge or self-learning bridge examines the source and destination addresses to form address or routing tables in memory.

ning tree algorithm. IBM Token Ring networks support an optional routing method known as *source routing*. If that routing method is not used, an IBM bridge can support transparent bridging. In addition, a recently adopted standard known as source routing transparent (SRT) bridging provides the ability for bridges to support both methods in constructing Ethernet and IBM Token Ring networks. The spanning tree algorithm used by transparent bridges, the source routing algorithm used by source routing bridges, and the operation of SRT bridges are discussed in detail later in this section.

Address/Routing Table Construction

In examining the construction of bridge address/routing tables for the network illustrated in Figure 5.3, we will assume each bridge operates as a transparent bridge. As frames flow on the Ethernet, bridge 1 examines the source address of each frame. Eventually after both stations A and B have become active, the bridge associates their address as being on port 1 of that device. Any frames with a destination address other than stations A or B are considered to be on another network. Thus, bridge 1 would eventually associate addresses C, D, E, and F with port 2 once it receives frames with those addresses in their destination address fields. Similarly, bridge 2 constructs its address/routing table. Since frames from Ethernet 1 and Token Ring 1 can have source addresses of A, B, C or D, eventually the address/routing table of bridge 2 associates those addresses with port 1 of that device. Since frames from Ethernet 1 or Token Ring 1 with a destination address of E or F are not on those local area networks, bridge 2 then associates those addresses with port 2 of that device.

Advantages   One of the key advantages of a transparent bridge is that it operates independent of the contents of the information field and is protocol independent. Since this type of bridge is self-learning, it requires no manual configuration and is essentially a "plug-and-work" device. Thus, this type of bridge is attractive for connecting a few local area networks together and is commonly sufficient for most small and medium-sized businesses. Unfortunately, its use limits the development of certain interconnection topologies, as we will soon see.

Disadvantages   To illustrate the disadvantages associated with transparent bridges, consider Figure 5.4, in which the three Ethernet local area networks are interconnected through the use of three bridges. In this example, the internet forms a circular or loop topology. Since a two-port transparent bridge views stations as either being connected to port 1 or port 2, a circular or loop topology will create problems. Those problems can result in an unnecessary duplication of frames which will not only degrade the overall level of performance of the internet but quite possibly confuse end stations. For example, consider a frame whose source address is A and whose destination address is F. Both bridge 1 and bridge 2 will forward the frame. Although bridge 1 will forward the frame to its appropriate network using the most direct route, the frame will also be forwarded by bridge 3 to Ethernet 2, resulting in a duplicate frame arriving at workstation F. At station F a mechanism would be required to reject duplicate frames. Even if such a mechanism is available, the additional traffic flowing across

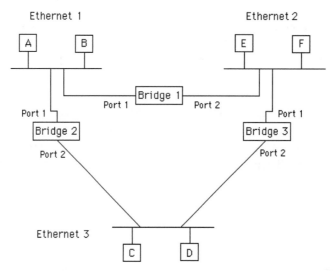

Figure 5.4 Transparent bridges do not support network loops. The construction of a circular or loop topology with transparent bridges can result in an unnecessary duplication of frames, and may confuse end stations. To avoid these problems, the Spanning Tree Protocol (STP) opens a loop by placing one bridge in a standby mode of operation.

multiple internet paths would result in an increase in network utilization approaching 100 percent. This in turn would saturate some networks, while significantly reducing the level of performance of other networks. For those reasons transparent bridging is prohibited from creating a loop or circular topology. However, transparent bridging supports concurrently active multiple bridges using an algorithm known as the spanning tree to determine which bridges should forward and which bridges should only filter frames.

Prior to discussing the operation of the spanning tree, let's focus our attention upon two additional limitations associated with bridges. Those limitations include the physical constraints associated with a bridge's RAM memory and the broadcast traffic generated by this communications device.

As the number of stations on bridged networks increases and the number of network segments bridged increases, the use of address/routing tables used to hold information increases. Unless a bridge has a tremendous amount of RAM storage, its address/routing tables will eventually fill and probably overflow, resulting in a loss of routing information. To alleviate this situation, some bridges periodically purge all entries and reconstruct their address/routing tables. Other bridges use a first-in/first-out (FIFO) purge method, periodically removing old entries from the table. Both methods can result in a new learning time being required to construct appropriate entries, and can also result in small internetwork transmission delays unless they broadcast frames with unknown destinations.

When a bridge is in its learning state, it does not know the specific port to forward a frame to. While the two port bridges shown in Figure 5.3 only require unknown destination frames to be forwarded onto a port other than their origination, suppose bridge 1 contained two additional ports (3 and 4) used to provide a connection to two additional networks. If a frame arrived on port 1, whose destination address was not contained in the address/routing table, the bridge would forward the frame onto all ports other than the port is was received on. This would result in unwanted broadcast traffic flowing onto two of three ports. Since each station on a network must examine each frame, this situation taxes station resources as well as generates network bandwidth with unnecessary traffic.

Spanning Tree Protocol

The problem of active loops was addressed by the IEEE Committee 802 in the 802.1D standard with an intelligent algorithm known as the *spanning tree protocol* (STP). The STP is based upon graph theory and converts a loop into a tree topology by disabling a link. This action ensures there is a unique path from any node in an internet to every other node. Disabled nodes are then kept in a standby mode of operation until a network failure occurs. At that time, the spanning tree protocol will attempt to construct a new tree using any of the previously disabled links.

Operation

To illustrate the operation of the spanning tree protocol, we must first become familiar with the difference between the physical and active topology of bridged networks. In addition, there are a number of terms associated with the spanning tree algorithm defined by the protocol we should become familiar with. Thus, we will also review those terms prior to discussing the operation of the algorithm.

Physical versus Active Topology In transparent bridging, a distinction is made between the physical and active topology resulting from bridged local area networks. This distinction enables the construction of a network topology in which inactive but physically constructed routes can be placed into operation if a primary route should fail and in which the inactive and active routes would form an illegal circular path violating the spanning tree algorithm if both routes were active at the same time.

Figure 5.5a illustrates one possible physical topology of bridged networks. The cost assigned to each bridge will be discussed later in this chapter. Figure 5.5b illustrates a possible active topology for the physical configuration shown at the top of that illustration.

When a bridge is used to construct an active path, it will forward frames through those ports used to form active paths. The ports through which frames are forwarded are said to be in a forwarding state of operation. Ports that cannot forward frames due to their operation forming a loop are said to be in a blocking state of operation.

Under the spanning tree algorithm, a port in a blocking state can be placed into a forwarding state and provides a path that becomes part of the active network topology. This new path must not form a closed loop and usually occurs due to the failure of another path, bridge component, or the reconfiguration of interconnected networks.

Spanning Tree Algorithm The basis for the spanning tree algorithm is a tree structure since a tree forms a pattern of connections that has no loops. The term *spanning* is used because the branches of a tree structure span or connect subnetworks.

Similar to the root of a tree, one bridge in a spanning tree network will be assigned to a unique position in the network. Known as the *root bridge*, this bridge is assigned as the top of

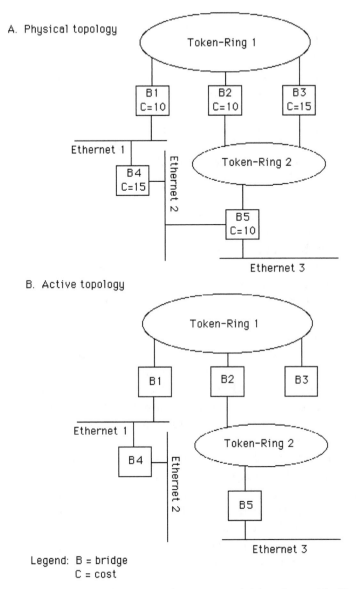

Figure 5.5 The placement of transparent bridges into a blocking state via the spanning tree algorithm results in an active topology that is a subset of the physical topology.

the spanning tree and has the potential to carry the largest amount of internet traffic due to its position.

Since bridges and bridge ports can be active or inactive, a mechanism is required to identify bridges and bridge ports. Each bridge in a spanning tree network is assigned a unique bridge identifier. This identifier is the MAC address on the bridge's lowest port number and a two-byte bridge priority level. The priority level is defined when a bridge is installed and functions as a bridge number. Similar to the bridge priority level, each adapter on a bridge which functions as a port has a two-byte port identifier. Thus, the unique bridge identifier and port identifier enables each port on a bridge to be uniquely identified.

Under the spanning tree algorithm, the difference in physical routes between bridges is recognized and a mechanism is provided to indicate the preference for one route over another. That mechanism is accomplished by the ability to assign a path cost to each path. Thus, you could assign a low cost to a preferred route and a high cost to a route you want to be used only in a backup situation.

Once path costs are assigned to each path in an internet, each bridge will have one or more costs associated with different paths to the root bridge. One of those costs is lower than all other path costs. That cost is known as the bridge's *root path cost* and the port used to provide the least path cost toward the root bridge is known as the *root port*.

As previously discussed, the spanning tree algorithm does not permit active loops in an interconnected network. To prevent this situation from occurring, only one bridge linking two networks can be in a forwarding state at any particular time. That bridge is known as the *designated bridge*, while all other bridges linking two networks will not forward frames and will be in a blocking state of operation.

Constructing the Spanning Tree The spanning tree algorithm employs a three-step process to develop an active topology. First, the root bridge is identified. In Figure 5.5b we will assume bridge 1 was selected as the root bridge. Next, the path cost from each bridge to the root bridge is determined and the minimum cost from each bridge becomes the root path cost. The port in the direction of the least path cost to the root bridge, known as the root port, is then determined for each bridge. If the root path cost is the same for two or more bridges linking LANs, then the bridge with the highest priority will be selected to furnish the minimum path cost. Once the paths are selected, the designated ports are activated.

In examining Figure 5.5a, let us now use the cost entries assigned to each bridge. Let us assume bridge 1 was selected as the root bridge as we expect a large amount of traffic to flow between Token Ring 1 and Ethernet 1 networks. Therefore, bridge 1 will become the designated bridge between Token Ring 1 and Ethernet 1 networks.

In examining the path costs to the root bridge, note that the path through bridge 2 was assigned a cost of 10, while the path through bridge 3 was assigned a cost of 15. Thus, the path from Token Ring 2 via bridge 2 to Token Ring 1 becomes the designated bridge between those two networks. Hence, Figure 5.5b shows bridge 3 inactive by the omission of a connection to the Token Ring 2 network. Similarly, the path cost for connecting the Ethernet 3 network to the root bridge is lower by routing through the Token Ring 2 and Token Ring 1 networks. Thus, bridge 5 becomes the designated bridge for the Ethernet 3 and Token Ring 2 networks.

Bridge Protocol Data Unit One question that has probably occurred to you by now is: How does each bridge know whether to participate in a spanned tree topology? Bridges obtain topology information by the use of *bridge protocol data unit* (BPDU) frames.

The root bridge is responsible for periodically transmitting a "HELLO" BPDU frame to all networks to which it is connected. According to the spanning tree protocol, HELLO frames must be transmitted every 1 to 10 seconds. The BPDU has the group MAC address 800143000000 which is recognized by each bridge. A designated bridge will then update the path cost and timing information and forward the frame. A standby bridge will monitor the BPDUs but does not update or forward them.

When a standby bridge is required to assume the role of the root or designated bridge as the operational states of other bridges change, the HELLO BPDU will indicate that a standby bridge should become a designated bridge. The process by which bridges determine their role in a spanning tree network is an iterative process. As new bridges enter a network they assume a listening state to determine their role in the network. Similarly, when a bridge is removed, another iterative process occurs to reconfigure the remaining bridges.

Although the STP algorithm procedure eliminates duplicate frame and degraded internet performance, it can be a hindrance in situations where multiple active paths between networks are desired. Another disadvantage of the spanning tree protocol is when it is used in remote bridges connecting geographically dispersed networks. For example, returning to Figure 5.4, suppose Ethernet 1 was located in Los Angeles, Ethernet 2 in New York, and Ethernet 3 in Atlanta. If the link between Los Angeles and New York was placed in a standby mode of operation, all frames from Ethernet 2 routed to Ethernet 1 would be routed through Atlanta. Depending upon the traffic between networks, this situation may require an upgrade in the bandwidth of the links connecting each network to accommodate the extra traffic flowing through Atlanta. Similarly, when using local bridges, additional traffic flowing via local bridges in interconnecting local area networks normally could result in an unacceptable level of performance occurring when LAN traffic is routed through an intermediate bridge.

Source Routing

Source routing is a bridging technique developed by IBM for connecting Token Ring networks. The key to the implementation of source routing is the use of a portion of the information field in the Token Ring frame to carry routing information and the transmission of "discovery" packets to determine the best route between two networks.

The presence of source routing is indicated by the setting of the first bit position in the source address field of a Token Ring frame to a binary one. When set, this indicates that the information field is preceded by a route information field (RIF) which contains both control and routing information.

The RIF Field

Figure 5.6 illustrates the composition of a Token Ring RIF. This field is variable in length and is developed during a discovery process which is described later in this section.

The control field contains information which defines how information will be transferred and interpreted as well as the size of the remainder of the RIF. The three broadcast bit positions indicate a nonbroadcast, all-routes broadcast, or single-route broadcast situation. A nonbroadcast designator indicates a local or specific route frame. An all-routes broadcast designator indi-

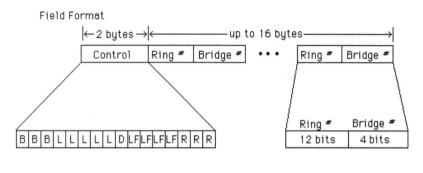

Figure 5.6   Token Ring route information field. The Token Ring route information field is variable in length.

cates that a frame will be transmitted along every route to the destination station. A single-route broadcast designator is used only by designated bridges to relay a frame from one network to another. In examining the broadcast bit settings shown in Figure 5.6, note that the letter X indicates a don't-care bit setting that can be either a 1 or 0.

The length bits identify the length of the RIF in bytes, while the D bit indicates how the field is scanned, left to right or right to left. Since vendors have incorporated different memory in bridges which may limit frame sizes, the LF bits enable different devices to negotiate the size of the frame. Normally a default setting indicates a frame size of 512 bytes. Each bridge can select a number and if supported by other bridges, that number is then used to represent the negotiated frame size. Otherwise, a smaller number used to represent a smaller frame size is selected and the negotiation process is repeated. Readers should note that a 1500-byte frame is the largest frame size supported by Ethernet IEEE 802.3 networks. Thus, a bridge used to connect Ethernet and Token Ring networks cannot support the use of Token Ring frames exceeding 1500 bytes.

Up to eight route number subfields, each consisting of a 12-bit ring number and a 4-bit bridge number, can be contained in the routing information field. This permits two to eight route designators, enabling frames to traverse up to eight rings across seven bridges in a given direction. Both ring numbers and bridge numbers are expressed as hexadecimal characters, with three hex characters used to denote the ring number and one hex character used to identify the bridge number.

Operation Example

As an illustration of the concept behind source routing, consider the internet illustrated in Figure 5.7. In this example, let us assume two Token Ring networks are located in Atlanta and one network is located in New York.

Each Token Ring and every bridge are assigned ring and bridge numbers. For simplicity, ring numbers R1, R2, and R3 were used, although as previously explained, those numbers are actually represented in hexadecimal. Similarly, for simplicity,

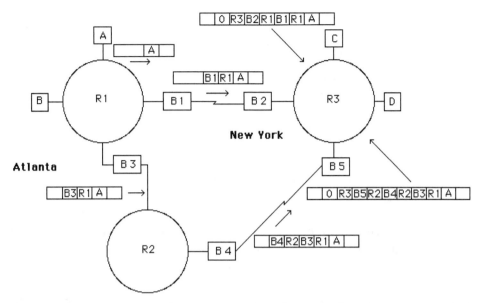

Figure 5.7 Source routing discovery operation. The route discovery process results in each bridge entering the originating ring number and its bridge number into the route information field.

bridge numbers are shown as B1, B2, B3, B4, and B5 instead of a hexadecimal character.

When a station wants to originate communications it is responsible for finding the destination by transmitting a discovery packet to network bridges and other network stations whenever it has a message to transmit to a new destination address. Assuming station A wishes to transmit to station C, it sends a route discovery packet which contains an empty route information field and its source address as indicated in the upper-left portion of Figure 5.7. This packet is recognized by each source routing bridge in the network. When received by a source routing bridge, the bridge enters the ring number from which the packet was received and its own bridge identifier in the packet's routing information field. The bridge then transmits the packet to all its connections with the exception of the connection on which the packet was received, a process known as *flooding*. Depending upon the topology of the interconnected networks, multiple copies of the discovery packet will more than likely reach the recipient. This is illustrated in the upper-right corner of Figure 5.7, in which two discovery packets reach station C. Here one packet contains the sequence R1B1R1B2R30, where the zero indicates there is no bridging in the last ring. The second packet contains the route sequence R1B3R2B4R2B5R30. Station C then picks the best route based upon either the most direct path or the earliest arriving packet and transmits a response to the discover packet originator. The response indicates the specific route to use and station A then enters that route into memory for the duration of the transmission session.

Under source routing, bridges do not keep routing tables like transparent bridges. Instead, tables are maintained at each station throughout the network. Thus, each station must check its routing table to determine the route frames must traverse to reach their destination station. This routing method results in source routing using distributed routing tables in comparison to the centralized routing tables used by transparent bridges.

Advantages

There are several advantages associated with the use of source routing. One advantage is the ability to construct mesh networks with loops for a fault-tolerant design, which cannot be accomplished with the use of transparent bridges. Another advantage is the inclusion of routing information in the information frames. Several vendors have developed network management software products which use that information to provide statistical information concerning internet activity. Those products may assist you in determining wide area network link utilization, the need to modify the capacity of those links, or whether one or more workstations are hogging communications between networks.

Disadvantages

Although the preceding advantages are considerable, they are not without a price. That price includes a requirement to specifically identify bridges and links, higher bursts of network activity, and an incompatibility between Token Ring and Ethernet networks. In addition, due to the structure of the Token Ring route information field, which supports a maximum of seven entries, routing of frames is restricted to crossing a maximum of seven bridges.

When using source routing bridges to connect Token Ring networks you must configure each bridge with a unique bridge/ring number. In addition, unless you wish to accept the default method by which stations select a frame during the route discovery process you will have to reconfigure your LAN software. Thus, source routing creates an administrative burden not present when using transparent bridges.

Due to the route discovery process, the flooding of discovery frames occurs in bursts when stations are powered on or after a power outage. Depending upon the complexity of an internet, the discovery process can degrade network performance. Perhaps the biggest problem is for organizations that require the interconnection of Ethernet and Token Ring networks.

A source routing bridge can only be used to interconnect Token Ring networks since it operates on route information field data which is not included in an Ethernet frame. Although transparent bridges can operate in Ethernet, Token Ring, and mixed environments, their use precludes the ability to construct loop or mesh topologies and inhibits the ability to establish operational redundant paths for load sharing. Another problem associated with bridging Ethernet and Token Ring networks also involves the route information field in a Token Ring frame. Unfortunately, different LAN operating systems use the RIF data in different ways. Thus, the use of a transparent bridge to interconnect Ethernet and Token Ring networks may require the same local area network operating system on each network. To alleviate these problems, several vendors introduced source routing transparent (SRT) bridges which function in accordance with the IEEE 802.1D standard that was approved during 1992.

Source Routing Transparent Bridges

A source routing transparent bridge supports both IBM's source routing and the IEEE transparent spanning tree protocol operations. This type of bridge can be considered two bridges in one and has been standardized by the IEEE 802.1 committee as the IEEE 802.1D standard.

Operation

Under source routing, the media access control packets contain a status bit in the source field which identifies whether source routing is to be used for a message. If source routing is indicated, the bridge forwards the frame as a source routing frame. If source routing is not indicated, the bridge determines the destination address and processes the packet using a transparent mode of operation, using routing tables generated by a spanning tree algorithm.

Advantages

There are several advantages associated with the use of source routing transparent bridges. First and perhaps foremost, its use enables different networks to use different local area network operating systems and protocols. This capability enables you to interconnect networks developed independently of one another and allows organization departments and branches to use LAN operating systems without restriction. Second and also very important, source routing transparent bridges can connect Ethernet and Token Ring networks while preserving the ability to mesh or loop Token Ring networks. Thus, its use provides an additional level of flexibility for network construction.

Translating Operations

When interconnecting Ethernet/IEEE 802.3 and Token Ring networks, the difference between frame formats requires the conversion of frames.

As previously noted in Chapter 3, there are several types of Ethernet frames, such as Ethernet, IEEE 802.3, Novell's Ethernet-802.3, and Ethernet-SNAP. The later two frames represent variations of the physical IEEE 802.3 frame format. Ethernet and Ethernet-802.3 do not use logical link control, while IEEE 802.3 CSMA/CD LANs specify the use of IEEE 802.2 logical link control. In comparison, all IEEE 802.5 Token Ring networks either directly or indirectly use the IEEE 802.2 specification for logical link control.

The conversion from IEEE 802.3 to IEEE 802.5 can be accomplished by discarding portions of the IEEE 802.3 frame not applicable to a Token Ring frame, copying the 802.2 LLC protocol data unit (PDU) from one frame to another, and inserting fields applicable to the Token Ring frame. Figure 5.8 illustrates the conversion process performed by a translating bridge linking an IEEE 802.3 network to an IEEE 802.5 network. Note that fields unique to the IEEE 802.3 frame are discarded, while fields common to both frames are copied. Fields unique to the IEEE 802.5 frame are inserted by the bridge.

Since an Ethernet frame, as well as Novell's Ethernet-802.3 frame, does not support logical link control, the conversion to IEEE 802.5 requires more processing. In addition, each conversion is more specific and may or may not be supported by a specific translating bridge. For example, consider the conversion of

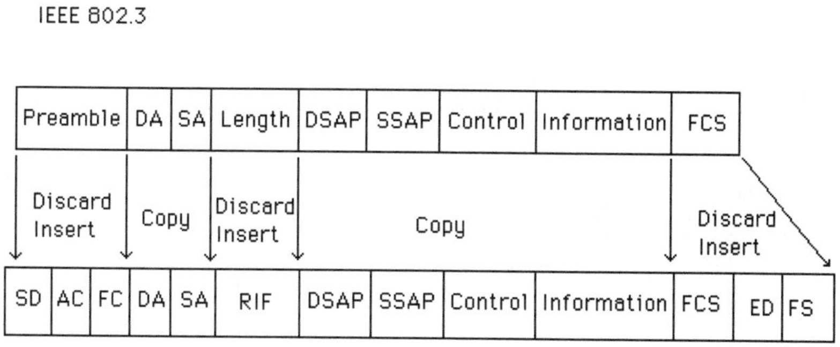

IEEE 802.3

Legend:

DA	Destination Address
SA	Source Address
AC	Access Control
FC	Frame Control
RIF	Routing Information Field
DSAP	Destination Service Access Point
SSAP	Source Service Access Point
ED	End Delimiter
FS	Frame Status Field

Figure 5.8   IEEE 802.3 to 802.% frame conversion.

Ethernet frames to Token Ring frames. Since Ethernet does not support LLC PDUs, the translation process results in the generation of a Token Ring–SNAP frame. This conversion or translation process is illustrated in Figure 5.9.

Figure 5.10 illustrates the conversion of IEEE 802.3 to FDDI frames. Note that both destination and source address fields must be bit reversed in each octet. When translating between Ethernet and FDDI, it is important to note that many bridges are limited to supporting FDDI RFC 1042 frame translation. Since all RFC 1042 frames are translated to IEEE 802.3 frames when bridged from an FDDI network to an Ethernet network, this means that Ethernet stations that transmit RFC 1042 frames, but cannot recognize IEEE 802.3 frames, in response will not be able to communicate with FDDI stations via a bridge. To overcome this problem requires the use of an Ethernet station that can recognize IEEE 802.3 and RFC 1042 encoded

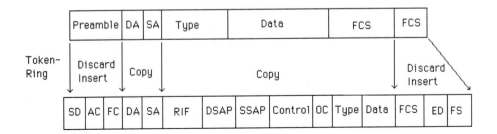

Legend:

DA	Destination Address
SA	Source Address
AC	Access Control
FC	Frame Control
RIF	Routing Information Field
DSAP	Destination Service Access Point
SSAP	Source Service Access Point
ED	End Delimiter
FS	Frame Status Field
OC	Organization Code

Figure 5.9 Ethernet to Token Ring frame conversion.

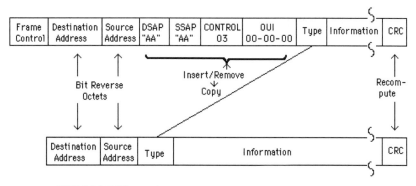

IEEE 802.3 Ethernet

Figure 5.10 IEEE 802.3 to FDDI RFC 1042 frame conversion.

frames. One example of this capability is Novell's ODI drivers used in NetWare 3.1X and 4.X.

In addition to IEEE 802.3 to FDDI RFC 1042 translation, many bridges support a variety of other Ethernet to FDDI translations. Some of those translations include Ethernet-SNAP to FDDI-SNAP, and Ethernet 802.3 to FDDI.

Bridge Utilization

A bridge can be used to interconnect separate local area networks to form several bridging topologies. Those topologies include serial, sequential, parallel, and star bridging structures. In addition, a version of parallel bridging can be used to form a backbone bridging structure.

Serial and Sequential Bridging

The top of Figure 5.11 illustrates the basic use of a bridge to interconnect two networks serially. Suppose monitoring of each network indicates a high level of intranetwork utilization. One possible configuration to reduce intra-LAN traffic on each network can be obtained by moving some stations off each of the two existing networks to form a third network. The three networks would then be interconnected through the use of an additional bridge as illustrated in the middle portion of Figure 5.11. This extension results in sequential or cascaded bridging and is

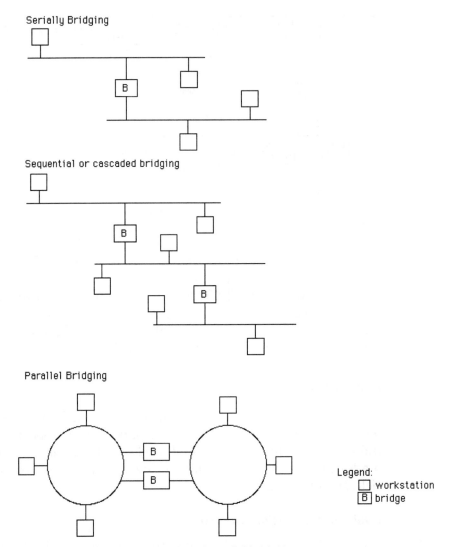

Figure 5.11 Serial, sequential, and parallel bridging.

appropriate when intra-LAN traffic is necessary but minimal. This internet topology is also extremely useful when the length of an Ethernet must be extended beyond the physical cabling of a single network. By appropriately locating servers within each network segment, you may be able to minimize inter-LAN transmission. For example, the first network segment could be used to connect marketing personnel, while the second and third segments could be used to connect engineering and personnel departments. Doing so might minimize the use of a server on one network by persons connected to another network segment. Both serial and sequential bridging are applicable to transparent, source routing, and source routing transparent bridges which provide neither redundancy nor the ability to balance traffic flowing between networks. Each of these deficiencies can be alleviated through the use of parallel bridging. However, this bridging technique creates a loop and is applicable only to source routing and source routing transparent bridges.

Parallel Bridging

The lower portion of Figure 5.11 illustrates the use of parallel bridges to interconnect two Token Ring networks. This bridging configuration permits one bridge to back up the other, providing a level of redundancy for linking the two networks as well as a significant increase in the availability of one network to communicate with another. For example, assume the availability of each bridge used at the top of Figure 5.11 (serial bridging) and bottom of Figure 5.11 (parallel bridging) is 90 percent. The availability through two serially connected bridges would be .9 × .9, or 81 percent. In comparison, the availability through parallel bridges would be 1 − (unavailability of bridge 1 × unavailability of bridge 2), or 1 − .1 × .1, which is 99 percent.

The dual paths between networks also improve inter-LAN communications performance as communications between stations on each network can be load balanced. Thus, the use of parallel bridges can be expected to provide a higher level of inter-LAN communications than the use of serial or sequential bridges. However, as previously noted, the use of this topology is not supported by transparent bridging.

Star Bridging

With a multiport bridge, you can connect three or more networks to form a star internet topology. The top portion of Figure 5.12 illustrates the use of one bridge to form a star topology by interconnecting four separate networks. This topology or a variation on this topology could be used to interconnect networks on separate floors within a building. For example, the top network could be on floor N + 1, while the bottom network could be on floor N − 1 in a building. The bridge and the two networks to the left and right of the bridge might then be located on floor N.

Although star bridging permits several networks located on separate floors within a building to be interconnected, all internet data must flow through one bridge which can result in both performance and reliability constraints to traffic flow. Thus, to internet separate networks on more than a few floors in a building you should consider the use of backbone bridging.

Backbone Bridging

The lower portion of Figure 5.12 illustrates the use of backbone bridging. In this example, one network runs vertically through a building with Ethernet "ribs" extending from the backbone onto each floor. Depending upon the amount of internet traffic and the vertical length required for the backbone network, it can be a conventional Ethernet bus-based network or a fiber optic backbone. Concerning the latter, you might consider the use of a 100-Mbps FDDI network whose use could serve as a superhighway to transport data between many individual Ethernet networks installed on separate floors within a building.

INTELLIGENT SWITCHES

Until the early 1990s, the primary method employed to overcome the effect of network congestion was segmentation, subdividing a network into two or more entities interconnected by a bridge or router. Today, the network manager and administrator have several options, including the use of a higher operating rate network such as Fast Ethernet or ATM or the use of intelligent switches. In this section we will focus on the latter, which are also referred to as switching hubs.

To obtain an appreciation for the role of intelligent switches, we will first review the operation of conventional hubs and the bandwidth constraints associated with their use. Once this is

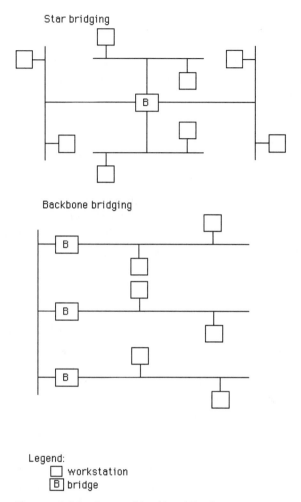

Figure 5.12   Star and backbone bridging.

accomplished, we will focus on the different operational methods supported by intelligent switching hubs, including the basic
switching methods supported by different products that fall into
this class of networking device. Using this information, as a
foundation we will explore the use of both Ethernet and Token
Ring intelligent switching hubs to obtain an understanding of
the key features built into many products and examine why the
presence of some features and the absence of others can result

in degraded performance instead of an expected improvement in performance. We will therefore examine how the use of certain intelligent switch features can result in network problems and how those problems can be alleviated through the use of other device features.

Conventional Hub Bottlenecks

Conventional hubs, which were developed to facilitate the cabling of network devices, also function as a bottleneck with respect to the use of network bandwidth. To obtain an appreciation for why conventional hubs function as network bottlenecks, we will discuss the operation of both Ethernet and Token Ring hubs, the latter of which is primarily referred to as a *multistation access unit* (MAU).

Ethernet Hub Operation

In an Ethernet environment a single LAN is usually referred to as a *segment*, with large networks typically composed of multiple segments connected by a bridge or router. The early implementations of Ethernet in the form of 10BASE-5 and 10BASE-2 coaxial cable–based networks resulted in the use of a common medium to which workstations are attached. This is illustrated in Figure 5.13, which shows the cabling structure of a coaxial based Ethernet network.

Based upon the fact that the bandwidth of the media is shared with only one user able to transmit at any given time, the Ethernet LAN segment shown in Figure 5.13 is commonly referred to as a shared-media, shared-bandwidth network.

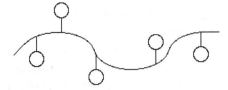

10BASE-5 and 10BASE-2 Etherent networks consist of a coaxial run to which network devices are attached.

Figure 5.13 A shared-media, shared-bandwidth Ethernet LAN segment.

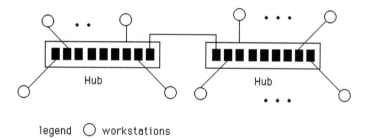

legend ○ workstations

Figure 5.14   A two hub 10BASE-T Ethernet network.

A change in the network topology and cabling structure of Ethernet resulted in the development of hub-centric 10BASE-T networks, in which cabling from individual network devices to dedicated ports on the hub resulted in a star-wiring configuration. When two or more hubs are interconnected to form a common network, the wiring topology resembles a star-bus structure, as illustrated in Figure 5.14. Although the wiring topology changed, the use of hubs did not alter the fact that the network remained a shared-media, shared-bandwidth network.

To illustrate the problem associated with the use of a shared-media, shared-bandwidth network, let's examine the operation of a conventional Ethernet hub. This type of hub simply duplicates nodes attached to the hub. Figure 5.15 illustrates the data flow when one workstation (node 1) transmits a frame to another workstation, file server, or another network device which is either connected to the same hub or to another hub which is

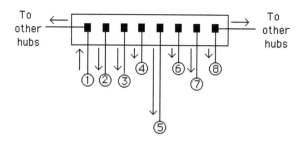

A conventional hub functions as a data regenerator, outputting an incoming frame received on one port onto all other ports.

Figure 5.15   Conventional hub dataflow.

connected to the hub the data originator is connected to. Since the hub functions as a data regenerator, the frame is repeated onto each connection to the hub, including interconnections to other hubs. This restricts data flow to one workstation at a time, since collisions occur when two or more attempt to gain access to the media at the same time.

Token Ring Hub Operation

Although data flow on a Token Ring network is circular, this type of network is also a shared-media, shared-bandwidth network. In a Token Ring network, environment hubs, referred to as multistation access units (MAUs), are connected via their Ring In and Ring Out ports to form a star-ring topology similar to that shown in Figure 5.16. The actual data flow of a frame is from one

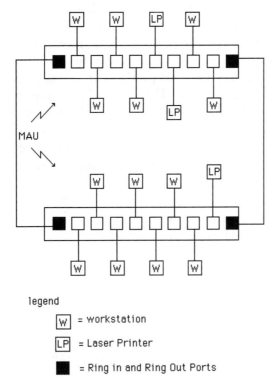

legend

W = workstation

LP = Laser Printer

■ = Ring In and Ring Out Ports

Figure 5.16 The connection of Token Ring MAUs forms a star-ring topology.

device to the next, flowing down the cable, called a lobe, connecting the device to the MAU port to an attached device and back to the port prior to flowing to the next port. Since only one frame can flow on the network at any point in time, access to the bandwidth is also shared. Thus, a Token Ring network also represents a shared-media, shared-bandwidth network.

Bottleneck Creation

Conventional Ethernet hubs create network bottlenecks because all traffic flows through a shared backplane in the hub. Thus, every device connected to an Ethernet hub competes for a slice of the bandwidth of the backplane. In a Token Ring environment devices compete to acquire a token, resulting in the sharing of network bandwidth in a similar manner. The end result of this bandwidth sharing is an average transmission rate per device that is many times below the operating rate of the network. For example, consider a departmental 10BASE-T network operating at 10 Mbps consisting of 12 interconnected 8-port hubs that supports a total of 96 devices. Then, the average slice of bandwidth available for each device is 10 Mbps/96 or approximately 104 kbps. Note that although each device transmits and receives data at the LAN operating rate of 10 Mbps, their average data transfer capability is approximately 104 kbps, since each device must compete with 95 other devices to obtain access to the network. Similarly, a 96-node Token Ring network would result in each device attached to that network having an average data transfer capability of 4 Mbps or 16 Mbps divided by 96, depending upon the operating rate of the network. This means that over a period of time, the addition of network users, introduction of one or more graphic-based applications, or growth in the use of current applications can result in a severely taxed network. When this type of situation occurs, you can consider a variety of techniques to enhance network performance such as network segmentation through the use of a bridge or router, migrating your existing infrastructure to a different and higher operating rate technology, or employing intelligent switching hubs, which is the focus of this section.

Switching Operations

The development of intelligent switching hubs has its foundation, similar to many other areas of modern communications, in telephone technology. Shortly after the telephone was invented, the switchboard was developed to enable multiple simultaneous conversations to occur without requiring telephone wires to be installed in a complex matrix between subscribers. Later, telephone office switches were developed to route calls based upon the telephone number dialed, followed in a similar manner by the development of bridges in a LAN environment. Bridges represent an elementary type of switch due to their limited number of ports and simplistic switching operation. That switching operation is based on whether the destination address in a frame "read" on one port is known to reside on that port.

Bridge Switching

Figure 5.17 illustrates the basic operation of a bridge. If you compare the operations performed by a bridge with respect to each port you will note they are nearly identical, with the only difference between the two operations concerning the port they forward frames to when the destination address of a frame is compared to a table of source addresses and no match occurs. When this situation occurs, the frame's destination is considered to reside on the network attached to the other port, as opposed to the port it was read from; hence it is forwarded through the bridge to the other port and placed onto the network connected to that port. If n networks are connected in serial via the use of $n - 1$ bridges and a frame is transmitted on the network at one end of the interconnected group of networks to the network on the opposite end of the interconnected group of LANs, each bridge would perform a similar forwarding operation until the frame traversed n bridges and was placed onto the last network in the interconnected series. The simplicity associated with the operation of bridges makes them a popular networking device. However, most bridges are limited to forwarding or "switching" frames on a serial basis, from one port to another. This restricts the forwarding rate to the lowest network operating rate. For example, the connection of a 10-Mbps Ethernet

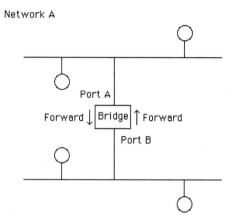

Network A

Port A

Forward ↓ | Bridge | ↑ Forward

Port B

Port A operation

1. Read source address of frames
   on LAN A to construct a table
   of source addresses.
2. Read destination address in
   frames and compare to addresses
   in source address table.
3. If address not in table, forward
   onto Port B, otherwise, do nothing.

Port B operation

1. Read source address of frames
   on LAN B to construct a table
   of source addresses.
2. Read destination address in
   frames and compare to addresses
   in source address table.
3. If address not in table, forward
   onto Port A, otherwise, do nothing.

Figure 5.17   Bridge switching operation.

network to a 16-Mbps Token Ring network via the use of a local bridge would reduce internetwork communications to a maximum operating rate of 10 Mbps, creating another network bottleneck.

The Switching Hub

Recognizing the limitations associated with the operation of bridges, vendors incorporated parallel switching technology into a device known as an *intelligent switching hub*. This device was based upon matrix switches which for decades have been successfully employed in telecommunications operations. By adding buffer memory to store address tables, frames flowing on LANs connected to different ports could be simultaneously read and forwarded via the switch fabric to ports connected to other networks.

Basic Components Figure 5.18 illustrates the basic components of a four-port intelligent switch. Although some switches function similar to bridges that read frames flowing on a network to construct a table of source addresses, other switches require their tables to be preconfigured. Either method allows the destination address to be compared to a table of destination addresses and associated port numbers. When a match occurs between the destination address of a frame flowing on a network connected to a port and the address in the port's address table, the frame is copied into the switch and routed through the switch fabric to the destination port, where it is placed onto the network connected to that port. If the destination port is in use due to a previously established cross-connection between ports,

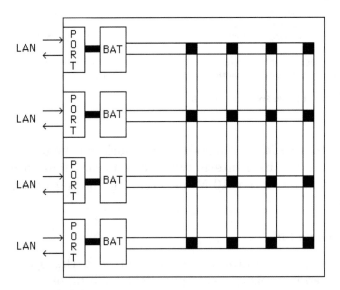

An intelligent switch consists of buffers and address tables (BAT), logic and a switching fabric which permits frames entering one port to be routed to any port in the switch. The destination address in a frame is used to determine the associated port with that address via a search of the address table, with the port address used by the switching fabric for establishing the cross connection.

Figure 5.18 Basic components of an intelligent switch.

the frame is maintained in the buffer until it can be switched to its destination.

Delay Times Switching occurs on a frame-by-frame basis, with the cross-connection torn down after being established for routing one frame. Thus, frames can be interleaved from two or more ports to a common destination port with a minimum of delay. For example, consider a maximum-length Ethernet frame of 1526 bytes composed of a 1500-byte data field and 26 overhead bytes. At a 10-Mbps operating rate, each bit time is $1/10^7$ seconds or 100 ns. For a 1526 byte frame the minimum delay time if one frame precedes it in attempting to be routed to a common destination becomes:

$$1526 \text{ bytes} \times \frac{8 \text{ bits}}{\text{byte}} \times \frac{100 \text{ ns}}{\text{bit}} = 1.22 \text{ ms}$$

This delay time represents blocking resulting from frames on two service ports having a common destination and should not be confused with another delay time referred to as *latency*. Latency represents the delay associated with the physical transfer of a frame from one port via the switch to another port and is fixed based upon the architecture of the switch. In comparison, blocking delay depends upon the number of frames from different ports attempting to access a common destination port and the method by which the switch is designed to respond to blocking. Some switches simply have large buffers for each port and service ports in a round-robin fashion when frames on two or more ports attempt to access a common destination port. This method of service does not show favoritism; however, it also does not consider the fact that some attached networks may have operating rates different from other attached networks. Other switch designs recognize that port buffers are filled based upon both the number of frames having a destination address of a different network and the operating rate of the network. Such switch designs use a priority service scheme based upon the occupancy of the port buffers in the switch.

Key Advantage of Use A key advantage associated with the use of intelligent switching hubs results from their ability to support parallel switching, permitting multiple cross-connections between source and destination to occur simultaneously. For example, if four 10BASE-T networks were connected to the four port switch shown in Figure 5.18, two simultaneous cross-connections, each at 10 Mbps, could occur, resulting in an increase in bandwidth to 20 Mbps. Here each cross-connection represents a dedicated 10-Mbps bandwidth for the duration of a frame. Thus, from a theoretical perspective, an N port switching hub supporting a 10-Mbps operating rate on each port provides a throughput up to $N/2 \times 10$ Mbps. For example, a 128-port switching hub would support a throughput up to $(128/2) \times 10$ Mbps or 640 Mbps, while a network constructed using a series of conventional hubs connected to one another would be limited to an operating rate of 10 Mbps, with each workstation on that network having an average bandwidth of 10 Mbps/128 or 78 kbps.

Through the use of intelligent switching hubs you can overcome the operating rate limitation of a local area network. In an Ethernet environment, the cross-connection through a switching hub represents a dedicated connection so there will never be a collision. This fact enabled many switching hub vendors to use the collision wire-pair from conventional Ethernet to support simultaneous transmission in both directions between a connected node and hub port, resulting in a full-duplex transmission capability that will be discussed in more detail later in this section. In fact, a similar development permits Token Ring switching hubs to provide full-duplex transmission since if there is only one station on a port there is no need to pass tokens and repeat frames, raising the maximum bidirectional throughput between a Token Ring device and a switching hub port to 32 Mbps. Thus, the ability to support parallel switching as well as initiate dedicated cross-connections on a frame-by-frame basis can be considered the key advantages associated with the use of intelligent switching hubs. Both parallel switching and dedicated cross-connections permit higher bandwidth operations. Now that we have an appreciation for the general operation of switching hubs, let's focus our attention upon the different switching techniques that can be incorporated into this category of communications equipment.

Switching Techniques

There are three switching techniques used by intelligent switching hubs: cross-point, also referred to as cut-through or on-the-fly; store-and-forward; and a hybrid method, which alternates between the first two methods based upon the frame error rate. As we will soon note, each technique has one or more advantages and disadvantages associated with its operation.

Cross-Point Switching

The operation of a cross-point switch is based upon an examination of the destination of frames as they enter a port on the switching hub. The switch uses the destination address as a decision criteria to obtain a port destination from a look-up table. Once a port destination is obtained a cross-connection through the switch is initiated, resulting in the frame being routed to a destination port where it is placed onto a network for which its frame destination address resides. In actuality there are usually two look-up tables in a switch. The first table, which is usually constructed dynamically, consists of source addresses of frames flowing on the network connected to the port. This enables the switch to construct a table of known devices. Then, the first comparison using the destination address in a frame is with the table of known source addresses. If the destination address matches an address in the table of known source addresses this indicates that the frame's destination is on the current network and no switching operation is required. If the frame's destination address does not match an address in the table of known source addresses this indicates that the frame is to be routed through the switch onto a different network. Then the switch will search a destination look-up table to obtain a port destination and initiate a cross-connection through the switch, routing the frame to a destination port where it is placed onto a network where a node with the indicated destination address resides.

Figure 5.19 illustrates the basic operation of cross-point or cut-through switching. Under this technique the destination address in a frame is read prior to the frame being stored (1). That address is forwarded to a look-up table (2) to determine the port destination address which is used by the switching fabric to ini-

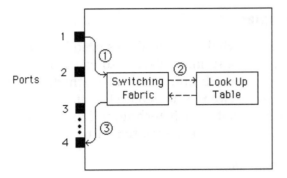

A cross-point or cut-through operating switch reads the destination address in a frame prior to storing the entire frame (1). It forwards that address to a look-up table (2) to determine the port destination address which is used by the switching fabric to provide a cross-connection to the destination port (3).

Figure 5.19   Cross-point/cut-through switching.

tiate a cross-connection to the destination port (3). Since this switching method only requires the storage of a small portion of a frame until it is able to read the destination address and perform its table look-up operation to initiate switching to an appropriate output port, latency through the switch is minimized.

Latency functions as a brake on two-way frame exchanges. For example, in a client-server environment the transmission of a frame by a workstation results in a server response. Thus, the minimum wait time is 2*latency for each client-server exchange, lowering the effective throughput of the switch. Since a cross-point switching technique results in a minimal amount of latency, the effect upon throughput of the delay attributable to a switching hub using this switching technique is minimal.

Store-and-Forward

In comparison to a cut-through switching hub, a store-and-forward switching hub first stores an entire frame in memory prior to operating on the data fields within the frame. Once the frame is stored, the switching hub checks the frame's integrity by performing a cyclic redundancy check (CRC) upon the contents of the frame, comparing its computed CRC against the CRC contained in the frame's frame check sequence (FCS) field. If the two match, the frame is considered to be error-free and additional processing and switching will occur. Otherwise, the frame is considered to have one or more bits in error and will be discarded.

In addition to CRC checking, the storage of a frame permits filtering against various frame fields to occur. Although a few manufacturers of store-and-forward intelligent switching hubs support different types of filtering, the primary advantage advertised by such manufacturers is data integrity. Whether this is actually an advantage depends upon how you view the additional latency introduced by the storage of a full frame in memory as well as the necessity for error checking. Concerning the latter, switches should operate error-free, so a store-and-forward switch only removes network errors which should be negligible to start with.

When a switch removes an errored frame, the originator will retransmit the frame after a period of time. Since an errored frame arriving at its destination network address is also discarded, many people question the necessity of error checking by a store-and-forward switching hub. However, filtering capability, if offered, may be far more useful as you could use this capability, for example, to route protocols carried in frames to destination ports far easier than by frame destination address. This is especially true if you have hundreds or thousands of devices connected to a large switching hub. You might set up two or three filters instead of entering a large number of destination addresses into the switch. When a switch performs filtering of protocols, it really becomes a router. This is because it is now operating at layer 3 of the OSI Reference Model.

Figure 5.20 illustrates the operation of a store-and-forward switching hub. Note that a common switch design is to use shared buffer memory to store entire frames which increases the latency associated with this type of switching hub. Since the minimum length of an Ethernet frame is 72 bytes, then the minimum one way delay or latency, not counting the switch over-

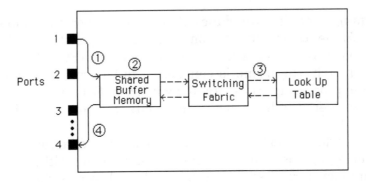

A store and forward switching hub reads the frame destination
address (1) as it is placed in buffer memory (2). As the entire
frame is being read into memory, a look up operation (3) is performed to obtain a destination port address. Once the entire
frame is in memory a CRC check is performed and one or more
filtering operations may be peformed. If the CRC check indicates
the frame is error-free, it is forwarded from memory to its'
destination address (4), otherwise it is disregarded.

Figure 5.20   Store-and-forward switching.

head associated with the look-up table and switching fabric operation, becomes:

$$96 \text{ μs} + 72 \text{ bytes} \times 8 \text{ bits/byte} \times 100 \text{ ns/bit}$$
or $\quad 9.6 \times 10^{-6} + 576 \times 100 \times 10^{-9}$
or $\quad 67.2 \times 10^{-6}$ seconds

Here 9.6 μs represents the Ethernet interframe gap, while
100 ns/bit is the bit duration of a 10-Mbps Ethernet LAN. Thus,
the minimum one-way latency of a store-and-forward Ethernet
switching hub is .0000672 seconds, while a round-trip minimum
latency is twice that duration. For a maximum-length Ethernet
frame with a data field of 1500 bytes, the frame length becomes
1526 bytes. Thus, the one-way maximum latency becomes:

$$96 \text{ μs} + 1526 \text{ bytes} \times 8 \text{ bits/byte} \times 100 \text{ ns/bit}$$
or $\quad 9.6 \times 10^{-6} + 12208 \times 100 \times 10^{-9}$
or $\quad .012304$ seconds

Hybrid

A hybrid switch supports both cut-through and store-and-forward switching, selecting the switching method based upon monitoring the error rate encountered by reading the CRC at the end of each frame and comparing its value to a computed CRC performed on-the-fly on the fields protected by the CRC. Initially the switch might set each port to a cut-through mode of operation. If too many bad frames are noted occurring on the port the switch will automatically set the frame processing mode to store-and-forward, permitting the CRC comparison to be performed prior to the frame being forwarded. This permits frames in error to be discarded without having them pass through the switch. Since the "switch," no pun intended, between cut-through and store-and-forward modes of operation occurs adaptively, another term used for the operation of this type of switch is *adaptive*.

The major advantages of a hybrid switch are that it provides minimal latency when error rates are low and discards frames by adapting to a store-and-forward switching method so it can discard errored frames when the frame error rate rises. From an economic perspective, the hybrid switch can logically be expected to cost more than a cut-through or store-and-forward switch as its software development effort is more comprehensive. However, due to the competitive market for communications products its price may be reduced below competitive switch technologies.

In addition to being categorized by their switching technique, switching hubs can be classified by their support of single or multiple addresses per port. The former method is referred to as port-based switching, while the latter switching method is referred to as segment-based switching.

Port-Based Switching

A switching hub which performs port-based switching only supports a single address per port. This restricts switching to one device per port; however, it results in a minimum amount of memory in the switch as well as provides for a relatively fast table look-up when the switch uses a destination address in a frame to obtain the port for initiating a cross-connect.

Figure 5.21 illustrates an example of the use of a port-based switching hub. In this example, M user workstations use the switch to contend for the resources of N servers. If M > N, then a switching hub connected to Ethernet 10-Mbps LANs can support a maximum throughput of $N/2 \times 10$ Mbps, since up to N/2 simultaneous client-server frame flows can occur through the switch.

It is important to compare the maximum potential throughput of a switch to its rated backplane speed. If the maximum potential throughput is less than the rated backplane speed, the switch will not cause delays based upon the traffic being routed through the device. For example, consider a 64-port switch that has a backplane speed of 400 Mbps. If the maximum port rate is 10 Mbps, then the maximum throughput assuming 32 active cross-connections were simultaneously established becomes 320 Mbps. In this example, the switch has a backplane transfer ca-

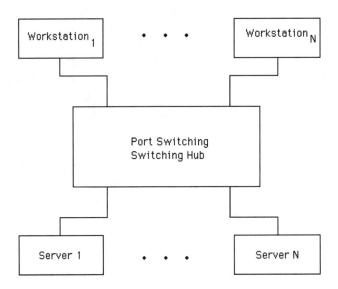

A port-based switching hub associates one address with each port, minimizing the time required to match the destination address of a frame against a table of destination addresses and associated port numbers.

Figure 5.21   Port-based switching.

pability sufficient to handle the worst-case data transfer scenario. Now let's assume that the maximum backplane data transfer capability was 200 Mbps. This would reduce the maximum number of simultaneous cross-connections capable of being serviced to 20 instead of 32 and adversely affect switch performance under certain operational conditions.

Since a port-based switching hub has to store only one address per port, search times are minimized. When combined with a pass-through or cut-through switching technique, this type of switch results in a minimal latency including the overhead of the switch in determining the destination port of a frame.

Segment-Based Switching

A segment-based switching technique requires a switching hub to support multiple addresses per port. Through the use of this type of switch, you achieve additional networking flexibility since you can connect other hubs to a single segment-based switching hub port.

Figure 5.22 illustrates an example of the use of a segment-based switching hub in an Ethernet environment. Although two segments in the form of conventional hubs with multiple devices connected to each hub are shown in the lower portion of Figure 5.22, note that a segment can consist of a single device, resulting in the connection of one device to a port on a segment switching hub being similar to a connection on a port switching hub. However, unlike a port switching hub, which is limited to supporting one address per port, the segment switching hub can, if necessary, support multiple devices connected to a port. Thus, the two servers connected to the switch at the top of Figure 5.22 could, if desired, be placed on a conventional hub or a high-speed hub, such as a 100BASE-T hub, which in turn would be connected to a single port on a segment switching hub.

In Figure 5.22, each conventional hub acts as a repeater and forwards every frame transmitted on that hub to the switching hub, regardless of whether the frame requires the resources of the switching hub. The segment switching hub examines the destination address of each frame against addresses in its look-up table, forwarding only those frames that warrant it. Other-

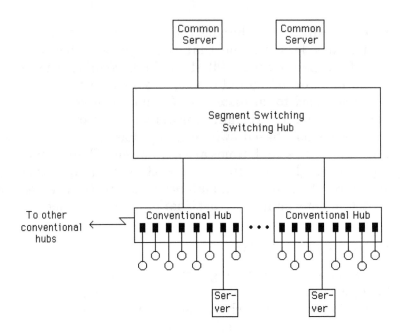

Through the use of a segment-based switching hub, you
can maintain servers for use by workstations on a common
network segment as well as provide address by all workstations to common severs.

Figure 5.22 Segment-based switching.

wise, frames are discarded as they are local to the conventional
hub. Through the use of a segment-based switching hub, you can
maintain the use of local servers with respect to existing LAN
segments as well as install servers whose access is common to all
network segments. The latter is illustrated in Figure 5.22 by the
connection of two common servers shown at the top of the switching hub. If you obtain a store-and-forward segment switching
hub which supports filtering, you could control access to common
servers from individual workstations or by workstations on a
particular segment. In addition, you can also use the filtering capability of a store-and-forward segment-based switching hub to
control access from workstations located on one segment to
workstations or servers located on another segment.

Switching Architecture

The construction of intelligent switches varies both among manufacturers as well as within some vendor product lines. Most switches are based upon the use of either Reduced Instruction Set Computer (RISC) microprocessors or Application Specific Integrated Circuit (ASIC) chips, while a few products use conventional Complex Instruction Set Computer (CISC) microprocessors.

Although there are a large number of arguable advantages and disadvantages associated with each architecture from the standpoint of the switch manufacturer that are beyond the scope of this book, there are also some key considerations that warrant discussion with respect to virtual LANs and virtual networking. Both RISC and CISC architectures enable switches to be programmed to make forwarding decisions based on either the data link layer or network layer address information. In addition, when there is a need to modify the switch so as to enable it to support a VLAN standard when the standard is promulgated, this architecture is easily upgradable.

In comparison to RISC- and CISC-based switches, an ASIC-based device represents the use of custom-designed chips to perform specific switch functions in hardware. Although ASIC-based switches are faster than RISC- and CISC-based switches, there is no easy way to upgrade this type of switch. Instead, the vendor will have to design and manufacture new chips and install the hardware upgrade in the switch.

In early 1997, most switches used an ASIC architecture as its speed enabled the support of cut-through switching. While ASIC-based switches provide the speed necessary to minimize latency, you should carefully check vendor upgrade support as most vLAN standards can be expected to require modifications to existing switches.

Now that we have an appreciation for the general operation and utilization of switching hubs, let's examine the high-speed connection of switch ports to 100BASE-T, FDDI, ATM, and other types of networks which can result in data flow compatability problems along with methods used to alleviate such problems. Once this is accomplished we will turn our attention to Ethernet and Token Ring networking techniques using different types of intelligent switches.

High-Speed Port Operation

There are several types of high-speed connections intelligent switches may support. Those high-speed connections include full-duplex Ethernet and Token Ring, a grouping of ports operating as an entity and referred to as a fat pipe, 100-Mbps 100BASE-T and FDDI, as well as ATM.

Full-Duplex Ethernet and Token Ring

The cross-connection between the origination and destination port occurs on a frame-by-frame basis with the switching fabric in the switch building and tearing down each connection. When the connection is established, other data sources routed to the same destination address are precluded by the switching fabric from interfering with the flow of data. Thus, this precludes the possibility of collisions occurring in an Ethernet environment. Recognizing this fact, switching hub designers were able to use the second wire-pair of conventional Ethernet previously used for collision recognition as a path for the simultaneous transmission in the opposite direction, in effect obtaining a full-duplex transmission capability. In a Token Ring environment, if there is only one station on a port the need to pass tokens and repeat frames is eliminated, permitting full-duplex operations. Support for full-duplex Token Ring operation is accomplished through the use of modified Token Ring adapter cards. Such modified adapters do not include a repeater path which is normally used to allow a frame appearing on the receive path of a lobe to be placed on its transmit path. Figure 5.23 compares the operation of conventional and full-duplex operating Token Ring adapter cards.

In examining the illustration in the left portion of Figure 5.23 note that although the title is "conventional," in reality a conventional Token Ring adapter permits both reception and transmission of data to occur at the same time. Although this is indeed a full-duplex operation, only received data can be simul-

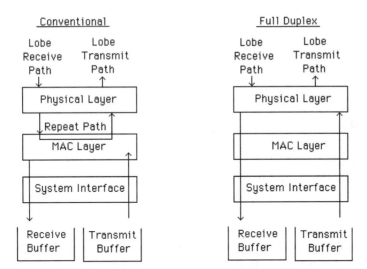

Figure 5.23   Comparing conventional and full-duplex Token Ring adapter card operators.

taneously placed onto the lobe's transmit path. If a workstation is receiving a frame and has data to send, the frame must circulate back to the originator and be converted into a token. Then, upon receipt of the token the workstation can transmit data. In comparison, when one Token Ring station is connected to a port on a Token Ring switch, as a frame is received the port can generate a new frame in the opposite direction, providing a true full-duplex operation in which different frames are simultaneously transmitted and received.

Although many vendors imply that the support of full-duplex transmission doubles the throughput of a 10BASE-T or Token Ring port to 20 or 36 Mbps, in actuality your ability to increase the throughput through a port depends upon the type of traffic supported by the port. For example, connecting a workstation to a full-duplex port would more than likely provide a negligible gain in throughput since most client-server communications are essentially half-duplex. However, the attachment of a server via a full-duplex port would enable the server to process query N while transmitting response N − 1 to query N − 1. Thus, you can obtain a degree of overlap of operations by using a server on a full-duplex switching hub port.

Fat Pipe

Fat pipe is a term used by some vendors to represent a group of N ports that operate together as an entity, providing a throughput of N × (port operating rate) or N × 2 × (port operating rate) if full-duplex transmission is supported by each port in the fat pipe group of ports. For example, consider an Ethernet switch with a fat pipe that can be constructed through a grouping of five 10-Mbps ports. This will provide a maximum throughput of 50 Mbps or 100 Mbps if each port supports full-duplex data transfer. However, as previously noted, your ability to obtain anywhere near a sustained level of full-duplex data transfer is doubtful.

Figure 5.24 illustrates a fat pipe formed by the grouping of five port connections which function as an entity. Note that in this example the fat pipe is used to provide a connection between a server and a switching hub, which is the primary application for the use of a fat pipe—providing nodes with a higher level of throughput. This is because access to modern servers as well as their ability to provide responses are a typical constraint of heavily utilized 10-Mbps Ethernet and 10-Mbps Token Ring networks.

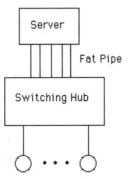

A fat pipe is a physical grouping of n ports that function as an entity.

legend ◯ workstations and/or servers

Figure 5.24   Using a fat pipe.

Once a frame destined for the server is received by the switching hub, it is subdivided and transmitted over five physical connections. Since the server must reconstruct the frame, special software is required to operate on the server. Thus, the software must be compatible with the LAN operating system used by the server.

One of the problems associated with the use of fat pipes as well as the use of different types of high-speed ports, such as 100BASE-T, FDDI, or ATM, is the situation where a workstation query results in a lengthy response from the server. To illustrate this problem, let's assume we are using an Ethernet switching hub with a workstation connected to a port at 10 Mbps while a server is connected to five 10-Mbps ports that form a fat pipe. Since the fat pipe response is at an operating rate of $n \times 10$ Mbps, while the workstation is connected to the hub at 10 Mbps, within a short period of time frames can be expected to overflow the port's receive buffer storage capacity, resulting in frame loss which requires the server to retransmit lost frames. To limit frame loss, vendors added buffer storage to their high-speed ports. However, no amount of buffer storage can prevent frame loss, resulting in some vendors adding flow control support to their switches. Prior to discussing the methods commonly used to regulate traffic between high-speed and lower-operating-rate ports, let's examine other common methods used by intelligent switch vendors to provide a high-speed data transfer capability between a switch port and an attached device.

100BASE-T

The inclusion of 100BASE-T port support is similar to a fat pipe; however, an increase in throughput now occurs via the use of a single port connection instead of multiple port connections. Similar to the operation of a fat pipe, the use of a 100BASE-T connection can occur in either a half- or full-duplex operating mode. In addition, frame loss via a 100BASE-T connection is compensated for by buffer memory within the switching hub but does not preclude the eventual loss of frames when a lengthy response to a query occurs.

FDDI and ATM Connections

FDDI and ATM ports are incorporated into some intelligent switching hubs to provide a high-speed data transfer capability between the switch and an attached device. Although many users employ high-speed ports for use with servers, such ports can also be used to develop a hierarchical network of conventional hubs, switching hubs, and high-speed backbone hubs. An example of the creation of a hub hierarchy is shown in Figure 5.25.

In the hub hierarchy illustrated in Figure 5.25, a FDDI hub is used to form a network consisting of three middle-tier switching hubs. The switching hubs in turn support port switching or port and segment switching, with the connection of conventional hubs forming the lower tier in the three-tier hub hierarchy. Through the use of one FDDI port on each switching hub access is obtained to an FDDI ring constructed through the use of an FDDI hub. Assuming each switching hub supports two different types of high-speed ports, the second port might be a 100BASE-T port used to provide access at 100 Mbps between the switch and an attached server. Thus, this configuration allows users at-

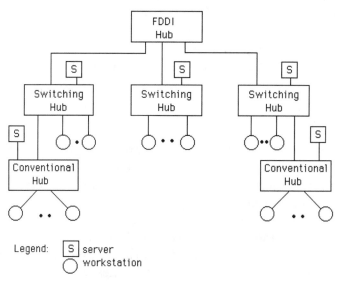

Figure 5.25 Creating a hub hierarchy.

tached to a conventional hub to access servers on that hub, access a server connected to the switching hub their conventional hub is connected to, or access a server connected to a different switching hub.

Although the FDDI operating rate is fixed at 100 Mbps, there are two ATM LAN operating rates you must consider. One rate is 25 Mbps, and the other rate is approximately 155 Mbps. Since the lower rate may provide only a marginal improvement over full-duplex 10BASE-T and full-duplex 16-Mbps Token Ring operations, it might be advisable to ignore that technology.

Flow Control

Flow control represents the orderly regulation of the transmission of information between devices, a necessity whenever there is a positive speed differential between the source and destination of information. Although some vendors include buffer storage to act as a temporary holding area until transmission ceases or the amount of data flow is reduced, no amount of buffer storage can guarantee data integrity. Thus, you can expect to lose frames if a switching hub does not provide flow control to regulate the flow of traffic between ports that have different operating rates.

The effect of frame loss depends upon the overall traffic supported by the hub. If you have several servers connected to high-speed ports and short queries result in lengthy transmissions, the loss of frames is compensated for by server retransmissions. Under certain situations the additional retransmissions lock out responses to other workstation queries and can actually result in a level of performance being less than that obtainable through the use of a conventional hub. For this reason the use of high-speed ports should normally be accompanied by the use of flow control, either the use of backpressure in an Ethernet environment or a server software module which works in tandem with the switch in both Ethernet and Token Ring environments.

Backpressure   *Backpressure* is a term used to represent the generation of a false collision signal. Since a collision signal causes an Ethernet workstation or server to delay further transmission based upon an exponential backoff algorithm, it provides a mechanism for implementing flow control. That is, once buffer storage in the hub reaches a predefined level of occupancy, the switch will generate a collision signal. As the transmitting device delays further transmission, the hub's destination port has the opportunity to empty the contents of its buffer, precluding data loss.

Since backpressure requires the use of a second wire pair, it is mutually exclusive with full-duplex transmission. If you require full-duplex transmission on a high-speed port and want to preclude the loss of frames via flow control, you must turn to the use of a server software module.

Server Software Module When this book was prepared, switching hub vendors indicated they were developing software to operate under NetWare and Windows NT that would regulate the flow of data between hub ports and servers. Once such products are available they will support full-duplex transmission as well as preclude frame loss, something currently lacking in the switching hub marketplace.

Token Ring Switching

Until now we have primarily focused our attention on Ethernet switches, using Ethernet segments to illustrate intelligent switch operations. Token Ring switches, in many ways, are similar to Ethernet switches; however, there are certain key differences between the two.

Port Switching

Due to the Token Ring protocol, stations gain access to a ring by acquiring a free token. A port-switching Token Ring switch forms a ring between the port and an attached station or network node. This type of Token Ring switch is also known as a Dedicated Token Ring and allows that station to obtain the full bandwidth of the ring instead of having to share it with other network users.

Bridging Support   Figure 5.26 illustrates a four-port Dedicated Token Ring (DTR) switch. In effect, the switch consists of four separate rings and will use bridging to provide a mechanism to transmit data from one ring to another. Concerning the method of bridging supported, unlike Ethernet, which is restricted to transparent bridging, Token Ring switches can also support source routing and source routing transparent bridging.

Switches supporting source routing operate at the data link layer of the OSI Reference Model. Such switches use source routing to make forwarding decisions on each frame it receives. That decision occurs relatively quickly, as the switch can use information in the routing information field to make its forwarding decisions. In comparison, when transparent bridging is used, forwarding decisions are based upon the switch first reading MAC address information in a frame and comparing that address to the tables of addresses it maintains to initiate its switching operation.

In examining Figure 5.26, note that the *data transfer unit* (DTU) provides the data highway which enables the transfer of information from one ring to another. To illustrate the connection of a ring to a switch port, small rings will be shown for each connection between a switch port and a workstation throughout the remainder of this book, with solid lines used to illustrate Ethernet switch connections.

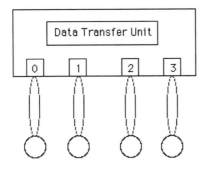

Figure 5.26   Dedicated Token Ring switching.

Full-Duplex Operations   A DTR method of operation is compatible with the original IEEE 802.5 standard. That standard requires half-duplex transmission since data is transmitted only when the ring is free of messages that a station may need to receive. This method of transmission was required to ensure that a transmitting station does not overwrite a message that has not yet reached its destination address. Under DTR, there are only two stations on the ring, the attaching station and the switch port. Since no data transmitted from one station to the other requires retransmission, both stations can transmit data as required. This new mode of Token Ring operation is defined by the 802.5r standard as Transmit Immediate (TXI). Under the TXI mode of operation, the requirement to acquire a token prior to being able to transmit is eliminated, allowing full-duplex transmission that doubles the bandwidth to 16 Mbps in each direction for a total of 32 Mbps per port.

In addition to port or DTR switching, Token Ring switches can be obtained that function as a segment switch. In doing so, the switch supports multiple stations beyond the two supported on a DTR switch; however, this results in the inability of the switch to support full-duplex transmission.

Switching Techniques

Similar to Ethernet switches, Token Ring switches support three switching techniques. Some Token Ring switches support cross-point or cut-through switching. Other switches employ store-and-forward switching, while a few switches support both methods. Concerning the latter, like their Ethernet relatives, they are commonly referred to as adaptive or hybrid switches.

Network Utilization

Unlike Ethernet, for which switches are commonly used to facilitate workgroup access to servers, in a Token Ring environment many organizations establish separate rings on floors and interconnect networks via bridging to backbone ring. In concluding this section, we will focus our attention upon the use of Ethernet and Token Ring switches and note several examples of their use.

Network Redistribution

Network redistribution involves the movement of bandwidth-intensive workstations off conventional hubs, connecting them directly to ports on an intelligent switch. Figure 5.27 illustrates an example of network redistribution through the use of an intelligent switching hub.

In the left portion of Figure 5.27 a conventional hub is shown providing support for n nodes to a common server. Assuming two workstations require access to a visual database, transmit or receive large files, or perform other bandwidth-intensive applications, those workstations were redistributed onto an intelligent switch, as shown in the right portion of Figure 5.27. Note that only one server is shown in the "after" network schematic, with the server relocated from the conventional hub to the intelligent switching hub, with the server connected to the intelligent switching hub by either a fat pipe or high-speed connection. If a conventional connection were used, the redistribution of work-

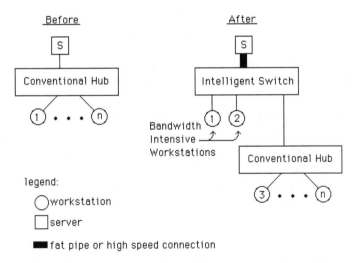

Through the movement of bandwidth intensive workstations off conventional hubs, you can minimize the effect of bottlenecks they cause on other workstations remaining connected to conventional hubs.

Figure 5.27   Network redistribution.

stations would have a negligible effect upon performance as access to the server would not increase, only enhancing any peer-to-peer communications that may occur.

Server Segmentation

Since access to data on servers is normally the reason why network performance degrades, another switching technique commonly used is to segment servers. Figure 5.28 illustrates an example of server segmentation obtained through the use of an intelligent switching hub.

In the top portion of Figure 5.28, two servers are shown on a network consisting of interconnected conventional hubs. In this example, access to either server is constrained by the operating rate of the network. For example, if the top portion of Figure 5.28 represented a 10BASE-T network, the maximum bandwidth to a server would be 10 Mbps, which is the operating rate of the LAN, while the average bandwidth would be 10 Mbps/n, where n represents the total number of nodes on the network.

Through the use of an intelligent switching hub servers can be placed on their own network segment, as illustrated in the lower portion of Figure 5.28. In addition, through the use of a fat pipe or high-speed connection between each server and the switch you can enhance access to each server.

If you simply moved each conventional hub onto a port on the switch, your ability to enhance network access would be limited. This limitation would result from the fact that the simultaneous access of workstations on different conventional hubs to different servers only provides the ability to double bandwidth. Thus, you would more than likely want to consider connecting high-activity workstations directly to the switch, as shown in the lower portion of Figure 5.28.

Network Segmentation

A third networking technique commonly associated with the use of intelligent switching hubs is network segmentation. Although the concept is similar to network segmentation performed by bridges and routers, the use of intelligent switches provides a significant increase in network configuration flexibility. To illus-

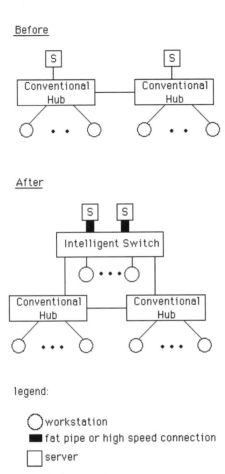

Figure 5.28 Server segmentation.

trate this increased flexibility consider Figure 5.29, in which one large Token Ring network was segmented into three via the use of a Token Ring switch.

Backbone Replacement

Our last network utilization example is focused upon a common use of Token Ring switches, replacing a backbone ring. The top of Figure 5.30 illustrates a common Token Ring implementation in which separate rings are established on different floors in a building with bridges connected to a backbone ring whose cable

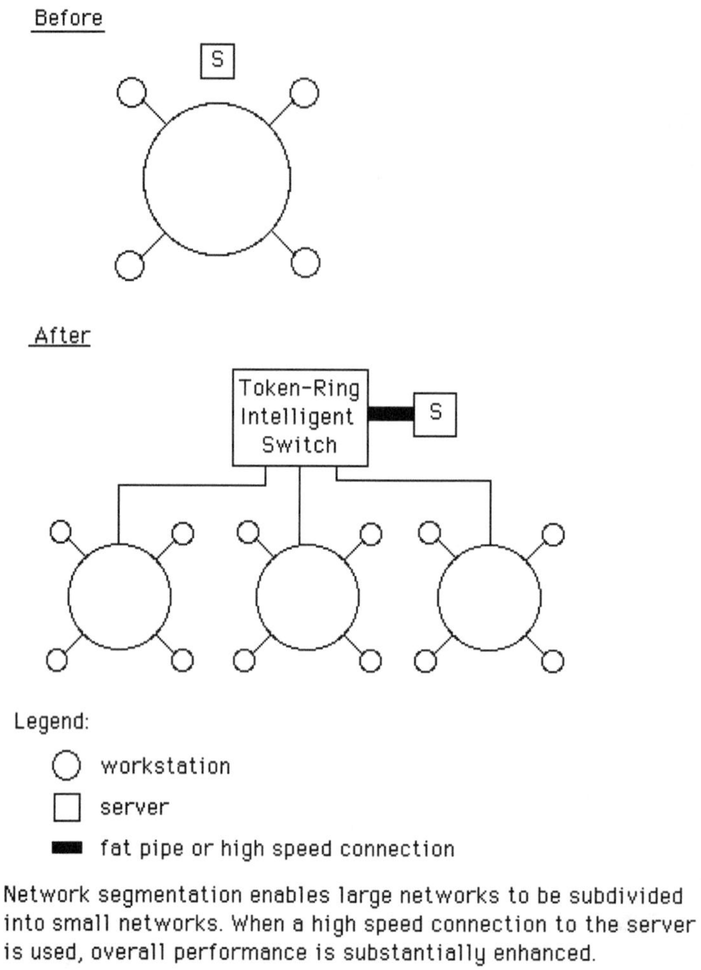

Before

After

Legend:

○ workstation

□ server

■ fat pipe or high speed connection

Network segmentation enables large networks to be subdivided
into small networks. When a high speed connection to the server
is used, overall performance is substantially enhanced.

Figure 5.29 Network segmentation of a large Token Ring network into three networks.

is usually run up an elevator shaft. Sometimes servers requiring common access from users on all rings are cabled to a MAU on the backbone ring with other servers primarily accessed by users on one ring attached to that ring. Thus, in the top portion of Figure 5.30, it was assumed that two servers were attached to local rings due to primary access from stations on those rings,

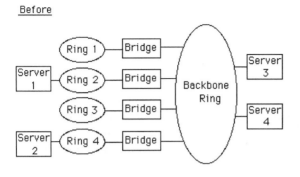

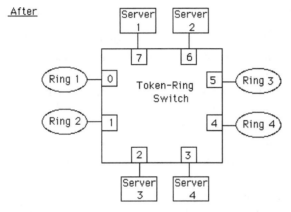

Figure 5.30 Backbone replacement.

while two servers requiring access from stations on most, if not all, rings were connected to the backbone ring.

The lower portion of Figure 5.30 illustrates the use of an eight-port Token Ring switch. Through the use of the switch, the bottleneck associated with a backbone ring for which only one station at a time can access a server connected to that ring is alleviated. For example, two simultaneous cross-connections between users on any ring and servers 3 and 4 can occur. In comparison, only one access to either server 3 or 4 at a time could occur when using the backbone ring shown at the top of Figure 5.30.

ROUTERS

By operating at the network layer, a router becomes capable of making intelligent decisions concerning the flow of information in a network. To accomplish this, routers perform a variety of functions that are significantly different from those performed by bridges. Unlike bridges, routers are addressable. Thus, routers examine frames that are directly addressed to them by looking at the network address within each frame to make their forwarding decision.

Basic Operation and Use of Routing Tables

To illustrate the basic operation of routers, consider the simple mesh structure formed by the use of three routers labeled R1, R2, and R3 in Figure 5.31a. In this illustration, three Ethernet networks are interconnected through the use of three routers.

The initial construction of three routing tables is shown in Figure 5.31b. Unlike bridges which learn MAC addresses, most routers are initially configured, with routing tables established at the time of equipment installation. Thereafter, periodic communication between routers dynamically updates routing tables to take into consideration changes in internet topology and traffic.

In examining Figure 5.31b, note that the routing table for router R1 indicates the routers it must communicate with to access each interconnected Ethernet network. Hence, router R1 would communicate with router R2 to reach Token Ring network 2 and communicate with router R3 to reach Token Ring network 3.

Figure 5.31c illustrates the composition of a packet originated by station S2 on Ethernet 1 that is to be transmitted to station S12 on Ethernet 2. Router R1 first examines the destination network address and notes it is on another network. Thus, the router searches its routing table and finds that the frame should be transmitted to router R2 to reach Ethernet network 2. Hence, router R1 forwards the frame to router R2. Router R2 then places the frame onto Ethernet network 2 for delivery to station S12 on that network.

Since routers use the network addresses instead of MAC ad-

A. Simple mesh structure

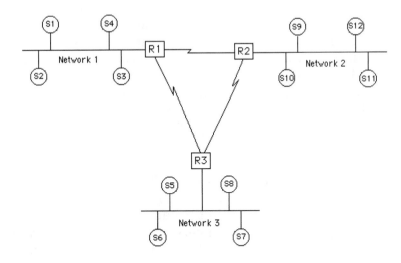

B. Routing tables

R1			R2			R3	
1	*		1	R1		1	R1
2	R2		2	*		2	R2
3	R3		3	R2		3	*

C. Packet composition

MAC	LLC	Destination 2.S12	Source 1.S2	DATA

Legend: [R] router   (S) network station

Figure 5.31 Basic router operation.

dresses for making their forwarding decisions, it is possible to have duplicate locally administered MAC addresses on each network interconnected by a router. In comparison, the use of bridges would require you to first review and then eliminate any duplicate locally administered addresses common to networks to be interconnected—a process that can be time consuming when large networks are connected.

Another difference between bridges and routers is the ability of a router to support the transmission of data on multiple paths between local area networks. Although a multiport bridge with a filtering capability can be considered to perform intelligent routing decisions, the result of a bridge operation is normally valid for only one point-to-point link within a wide area network. In comparison, a router may be able to acquire information about the status of a large number of paths and select an end-to-end path consisting of a series of point-to-point links. In addition, most routers can fragment and reassemble data. This permits packets to flow over different paths and to be reassembled at their final destination. With this capability a router can route each packet to its destination over the best possible path at a particular instant in time and dynamically change paths to correspond to changes in network link status on traffic activity.

For example, each of the routing tables illustrated in Figure 5.32b can be expanded to indicate a secondary path to each network. Thus, while router R1 would continue to use the entry of R2 as its primary mechanism to reach network 2, a secondary entry of R3 could be established to provide an alternative path to network 2 via routers R3 and R2 rather than directly via router R2.

Networking Capability

To better illustrate the networking capability of routers, consider Figure 5.32, which shows three geographically dispersed locations that have a total of four Ethernet and three Token Ring networks interconnected through the use of four routers and four wide area network transmission circuits or links. For simplicity, the use of modems or DSUs on the wide area network is not shown. This illustration will be referenced several times in this section to denote different types of router operations.

In addition to supporting a mesh structure that is not obtainable from the use of transparent bridges, the use of routers offers other advantages in the form of addressing, message processing, link utilization, and priority of service. Routers are known to stations that use their service. Hence, packets can be directly addressed to a router. This eliminates the necessity for the device to examine in detail every packet flowing on a network and re-

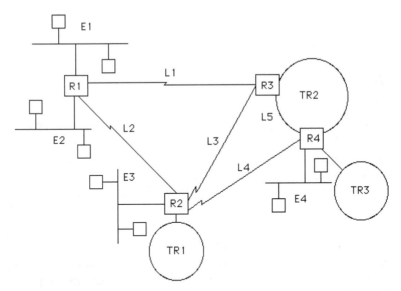

Figure 5.32 Router operation. Routers enable the transmission of data over multiple paths, alternate path routing, and the use of a mesh topology that transparent bridges cannot support.

sults in the router only having to process messages that are addressed to it by other devices. Concerning link utilization, assume a station on E1 transmits to a station on TR3. Depending upon the status and traffic on network links, packets could be routed via L1 and use TR2 to provide a transport mechanism to R4, from which the packets are delivered to TR3. Alternatively, links L2 and L4 could be used to provide a path from R1 to R4. Although link availability and link traffic usually determines routing, routers can support prioritized traffic and may store low-priority traffic for a small period of time to allow higher-priority traffic to gain access to the wide area transmission facility. Due to these features, which are essentially unavailable with the use of bridges, the router is a more complex and costlier device.

Communication, Transport, and Routing Protocols

For routers to be able to operate in a network they must normally be able to speak the same language at both the data link and network layers. The key to accomplishing this is the ability of routers to support common communication, transport, and routing protocols.

Communication Protocol

Communication protocols support the transfer of data from a station on one network to a station on another network at the OSI network layer. Several common protocol implementations with respect to the OSI Reference Model, which includes Novell's NetWare, use IPX as their network communications protocol, while IBM LANs use the PC LAN Support Program and Microsoft's LAN Manager uses the Internet Protocol (IP). This means that a router linking networks based upon Novell, IBM, and Microsoft LAN operating systems must support those three communication protocols. Thus, router communication protocol support is a most important criterion in determining if a particular product is capable of supporting your internetworking requirements.

Routing Protocol

The routing protocol references the method used by routers to exchange routing information and forms the basis for providing a connection across an internet. In evaluating routers, it is important to determine the efficiency of the routing protocol, its effect upon the transmission of information, the method used and memory required to construct routing tables, and the time required to dynamically adjust those tables. Examples of router-to-router protocols include Xerox Network Systems' (XNS) Routing Information Protocol (RIP) and the Transmission Control Protocol/Internet Protocol's (TICP/IP) RIP, Open Shortest Path First (OSPF), and Hello routing protocols. Due to the importance of routing protocols, we will examine their operation in some detail later in this section.

Transport Protocol

The transport protocol represents the format by which information is physically transported between two points. Examples of transport protocols include Token Ring and Ethernet MAC for LANs as well as such WAN protocols as X.25 and Frame Relay.

There are a wide variety of communication and transport protocols in use today. Some of these protocols were designed specifically to operate on local area networks, such as Apple Computer's AppleTalk. Other protocols, such as X.25 and Frame Relay, were developed as wide area network protocols.

Sixteen popular communication and transport protocols are listed below. Many routers support only a subset of these protocols.

AppleTalk
Applo Domain VINES
Banyan
CHAOSnet
DECnet Phase IV
DECnet Phase V
DDN X.25
Frame Relay
ISO CLNS
HDLC
NOVELL IPX
SDLC
TCP/IP
Xerox XNS
X.25
Ungermann-Bass Net/One

Types of Routing Protocols

The routing protocol is the key element to transferring information across an internet in an orderly manner. The protocol is responsible for developing paths between routers, using a predefined mechanism.

There are two types of routing protocols: interior and exterior domain. Here, we use the term *domain* to refer to the connection of a group of networks to form a common entity, such as a corporate or university enterprise network.

Interior Domain

An interior domain routing protocol is used to control the flow of information within a series of separate networks that are interconnected to form an internet. Thus, interior domain routing protocols provide a mechanism for the flow of information within a domain and are also known as intradomain routing protocols. Such protocols create routing tables for each autonomous system within the domain, using such metrics as the hop count or time delay to develop routes from one network to another within the domain. Examples of interior domain routing protocols include RIP, OSPF, and Hello.

Exterior Domain

Exterior domain routing protocols are used to connect separate domains together. Thus, they are also referred to as interdomain routing protocols. Example of interdomain routing protocols include the Exterior Gateway Protocol (EGP), the Border Gateway Protocol (BGP), and the Inter-Domain Routing Protocol (IDRP). Unlike interior domain routing protocols, which are focused on the construction of routing tables for data flow within a domain, interdomain routing protocols specify the method by which routers exchange information concerning what networks they can reach on each domain.

Protocol Operation

As previously discussed, interior domain routing protocols govern the flow of information between networks. Thus, this represents the type of routing protocol that is of primary interest to most organizations. Interior domain routing protocols can be further subdivided into two broad categories based upon the method they use for building and updating the contents of their routing tables—vector distance and link state.

Vector Distance Protocol

A vector distance protocol constructs a routing table in each router and periodically broadcasts the contents of the routing table across the internet. When the routing table is received at another router, that device examines the set of reported network destinations and the distance to each destination. The receiving router then determines if it knows a shorter route to a network destination, finds a destination it does not have in its routing table, or finds a route to a destination through the sending router where the distance to the destination changed. If any one of these situations occurs the receiving router will change its routing tables.

The term *vector distance* relates to the information transmitted by routers. Each router message contains a list of pairs known as vector and distance. The vector identifies a network destination, while the distance is the distance in hops from the router to that destination.

Figure 5.33 illustrates the initial distance vector routing table for routers R1 and R2 illustrated in Figure 5.32. Each table contains an entry for each directly connected network and is broadcast periodically throughout the internet. Here the distance column indicates the distance to each network from the router in hops.

At the same time router R1 is constructing its initial distance vector table other routers are performing a similar operation. The lower portion of Figure 5.33 illustrates the composition of the initial distance vector table for router R2.

As previously mentioned, under a distance vector protocol the contents of each router's routing table are periodically broadcast. Assuming routers R1 and R2 broadcast their initial

a. Router R1

Destination	Distance
EI	0
E2	0

b. Router R2

Destination	Distance
E3	0
TR1	0

Figure 5.33   Initial distance vector routing tables.

a. Router R1

Destination	Distance	Route
EI	0	direct
E2	0	direct
E3	1	R2
TR1	1	R2

b. Router R2

Destination	Distance	Route
E1	1	R1
E2	1	R1
E3	0	direct
TR1	0	direct

Figure 5.34   Initial routing table update.

distance vector routing tables, each router uses the received routing table to update its initial routing table. Figure 5.34 illustrates the result of this initial routing table update process for routers R1 and R2.

As additional routing tables are exchanged the routing table in each router will converge with respect to the internet topology. However, to insure each router knows the state of all links, routing tables are periodically broadcast by each router. Although this process has a minimal effect upon small networks, its use with large networks can significantly reduce available bandwidth for actual data transfer. This is because the transmission of lengthy router tables will require additional transmission time in which data cannot flow between routers.

Popular vector distance routing protocols include the TCP/IP Routing Information Protocol (RIP), the AppleTalk Routing Table Management Protocol (RTMP), and Cisco's Interior Gateway Routing Protocol (IGRP).

Routing Information Protocol   Under RIP, participants are either active or passive. Active participants are normally routers which transmit their routing tables, while passive machines listen and update their routing tables based upon information supplied by other devices. Normally, host computers operate as passive participants while routers operate as active participants.

Under RIP, an active router broadcasts its routing table every 30 seconds. Each routing table entry contains a network address and the hop count to the network. However, unlike the previous vector distance example in which a directly connected network has a hop count distance of 0, RIP uses a hop count of 1. Similarly, RIP uses a hop count of 2 for networks that are reachable through one router.

One key limitation of RIP is the maximum hop distance it supports. This distance is 16 hops, which means an alternative protocol must be used for large networks.

Link State Protocols

A link state routing protocol addresses the traffic problem associated with large networks that use a vector distance routing protocol. It does this by transmitting routing information only when there is a change in one of its links. A second difference between vector difference and link state protocols concerns the manner in which a route is selected when multiple routes are available between destinations. For a vector distance protocol the best path is the one that has the fewest number of intermediate routers on hops between destinations. In comparison, a link state protocol can use multiple paths to provide traffic balancing between locations. In addition, a link state protocol permits routing to occur based upon link delay, capacity, and reliability. This provides the network manager with the ability to specify a variety of route development situations.

SPF Algorithms Link state routing protocols are implemented through the use of a class of algorithms known as Shortest Path First (SPF). Unfortunately, the name associated with this class of algorithms is a misnomer as routing is not based upon the shortest path.

The use of SPF algorithms requires each participating router to have complete knowledge of the internet topology. Each router participating in an SPF algorithm then performs two tasks—status testing of neighboring routers and periodically transmitting link status information to other routers.

To test neighboring routers a short message is periodically transmitted. If the neighbor replies the link is considered to be up. Otherwise, the absence of a reply after a predefined period of time indicates that the link is down.

To provide link status information, each router will periodically broadcast a message which indicates the status of each of its links. Unlike the vector distance protocol, in which routes are specified, an SPF link status message simply indicates whether or not communications are possible between pairs of routers. Using information in the link status message routers are able to update their network map.

In comparison to vector distance protocols, in which tables are required to be exchanged, link state protocols such as SPF algorithms exchange a much lower volume of information in the form of link status queries and replies. Then, SPF participating routers simply broadcast a status of each of their links that other routers use to update their internet map. This routing technique permits each router to compute routes independently of other routers and eliminates the potential for table flooding that can occur when a vector state protocol is used to interconnect a large number of networks.

Filtering

The filtering capability of routers is primarily thought of as a mechanism to implement security. Although filtering does indeed provide a mechanism to implement network security, it also provides a mechanism to regulate network traffic. Through the regulation of network traffic you may be able to predefine routes for particular types of packets, protocols, and addresses, as well as different combinations of the preceding. Thus, filtering also provides a virtual network creation capability as well as a mechanism to extend virtual networking to distant locations.

The filtering capability of routers is highly dependent upon the functionality of a router as well as the ingenuity of the router manager or administrator. To illustrate the latter, we will define a few generic router-filtering functions so we can illustrate how those functions can be applied to achieve a variety of filtering results that could satisfy different organizational requirements. Although the router-filtering functions we will define are not applicable to a specific router, most routers will support the functions we will cover. Thus, the filtering examples presented in this section represent practical examples that illustrate how you can control network traffic.

The key to the functionality of a router's filtering capability is the router's ability to "look" inside the composition of packets. Most routers, at a minimum, provide filtering based upon the examination of the contents of the destination and source addresses transported by a packet. Other routers provide a filtering capability based upon the Ethernet protocol value carried in the type/length field and the DSAP and SSAP values carried in the data field. This additional capability provides you with the ability, for example, to enable or disable Novell IPX traffic between certain router ports, enable or disable TCP/IP traffic between the same or different router ports, and regulate other protocols that may be carried to and from an Ethernet LAN.

Figure 5.35 illustrates the connection of an Ethernet network to a four-port router. In this example, ports 1, 2, and 3 can represent connections to other routers via wide area network transmission facilities or to other LANs a short distance away. Since we are primarily interested in how we can use filtering as a mechanism to regulate traffic, it is more important to focus our attention upon the flow of data between router ports than the devices connected to each hub. However, since we need a point of reference, we will discuss traffic routed to and from the Ethernet network connected to port 0 in Figure 5.35.

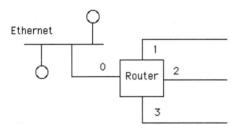

Figure 5.35 Through filtering you can implement security as well as regulate network traffic.

Filtering Expressions

Most routers perform filtering based upon specified patterns linked by logical operators. Thus, you would first specify one or more patterns to be filtered and then link multiple patterns or prefix a single pattern with an appropriate logical operator. Prior to actually creating a filter pattern, it is important to note how the manufacturer of the router implements filtering. Some vendors enable everything, requiring you to preclude certain data flows by filtering. Other vendors inhibit everything, only permitting data flow based upon positive filters. For our examples, we will presume the manufacturer of our router permits or enables all data flow unless it is specifically precluded.

Filtering Examples

For our first example, let's assume you have a Unix server connected to the Ethernet LAN and do not want IP traffic from port 2 to flow to the server. Assuming P1 (pattern 1) = IP, originating port is PORT2 and destination port is PORT0, you would set up the filter as follows:

```
Originate        Destination      Action
P1 AND PORT2        PORT0          Disable
```

Thus, any IP frames received on port 2 and destined for port 0 would be filtered or blocked.

Now let's assume you do not want to transfer Ethernet broadcast packets beyond that network. To do so you would set the pattern (P1) to recognize a destination address of FF-FF-FF-FF-FF-FF, which is the Ethernet broadcast address. Then, you would set up the filter as follows:

```
Originate        Destination                     Action
P1 AND PORT0     PORT1 OR PORT2 OR PORT3         Enable
```

For our last example, let's assume router-filtering patterns and ports support the use of the logical NOT operator. Then, you could set up the filter for the preceding example as follows:

```
Originate         Destination      Action
P1 AND PORT0       NOT PORT0       Enable
```

Although the three examples illustrate but a fraction of router-filtering capability, they illustrate several important concepts. First, by filtering on source and/or destination addresses and protocols, it becomes possible to enable or disable traffic. Secondly, by reaching into the frame router, filtering permits you to enable or disable the flow of specific protocols. The latter is an important consideration when connecting a LAN to the Internet, since many organizations do not wish to provide access to their computer systems connected to the LAN by anyone that has Internet access.

By carefully using the filtering capability of a router, you can construct a *firewall* to protect your LAN from unwanted access. Although many trade publications refer to a firewall as a stand-alone computer system located between an organization's LAN and router, in actuality the filtering capability of a router may be sufficient to perform firewall functions. Of key interest when connecting a router to the Internet is the ability of the router to filter based upon logical ports carried by TCP/IP. This is because most Internet applications, such as Simple Mail Transfer Protocol (SMTP), File Transfer Protocol (FTP), and similar applications, are based upon the use of predefined ports.

vLAN Construction Basics

6

In this chapter we build upon our knowledge of LANs and LAN equipment operations presented in previous chapters to obtain a firm understanding of virtual LAN construction methods. In doing so we will examine how vLANs can be implicitly formed at layers 1 through 3 of the OSI Reference Model, as well as the constraints and limitations associated with each method of virtual LAN construction.

In addition, we will discuss the operation of different vendor equipment which enables users to construct "rule-based" virtual LANs. This rule-based capability is similar to bridge and router filtering capability, enabling vLAN construction to be accomplished on an almost infinite number of criteria. Although our examination of vLAN construction will discuss explicit tagging, we will defer a detailed discussion of this topic to Chapter 7 in recognition of tagging methods falling into de facto and de jure categories of standards.

PORT-GROUPING VLANS

As its name implies, a port-grouping vLAN represents a virtual LAN created by defining a group of ports on a switch or router to form a broadcast domain. Thus, another common name for this type of vLAN is a *port-based virtual LAN*. The hardware used to form a port-grouping vLAN can range in scope from an intelligent wiring hub to a switch or sophisticated router; however, due to the evolution in the design of network hubs as well as cost constraints, this method of vLAN creation is commonly based upon the use of an intelligent wiring hub.

Using Intelligent Wiring Hubs

In a conventional Ethernet hub, data received on one port is repeated onto all other ports. This results in the use of a single common channel on the backplane of the hub to transmit data to all ports. A few years ago vendors borrowed a technique commonly associated with time division multiplexing, partitioning the backplane channel by time to allow devices to access different "channels" produced by time. The resulting intelligent wiring hub lacks the switching capability associated with LAN switches; however, by associating ports to channels, a vLAN configuration capability is obtained.

Operation

When an intelligent wiring hub with vLAN creation capability is used, you obtain the capability to dynamically associate ports with portions of the hub's backplane channel. The backplane represents the hub's traffic highway and an intelligent hub with vLAN creation capability subdivides the backplane by time, enabling ports to be associated with derived subchannels of bandwidth. Through the assignment of ports to specific time slots, different network segments are created, with each segment being equivalent to a workgroup.

vLAN Creation

Figure 6.1 illustrates an example of the establishment of several virtual LANs using port grouping on an intelligent hub. In Figure 6.1 the backplane's transmission capability is shown segmented into three virtual LAN time slots that repeat in sequence. Hub ports 1 and 3 are assigned to the first time slot, which equates to

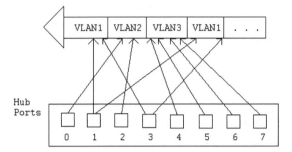

Figure 6.1 Port-group vLAN via an intelligent hub.

the first virtual LAN, while ports 0 and 2 are assigned to the second vLAN. The remaining ports, 4 through 7, are assigned to the third virtual LAN. In examining the backplane time slots, note that the fourth slot represents vLAN1 as there are a total of three virtual LANs. After the time slot for vLAN3 occurs, it is followed by the repeating sequence vLAN1, vLAN2, and so on. To illustrate that the same ports are associated with each vLAN unless a configuration change occurs, you will note that lines were drawn from ports 1 and 3 to each time slot labeled vLAN1.

Although the assignment of ports to time slots occurs electronically, in examining Figure 6.1 you will note that the lines routed from hub ports to the various time slots on the hub's backplane resemble the wiring of a patch panel. In effect, we can say that the creation of vLANs through the use of an intelligent hub represents a software-configurable wiring patch panel.

Advantages

The key advantages associated with the use of intelligent wiring hubs for the creation of vLANs are their cost and ease of use.

Cost Considerations An intelligent wiring hub can be considered to represent a low-cost port-switch. As such, the cost per port can be under $100.

Ease of Use The creation of vLANs using an intelligent wiring hub occurs through the use of a command or graphic user interface management port. For example, assume you wish to create a virtual LAN consisting of ports 0, 1, 2, 3, and 4. Some intelligent wiring hubs include an "ASSIGN" statement, where the format of the statement is:

$$\text{ASSIGN} \begin{cases} \text{port } n_1, \ n_2, \ . \ . \ n_n \\ \text{port } n_1, \ . \ . \ n_n \end{cases} \text{to VLAN}n$$

Using this format and assuming you wish to configure ports 0, 1, 2, 3, and 4 to represent a broadcast domain associated with VLAN1, you could use either of the two following ASSIGN statements:

```
ASSIGN PORT 0,1,2,3 TO VLAN1
ASSIGN PORT 0..3 TO VLAN1
```

Note that the first use of the ASSIGN statement requires all ports that form the vLAN to be entered. In comparison, the second format permits a group of contiguous ports to be specified similar to the manner by which a range is specified in Lotus 1-2-3.

Disadvantages

There are three primary disadvantages associated with vLANs created through the use of intelligent wiring hubs. Among those disadvantages are the inclusion of workstations being limited to those that can be directly connected to the hub, an inability to extend networking beyond the hub, and the manner by which configuration changes are effected.

Direct Connection and Extended Networking Since the creation of virtual LANs using a wiring hub is based upon the use of the hub's backplane, this restricts members of the vLAN to workstations that can be directly connected to the hub. In addition, since hub backplanes are independent of one another, this also means that workgroups resulting from the creation of a broadcast domain are limited to a single hub, inhibiting the connection of a hub-based vLAN to a wider network. Thus, a port-switched vLAN created from the use of a wiring hub is cut off from an extended network and requires the use of a bridge or router to obtain interoperability.

Configuration Changes Another problem associated with the formation of vLANs based upon port groupings concerns their configuration. Whenever a user requires recabling, a configuration change is also required to update the vLAN.

Although the problems and limitations associated with the use of port grouping are considerable, this method of defining vLAN membership is quite common. For many small organizations it can provide an easy-to-implement solution to virtual networking requirements.

Using LAN Switches

As noted in Chapter 5, a LAN switch is a much more sophisticated device than a wiring hub as it includes hardware which enables frames arriving on any port to be output to any other port. Although most switches were originally designed to operate on MAC addresses contained in frames, it was a relatively easy process for switch manufacturers to add vLAN creation based upon ports grouped into a domain.

Operation

Figure 6.2 illustrates the use of an intelligent LAN switch to create two vLANs based upon port groupings. In this example the switch was configured to create one virtual LAN consisting of ports 0, 1, 5, and 6, while a second virtual LAN was created based upon the grouping of ports 2, 3, 4, and 7 to form a second broadcast domain.

Port versus Segment Switching In examining the vLANs created by grouping ports through the use of a LAN switch, note that although a segment-based switch is shown in Figure 6.2, this method of vLAN creation is also applicable to a port-based switch. When a port-based switch is used, only one station per port can be linked into a vLAN broadcast domain. In comparison, when a segment-based switch is used, multiple stations connected to a port will be grouped into a virtual LAN.

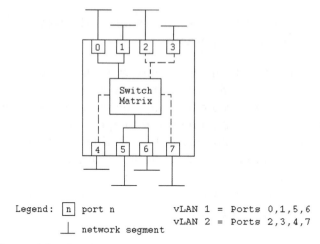

Legend: [n] port n

⊥ network segment

vLAN 1 = Ports 0,1,5,6
vLAN 2 = Ports 2,3,4,7

Figure 6.2 Creating port-grouping vLANs using a LAN switch.

Advantages

Advantages associated with the use of LAN switches for creating vLANs include the ability to use the switching capability of the switch, the ability to support multiple stations per port, and internetworking capability.

Switch Capability The capability of a LAN switch can include any of the large number of features discussed in Chapter 5, such as the use of fat pipes and flow control, to alleviate the potential loss of data due to a speed mismatch between ports. Thus, the use of a LAN switch to form vLANs based upon port grouping also provides a wealth of features beyond those of a conventional wiring hub.

Network Expansion In comparison to the use of intelligent wiring hubs, the use of LAN switches provides the capability to expand a virtual network beyond one device. For example, some vendors enable switches to be interconnected so that a port-based vLAN can span hundreds of ports on multiple switches. This is commonly accomplished through the use of a management console which enables interswitch communications to be defined so that a vLAN broadcast domain can be created using ports on multiple switches linked together.

Disadvantages

Although the use of a LAN switch provides a number of advantages over the use of a wiring hub with respect to the creation of vLANs, it also has certain disadvantages associated with it. Those disadvantages include the cost of LAN switches and the inability to associate multiple vLANs to a network segment connected to a switch port.

Cost Considerations In comparison to the use of an intelligent wiring hub, the use of a LAN switch is considerably more expensive. This additional expense results from the fact that the switch is a much more sophisticated device than an intelligent wiring hub.

vLAN Port Support Another limitation which is associated with both intelligent wiring hubs and LAN switches used to create port-based vLANs is the fact that they are limited to supporting one vLAN per port. This means that moves from one vLAN to another affect all stations connected to a particular port. This also means that a station requiring access to more than one vLAN must do so via router or by using multiple network interface cards if the station can support the use of multiple cards.

Supporting Inter-vLAN Communications

The use of multiple network interface cards provides an easy-to-implement solution to obtaining an inter-vLAN communications capability when only a few vLANs must be linked. This method of inter-vLAN communications is applicable to all methods of vLAN creation; however, when a built-in routing capability is included in a LAN switch, you would probably prefer to use the routing capability rather than obtain and install additional hardware.

Figure 6.3 illustrates the use of a server with multiple network interface cards to provide support to two port-based vLANs. Not only does this method of multiple vLAN support require additional hardware and the use of multiple ports on a switch or wiring hub, but, in addition, the number of NICs that can be installed in a station is typically limited to two or three. Thus, a large switch with hundreds of ports configured for supporting

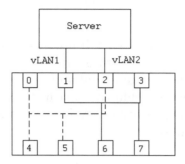

```
By installing multiple network adapter cards in a server or
workstation, a LAN device can become a member of multiple
vLANs.
```

Figure 6.3 Overcoming the port-based constraint where stations can only join a single vLAN.

three or more vLANs may not be capable of enabling a common server to support all stations connected to the switch.

MAC-BASED SWITCHING

A second type of vLAN creation is based upon the burned-in universally administered or software configured locally administered address of each device connected to a switch. Known as MAC-based switching in recognition of the use of media access control addresses, this method of vLAN creation is also referred to as a layer-2 vLAN, since the vLAN creation occurs at the data link layer. MAC-based switching requires a true switching hub or router as the hardware platform. That platform uses software to associate MAC addresses with a broadcast domain which in turn forms a virtual LAN.

When MAC addresses are associated with the creation of virtual LANs, a vLAN-capable switch can provide a high degree of versatility. For example, selective users on a segment connected to a port, as well as individual workstations connected to other ports on a switch, can be configured into a broadcast domain representing a virtual LAN. To illustrate the advantages and disadvantages associated with layer-2 vLANs, let's first focus our attention upon the use of a LAN switch which supports layer-2 vLAN creation.

Operational Example

Figure 6.4 illustrates the use of an 18-port switch to create two virtual LANs. In this example, 18 devices are shown connected to the switch via 6 ports, with 4 ports serving individual network segments. Thus, the LAN switch in this example is more accurately referenced as a segment switch with a MAC or layer-2 vLAN capability. This type of switch can range in capacity from small 8- or 16-port devices capable of supporting segments with up to 512 or 1024 total addresses to large switches with hundreds of ports capable of supporting thousands of MAC addresses. For simplicity of illustration, we will use the 6-port seg-

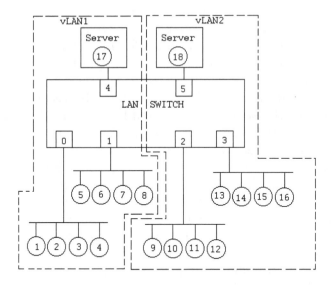

Legend:

$\boxed{n}$ port n

$\widehat{n}$ MAC address

A Layer-2 vLAN uses MAC addresses to construct broadcast domains that form a virtual LAN.

Figure 6.4   Layer-2 vLAN.

ment switch to denote the operation of layer-2 vLANs as well as their advantages and disadvantages.

In turning our attention to the vLANs shown in Figure 6.4, note that we will use the numeric or node addresses shown contained in circles as MAC addresses for simplicity of illustration. Thus, addresses 1 through 8 and 17 would be grouped into a broadcast domain representing vLAN1, while addresses 9 through 16 and 18 would be grouped into a second broadcast domain to represent vLAN2. At this point in time you would be tempted to say "so what," as the use of MAC addresses in creating layer-2 vLANs resembles precisely the same effect as if you used a port-grouping method of vLAN creation. For example, using an intelligent hub with vLAN creation based upon port grouping would result in the same vLANs as those shown in Figure 6.4 when ports 0, 1, and 4 are assigned to one virtual LAN and ports 2, 3, and 5 to the second.

To indicate the greater flexibility associated with the use of equipment that supports layer-2 vLAN creation, let's assume users with network node addresses 7 and 8 were just transferred from the project associated with vLAN1 to the project associated with vLAN2. If you were using a port-grouping method of vLAN creation, you would have to physically recable nodes 7 and 8 to either the segment connected to port 2 or the segment connected to port 3. In comparison, when using a segment switch with a layer-2 vLAN creation capability, you would use the management port to delete addresses 7 and 8 from vLAN1 and add them to vLAN2. The actual effort required to do so might be as simple as dragging MAC addresses from one vLAN to the other when using a GUI interface to entering one or more commands when using a command line management system. The top of Figure 6.5 illustrates the result of the previously mentioned node transfer. The lower portion of Figure 6.5 shows the two vLAN layer-2 tables, indicating the movement of MAC addresses 7 and 8 to vLAN2.

Although the reassignment of stations 7 and 8 to vLAN2 is easily accomplished at the MAC layer, it should be noted that the "partitioning" of a segment into two vLANs can result in upper-layer problems. This is because upper-layer protocols, such as IP, require all stations on a segment to have the same network address. Some switches overcome this problem by dynamically altering the network address to correspond to the vLAN on which the station resides. Other switches without this capability restrict the creation of MAC-based vLANs to one device per port, in effect limiting the creation of vLANs to port-based switches.

Advantages

MAC-based vLAN creation provides several advantages over a port-grouping vLAN creation method. Those advantages include additional flexibility with respect to the reassignment of stations from one vLAN to another, greater bandwidth, and additional expandability.

Flexibility

As indicated by the movement of network nodes illustrated in Figure 6.5, a key advantage associated with the use of a layer-2 vLAN creation is flexibility. That is, unlike a port-grouping method of vLAN creation which requires the recabling of workstations when workstation users are reassigned to a different vLAN, a layer-2 vLAN enables such reassignments via a command line entry or drag and move operation when using a GUI. In addition, if you simply wish to move a workstation to a different location, but wish to maintain the station's membership in the assigned vLAN, a switch performing layer-2 vLAN creation will automatically retain the station's membership. This is because membership is by MAC address, which enables the switch to retain the workstation's vLAN membership.

Bandwidth and Expandability

Other advantages of layer-2 vLAN switches concern bandwidth and expandability. As membership in a workgroup grows and its bandwidth requirements increase, the use of a layer-2 LAN switch enables workgroup members to be placed on multiple network segments while maintaining vLAN broadcast domains. In doing so the addition of extra servers to the switch which are configured into the same vLAN domain results in the ability of

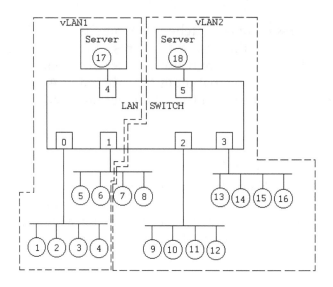

Legend: ⬜ n port n

⃝ n MAC address n

vLAN1 = 1, 2, 3, 4, 5, 6, 17

vLAN2 = 7, 8, 9, 10, 11, 12, 13, 14, 15, 16, 18

Figure 6.5 Moving stations when using a layer-2 vLAN.

multiple client-server operations to occur, which provides additional bandwidth. An example of this situation is illustrated in Figure 6.6. In this example a new server with the MAC address of 18 was added to vLAN1. Two in-progress client-server communications are shown occurring on vLAN1, in effect doubling the bandwidth available for users associated with that virtual LAN. In comparison, perhaps because of an absence of a requirement for additional performance, only one server is connected to vLAN2, which restricts the bandwidth available for users associated with virtual LAN.

Disadvantages

Although MAC-based vLAN creation provides more flexibility and greater expandability than the port-based vLAN creation

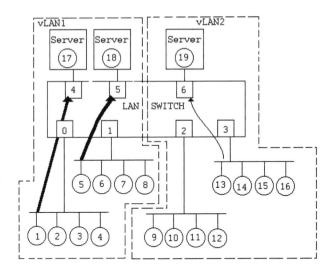

Legend: ⬚n port n

(n) MAC address n

vLAN1 = 1, 2, 3, 4, 5, 6, 7, 8, 17, 18

vLAN2 = 7, 8, 9, 10, 11, 12, 13, 14, 15, 16, 19

Figure 6.6 The use of a switch to form layer-2 vLANs can provide additional bandwidth by supporting multiple client-server operations.

method, there are certain limitations associated with the MAC-based vLAN creation process. Those limitations include the use of MAC addresses, which are not very intuitive, interswitch communications, the configuration of switches, and the difficulty associated with attempting to support mobile users attaching to fixed docking stations.

MAC Address Lists

The creation of a MAC address list can represent a time-consuming effort. This is because a MAC address is a sequence of hexadecimal numbers burned into the network interface card and used as such when universally administered addressing is employed or obtained from a configuration file when locally administered addressing is employed. For either situation, obtaining MAC addresses may require a visit to each workstation. The entry of those addresses into switch tables can be a long and tedious task.

Interswitch Communications

Similar to the port-grouping method of vLAN creation, a layer-2 vLAN is normally restricted to a single switch; however, some vendors include a management platform which enables multiple switches to support MAC addresses between closely located switches. Unfortunately, neither individual nor closely located switches permit an expansion of vLANs outside of the immediate area, resulting in the isolation of the virtual LANs from the rest of the network. This deficiency can be alleviated in two ways. First, for inter-vLAN communications you could install a second adapter card in a server and associate one MAC address with one vLAN while the second address is associated with the second virtual LAN. While this method is appropriate for a switch with two vLANs, you would require a different method to obtain interoperability when communications are required between a large number of virtual LANs. Similar to correcting the interoperability problem with the port-grouping method of vLAN creation, you would have to use routers to provide connectivity between layer-2 vLANs and the rest of your network.

Router Restrictions

When using a router to provide connectivity between vLANs, there are several restrictions you must consider. Those restrictions typically include a requirement to use a separate switch port connection to the router for each virtual LAN and the inability to assign portions of segments to different vLANs. Concerning the former, unless the LAN switch either internally supports layer-3 routing or provides a "trunking" or "aggregation" capability that enables transmission from multiple vLANs to occur on a common port to the router, one port linking the switch to the router will be required for each vLAN. Since router and switch ports are relatively costly, internetworking of a large number of virtual LANs can become expensive. Concerning the latter, this requirement results from the fact that in a TCP/IP environment routing occurs between segments. An example of inter-vLAN communications using a router is illustrated in Figure 6.7.

When inter-vLAN communications are required, the layer-2 switch transmits packets to the router via a port associated with the virtual LAN workstation requiring such communications. The router is responsible for determining the routed path to provide inter-vLAN communications, forwarding the packet back to the switch via an appropriate router to switch interface. Upon receipt of the packet the switch uses bridging to forward the packet to its destination port.

Returning to Figure 6.7, a workstation located in vLAN1 requiring communications with a workstation in vLAN2 would have its data transmitted by the switch on port 5 to the router. After processing the packet the router would return the packet to the switch, with the packet entering the switch on port 6. Thereafter, the switch would use bridging to broadcast the

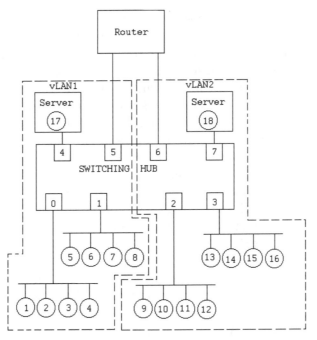

Figure 6.7 Inter-vLAN communications requires the use of a router.

packet to ports 2, 3, and 7 where it would be recognized by a destination node in vLAN2 and copied into an appropriate network interface card.

Although routing enables inter-vLAN communications, there are several disadvantages associated with the configuration shown in Figure 6.7. First, routers on a per-port cost basis are considerably more expensive than switches. Thus, the support of a large number of virtual LANs can become a budget buster. Second, from a performance perspective, the switch must forward each inter-vLAN packet twice. First the packet is forwarded from the originating node to the switch port cabled to the router that represents the originating vLAN switch to router connection. Next, the packet received from the router must be forwarded to its appropriate destination node. A third problem is the addition of the router which adds another device to configure and manage.

Configuration and Support

Two additional disadvantages associated with using MAC addresses to form vLANs include the configuration of switches and the inability to support the random use of docking stations. Concerning the configuration of switches, while this may not be a labor-intensive operation for a small switch, a very large network containing hundreds or thousands of users can require a considerable amount of setup time. To overcome this problem, some switches include an auto-setup feature which first initializes each subnet to a default vLAN and provides graphical tools to facilitate modifying those settings.

In today's mobile environment, many organizations use docking stations with built-in LAN adapters to provide network connectivity while employees move about the office, perform sales calls, and work at home using notebooks that mate into the docking stations upon their return to the office. Since the MAC address is burned into the LAN adapter, this means that a user who utilizes a different docking station than the one associated with the virtual LAN they belong to may not be able to join the intended vLAN. Although this problem could be alleviated by reconfiguring the switch, rather than perform this operation each time you could override universally administered addressing and use a configuration file in the notebook computer to establish a locally administered address. Then each time the notebook moves to a different docking station it would retain a fixed MAC address.

LAYER-3-BASED VLANS

A layer-3-based vLAN is constructed using information contained in the network layer header of packets. As such, this precludes the use of LAN switches that operate at the data link layer from being capable of forming layer-3 vLANs. Thus, layer-3 vLAN creation is restricted to routers and LAN switches that provide a layer-3 routing capability.

Through the use of layer-3 operating switches and routers there are a variety of methods that can be used to create layer-3 vLANs. Some of the more common methods supported resemble the criteria by which routers operate, such as IPX network numbers and IP subnets, AppleTalk domains, and layer-3 protocols.

The actual creation options associated with a layer-3 vLAN can vary considerably based upon the capability of the LAN switch or router used to form the virtual LAN. For example, some hardware products permit a subnet to be formed across a number of ports and may even provide the capability to allow more than one subnet to be associated with a network segment connected to the port of a LAN switch. In comparison, other LAN switches may be limited to creating vLANs based upon different layer-3 protocols.

Subnet-Based vLANs

Figure 6.8 illustrates the use of a layer-3 LAN switch to create two virtual LANs based upon IP network addresses. In examining the vLANs created through the use of the LAN switch, note that the first virtual LAN is associated with the subnet 198.78.55, which represents a Class C IP address, while the second vLAN is associated with the subnet 198.78.42, which represents a second Class C IP address. Also note that since it is assumed that the

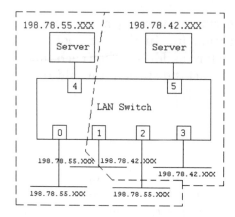

Figure 6.8 vLAN creation based upon IP subnets.

LAN switch supports the assignment of more than one subnet per port, port 1 on the switch consists of stations assigned to either subnet. While some LAN switches support this subnetting capability, it is also important to note that other switches do not. Thus, a LAN switch that does not support multiple subnets per port would require stations to be recabled to other ports if it was desired to associated them to a different virtual LAN.

Advantages

Three of the major advantages associated with layer-3 vLANs using subnetting include their flexibility, configuration, and inter-vLAN communications capability. Concerning the flexibility of layer-3 vLANs, as a user moves to another segment but retains his or her subnet number, many switches will "follow" the relocation, permitting moves to be accomplished without requiring the reconfiguration of a LAN switch.

The configuration of vLANs can be automatically formed, unlike port and MAC-based virtual networks whose setup can be tedious and time consuming. Thus, the cost of support of a layer-3 vLAN may be less than other types of virtual networks, and by itself can represent an important acquisition consideration.

The third advantage of a layer-3 vLAN is the fact that it supports routing. This means that it implicitly supports inter-vLAN communications, eliminating the necessity to obtain a separate router to support this capability.

Disadvantages

Although layer-3 vLANs using subnetting as a virtual LAN creation criterion address the flexibility problems of port-based vLANs and the configuration problems of MAC based vLANs, they are not problem free. Two limitations associated with vLANs using subnetting include the configuration required to ensure network stations are using the correct protocol and network address, and the inability of some switches to support multiple subnets on a port. Although the second limitation can be overcome through the selection of a more capable LAN switch, the first limitation is associated with all types of layer-3 vLANs.

Protocol-Based vLANs

In addition to forming virtual LANs based upon a network address, the use of the layer-3 transmission protocol as a method for vLAN creation provides a mechanism which enables vLAN formation to be based upon the layer-3 protocol. Through the use of this method of vLAN creation, it becomes relatively easy for stations to belong to multiple vLANs. To illustrate this concept, consider Figure 6.9, which illustrates the creation of two vLANs based upon their layer 3 transmission protocol. In examining the stations shown in Figure 6.9, note that the circles with the uppercase I represent those stations configured for membership in the vLAN based upon the use of the IP protocol, while those stations represented by circles containing the uppercase X are configured for membership in the vLAN which uses the IPX protocol as its membership criterion. Similarly, stations represented by circles containing the characters I/X operate dual protocol stacks, which enable such stations to become members of both vLANs.

Two servers are shown at the top of the LAN switch illustrated in Figure 6.9. One server is shown operating dual IPX/IP stacks which results in the server belonging to both vLANs. In comparison, the server on the upper right of the switch is con-

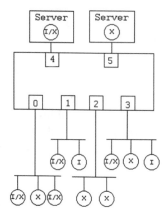

```
I = vLAN1 membership  X = vLAN2 membership
I/X = membership in both LANs
```

```
Legend:

 n   port n

 I   IP  Protocol used by station

 x   IPX Protocol used by station

I/X  IPX and IP Protocols used by station
```

Figure 6.9 vLAN creation based upon protocol.

figured to support IPX and could represent a NetWare file server restricted to membership in the vLAN associated with the IPX protocol.

Advantages

Similar to layer-3 vLANs that use subnetting, a major benefit associated with vLAN creation based upon protocol is networking flexibility. This flexibility enables stations to be moved from one network segment to another without losing vLAN membership. Another aspect associated with networking flexibility is the ability to obtain the bandwidth advantages associated with the use of LAN switches while tailoring traffic to support different services. For example, assume a requirement to connect stations on vLAN1 to the Internet develops. To support this new requirement you could add a port to the LAN switch and

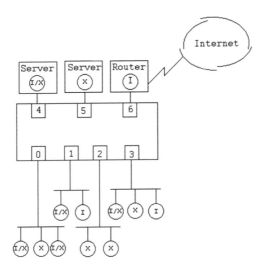

I = vLAN1 membership X = vLAN2 membership
I/X = membership in both LANs

Legend:

  n   port n

  I   IP Protocol used by station

  x   IPX Protocol used by station

  I/X IPX and IP Protocols used by station

Figure 6.10 Expanding a vLAN to support Internet access.

connect a router to that port. Figure 6.10 illustrates the expanded LAN switch with a router connected to port 6 of the switch. Note that although you might be tempted to anticipate bandwidth problems resulting from the connection of the Internet to vLAN1, only inbound traffic directed to the network address associated with the IP-based vLAN is broadcast to the vLAN domain. In addition, as with most router-based Internet connections, you can use the filtering capability of the router to limit inbound traffic to the vLAN. In the outbound direction, only IP traffic with a network address differing from the address associated with vLAN1 will be forwarded by the router to the Internet. Thus, the basic operational capability of the router can be used to limit both inbound and outbound traffic to and from the virtual LAN connected to the Internet via the router.

Other advantages associated with the use of layer-3 protocols for vLAN creation are similar to the advantages described for subnet-based vLANs. That is, those advantages include the automatic configuration of the switch and an implicit inter-vLAN communications capability.

Disadvantages

Layer-3 vLANs that use protocols for their creation method have similar disadvantages as subnet-based vLANs. That is, you must obtain equipment that supports the use of protocols for vLAN creation as well as verifies that stations are configured correctly.

RULE-BASED VLANS

A recent addition to vLAN creation methods is based upon the ability of LAN switches to look inside packets and use predefined fields, portions of fields, and even individual bit settings as a mechanism for the creation of a virtual LAN.

Capabilities

The ability to create virtual LANs via a rule-based methodology provides, no pun intended, a virtually unlimited virtual LAN creation capability. To illustrate a small number of the almost unlimited methods of vLAN creation, consider Table 6.1, which lists eight examples of rule-based vLAN creation methods. In examining the entries, note that in addition to creating vLANs via the inclusion of specific field values within a packet, such as all IPX users with a specific network address, it is also possible to create vLANs using the exclusion of certain packet field values. The latter capability is illustrated by the next-to-last example in Table 6.1, which forms a vLAN consisting of all IPX traffic with a specific network address but excludes a specific node address.

Table 6.1 Rule-Based vLAN Creation Examples

All IP users with a specific IP subnet address.

All IPX users with a specific network address.

All network users whose adapter cards were manufactured by the XYZ Corporation.

All traffic with a specific Ethernet type field value.

All traffic with a specific SNAP field value.

All traffic with a specific SAP field value.

All IPX traffic with a specific network address but not a specific node address.

A specific IP address.

Multicast Support

One rule-based vLAN creation example that deserves a degree of explanation to understand its capability is the last entry in Table 6.1. Although you might be tempted to think that the assignment of a single IP address to a vLAN represents a typographical mistake, in actuality it represents the ability to enable network stations to dynamically join an IP multicast group without adversely affecting the bandwidth available to other network users assigned to the same subnet, but located on different segments attached to a LAN switch. To understand why this occurs, let me digress and discuss the concept associated with IP multicast operations.

IP multicast references a set of specifications that allows an IP host to transmit one packet to multiple destinations. This one-to-many transmission method is accomplished by the use of Class D IP addresses (224.0.0.0 to 239.255.255.255), which are mapped directly to data link layer-2 multicast addresses. Through the use of IP multicasting, a term used to reference the use of Class D addresses, the need for an IP host to transmit multiple packets to multiple destinations is eliminated. This in turn permits more efficient use of backbone network bandwidth; however, the arrival of IP Class D addressed packets at a network destination, such as a router connected to an internal corporate network, can result in a bandwidth problem. This is because multicast transmission is commonly used for audio and/or video distribution of educational information, videoconferencing, news feeds, and financial reports, such as delivering stock prices. Due to the amount of traffic associated with multicast transmission, it could adversely affect multiple subnets linked together by a LAN switch that uses subnets for vLAN creation. By providing a "registration" capability that allows an individual LAN user to become a single user vLAN associated with a Class D address, Class D packets can be routed to a specific segment even when several segments have the same subnet. Thus, this limits the effect of multicast transmission to a single segment.

Advantages

The major advantages associated with a rule-based method of vLAN creation include its easy use of configuration and its operational flexibility. A rule-based creation method is similar to the manner by which filters are created when bridges and routers are used. Thus, the ability to configure one or more vLANs is relatively easy. Concerning flexibility, the ability to create vLANs based upon the value of a portion of a packet or the value of several fields or portions of packet fields makes vLAN creation able to satisfy just about any networking requirement a LAN manager or administrator may have. Thus, a rule-based vLAN creation capability should provide the most flexible method for creating virtual LANs.

Disadvantages

The major disadvantages associated with the use of a rule-based vLAN creation method include the configuration of vLANs and the efficiency of the switch. Due to the potential for creating vLANs based upon the value of a bit within a field of a packet, it can become a laborious task to correctly configure a complex vLAN association. Concerning switch efficiency, as the number of rules associated with the creation of a vLAN increases, the examination effort required for packets flowing through the switch increases. This in turn can result in an increase in packet latency through the LAN switch performing the rule-based comparisons.

COMPARING VLAN CREATION FEATURES

In this concluding section we will turn our attention to comparing the features and operational capabilities associated with the four major methods used to create vLANs. Table 6.2 provides a summary comparison of the features and operational capability of port-grouping, MAC-based, layer-3-based, and rule-based vLAN creation methods. Due to a few subtle differences between the use of wiring hubs and LAN switches for the creation of port-grouping vLANs, that vLAN creation category was subdivided to reference the use of wiring hubs and LAN switches.

Table 6.2 vLAN Assignment Method Comparison

	Port-grouping		MAC-based	Layer-3-based	Rule-based
	Wirehub	*Switch*	*MAC-based*	*Layer-3-based*	*Rule-based*
Connectivity beyond the workgroup	No*	No*	No*	Yes	Yes
Ease of station assignment	Easy	Easy	Difficult	Easy-Difficult	Easy-Difficult
Flexibility	None	None	Moderate	Moderate	High
Improved workgroup bandwidth	None	Yes	Yes	Yes	Yes
Multicast support	Inefficient	Inefficient	Inefficient	Efficient	Efficient
Multiple vLANs per port	No	No	Possible	Possible	Possible
Security	High	High	Low-High	Low-High	Selectable
vLAN spanning switches	No	Possible	Possible	Yes	Yes

*Installation of multiple adapters permits connectivity to other workgroups.

Connectivity Beyond the Workgroup

As indicated by the footnote in Table 6.2, both port-grouping and MAC-based methods of vLAN creation can provide for station connectivity beyond a workgroup by the installation of multiple adapters in the station. In comparison, the use of a layer-3 vLAN creation method implies a built-in routing capability which allows connectivity beyond a station's workgroup.

Ease of Station Assignment

Port-grouping is a relatively simple method of assigning stations to vLANs. Thus, this technique is easy to administer. In comparison, locating and entering MAC addresses can be a time-consuming and tedious task, resulting in the "difficult" entry in the table. Both layer-3 and rule-based vLAN creation methods can range from easy to difficult with respect to the ease of station assignments, with the level of difficulty based upon the actual assignment method used.

Flexibility

If we define flexibility as the ability to vary the composition of a vLAN according to organizational changes, we can say that port grouping represents an inflexible method of vLAN creation. In comparison, MAC-based and layer-3-based vLAN creation methods permit stations to physically move without requiring the reconfiguration of hardware. Thus, those methods of vLAN creation can be considered to provide a moderate level of flexibility. Since a rule-based vLAN creation method permits a high degree of tailoring of the composition of packets to an organization's vLAN creation requirements, it provides higher degree of flexibility.

Improved Workgroup Bandwidth

With the exception of the use of a wiring hub, all vLAN assignment methods listed in Table 6.2 permit the use of a LAN switch. Since a LAN switch enables multiple client-server sessions to occur simultaneously, its use can result in improved workgroup bandwidth.

Multicast Support

To effectively support the association of Class D addresses to the data link layer address requires the use of a routing capability. Thus, both layer-3 and rule-based vLAN creation methods provide an efficient method of multicast support. In addition, since a rule-based vLAN creation method also provides the ability to associate a single segment to a Class D address even when multiple segments have the same subnet, this method of vLAN creation becomes very efficient with respect to multicast support.

Multiple vLANs per Port

Although the ability to have multiple vLANs on a port is common to MAC, layer-3, and rule-based vLAN creation methods, a word of caution is warranted. As previously noted in this chapter, not all LAN switches have this capability. Thus, it is important to verify the capability of the switch to support this feature if this feature is required to satisfy your organization's operational requirements.

Security

The use of a port-grouping vLAN creation method provides the highest level of security since all stations on a segment must reside on the same vLAN. In comparison, MAC and layer-3-based vLAN creation methods that permit multiple vLANs per switch port would have a low level of security, while those vLAN creation methods that do not support multiple vLANs per port would have a high level of security. The reason multiple vLANs on a segment connected to a switch port results in a low level of security is due to the fact that users associated with one vLAN could use a protocol analyzer to read frames associated with another vLAN. Thus, the ability to associate multiple vLANs to a switch port can result in a security loophole. Due to the ability of a rule-based vLAN creation method to allow the manager to create the membership criteria, security is selectable under that vLAN creation method.

vLAN Spanning

The expansion of a vLAN across multiple switches is not possible when intelligent wiring hubs are used. In comparison, the use of a LAN switch for creating a vLAN based upon port-grouping, as well as the creation of a vLAN using a MAC-based creation method, may allow the expansion of the vLAN beyond a single switch. To do so, switches will commonly use a management port connection to interconnect switches, which allows table entries to be transferred between switches as well as allows for the transmission of frames between switches. Since layer-3 and rule-based vLAN creation methods employ routing, they enable multiple switches to be linked together.

7

Standards

As an emerging technology, you would more than likely expect vLANs to be awaiting the development of standards. Your expectation is quite correct, as when this book was prepared a considerable amount of effort remained to be expended by the IEEE committee involved in developing vLAN standards.

Rather than simply stating that standards are being developed, I decided to include this chapter as a mechanism to provide readers with information on two types of vLAN standards—de facto and de jure. The first type of standard to be covered in this chapter, de facto, represents a method for providing interoperability between vLANs formed by the use of switches from a leading router and switch manufacturer. Due to the market dominance of Cisco Systems, we can consider the method by which its switches and routers recognize vLANs as a de facto standard. Thus, in the first portion of this chapter we will focus on the Cisco Inter-Switch Link (ISL) protocol specification and that vendor's modification of the IEEE 802.10 security protocol. ISL is used by Cisco as a transport mechanism across Fast Ethernet, while the 802.10 protocol was modified by that vendor to provide a vLAN interswitch communications capability across FDDI backbones. In the second part of this chapter we will turn our attention to the de jure standard being developed by the IEEE. In doing so we will focus on the evolving IEEE 802.1Q standard.

DE FACTO STANDARDS

In this section we will examine two interswitch protocols developed by Cisco Systems that promote vLAN communications across shared LAN backbone technologies. Each protocol can be considered to represent a de facto standard based upon several factors: the vendor's stance in the marketplace, its proactive approach toward vendor interoperability by sharing its specifications with other vendors, and its effort in working with IEEE standards groups concerning the development of vLAN standards. Since formal standards may be several years or more from ratification, Cisco's efforts in developing its ISL protocol and modifying the 802.10 standard may continue to provide a de facto vLAN interoperability standard for the foreseeable future.

The ISL Protocol

To obtain the ability to enable vLANs to span more than one switch, Cisco Systems developed its Inter-Switch Link (ISL) protocol as a mechanism to convey virtual LAN associations across Fast Ethernet backbone networks. ISL actually represents a frame format and protocol which enables Ethernet, FDDI, and Token Ring frames to be transported between switches in addition to transporting their vLAN associations. Thus, ISL enables switches to support the connection of a variety of different LAN modules while supporting the association of vLANs between switches.

Overview

Through the use of ISL, vLANs are explicitly identified at layer 2 via a packet-tagging process. Using explicit tagging, a switch encapsulates a frame and adds a header to each received packet which includes a field that identifies the packet's vLAN membership. This information enables the packet to be forwarded to appropriate switches and routers based upon the value of the vLAN membership identifier and the packet's MAC address. Once the packet reaches its destination, the header is removed and it is forwarded to the receiving device.

Frame Flow

Figure 7.1 illustrates the flow of ISL frames between two Cisco switches to communicate vLAN associations between those switches. Under ISL, each packet that enters a switch from a non-interswitch port that is associated with a vLAN is encapsulated into an ISL packet. That packet is then forwarded only to those switches and interconnected links that have the same vLAN address. Thus, this transmission technique can considerably reduce the flow of unnecessary broadcasts between switches and switches and routers.

Frame Composition

The ISL frame consists of three primary fields—a header, the encapsulated frame, and a 32-bit *cyclic redundancy check* (CRC) appended to the end of the frame. Figure 7.2 illustrates the format of the ISL frame showing the fields within the frame and the size of each field indicated in bits placed in parenthesis in each field. In the remainder of this section we will examine the contents and use of each field.

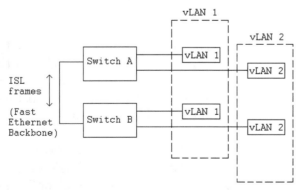

Figure 7.1 Using ISL to communicate vLAN associations.

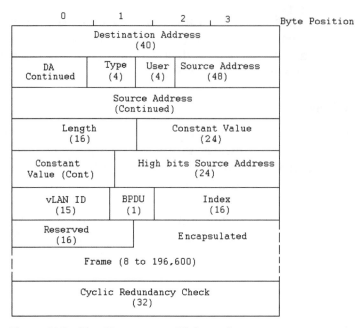

Figure 7.2 The Cisco systems ISL frame format.

Destination Address Field The destination address field is 40 bits in length and represents the destination address of the frame. Since a vLAN frame must be transmitted to a broadcast domain, the address represents a multicast address. Cisco currently sets that address to hex 01-00-0C-00-00 and the contents of that field is used to inform the receiver that an ISL-formatted frame is being received.

Type Field The purpose of the type field is to indicate the type of frame encapsulated within the ISL frame. Currently, four type codes have been defined as indicated in Table 7.1. Since a 4-bit field enables 16 type codes to be defined, support for additional encapsulations can be added in the future.

User Field The user field represents a 4-bit extension to the type field which enables variations to the basic encapsulated frame types listed in Table 7.1 to be defined. Such definitions can be used to indicate variations in different types of encapsulated

Table 7.1 Type Field Definitions

Type Code	Meaning
0000	Ethernet
0001	Token Ring
0010	FDDI
0011	ATM

frames or to define priorities to an encapsulated packet. For encapsulated Ethernet frames, user field bits 0 and 1 are used to indicate the priority of the encapsulated frame as it flows through one or more switches. Table 7.2 indicates the assignment of user field bits for encapsulated Ethernet frames. Note that an X in the field value represents a don't care condition.

The use of user field bits by a switch does not guarantee that a priority assignment will be honored. This is because the bit settings are used by a switch only when data can be forwarded more quickly, and the interpretation of the contents of the field does not guarantee that a frame will always have a quick path through a switch.

Source Address Field   The source address field is six bytes or 48 bits in length and contains the MAC address of the switch port transmitting the frame. Although monitoring of the values of this field can be used to determine interswitch traffic, the receiving device can ignore the contents of this field.

Length Field   The length field is two bytes or 16 bits in length. The value of this field is used to indicate a portion of the length

Table 7.2 User Field Priority Assignments

User Field Bit Settings	Meanings
XX00	Normal Priority
XX01	Priority 1
XX10	Priority 2
XX11	Highest Priority

of the ISL packet in bytes. That length excludes the destination address, type, user, source address, length, constant value, and CRC fields. Thus, the length field excludes 18 bytes in the header and represents the total length of the ISL packet minus 18 bytes.

Constant Value Field Following the length field, the ISL packet header contains a three-byte or 24-bit field that has a constant value. The value of that field is hex AA-AA-03.

High-Bits Source Address Field The high-bits source address field consists of three bytes or 24 bits. This field is used to represent the manufacturer portion of the source address field and is set to the value hex 00-00-0C.

vLAN Field The vLAN field is 15 bits in length and indicates the virtual LAN ID of the packet. In Cisco terminology, the value of this field is used to refer to the "color" of the packet.

Bridge Protocol Data Unit (BPDU) Field The BPDU field is one bit in length and is toggled to 1 when a bridge protocol data unit is encapsulated in an ISL packet. As previously indicated in this book, BPDUs are employed by the spanning tree algorithm to determine the topology of a network.

Index Field The index field is two bytes or 16 bits in length. The contents of this field is used to indicate the port index of the source of the packet as it exits a switch. The contents of this field is used for diagnostic purposes and can be set to any value by other devices and is ignored in received packets.

Reserved Field The reserved field is two bytes or 16 bits in length. This field is used when a Token Ring or an FDDI frame is encapsulated. When a Token Ring frame is encapsulated, its AC and FC field values are placed in the reserved field. When an FDDI frame is encapsulated, the FC field value of the FDDI frame is placed in the least significant byte of the reserved field. For other types of encapsulated frames the value of the reserved field is set to zero.

Encapsulated Frame Following the previously described ISL header fields is the encapsulated frame. That frame can vary in length from 1 to 24575 bytes to accommodate Ethernet, Token Ring, and FDDI frames. Included in the encapsulated frame is its own CRC value. Once an ISL packet is received at a switch the header and trailing CRC can be stripped, regenerating the original frame. That frame would then be used by the switch based upon certain values in the header, such as the vLAN identification.

CRC Field The CRC appended to the end of an ISL packet is calculated on the entire packet, from its destination address field through the entire encapsulated frame. The receiving station checks this CRC field value by recomputing its own CRC. If the two do not match the frame is discarded.

It is important to note that by itself ISL is restricted to providing a mechanism for vLANs to be extended from one switch to another. However, the ability to communicate between logically defined vLANs is a layer-3 function that requires routing. Thus, the ability for vLAN membership to span switches and for devices to become members of multiple vLANs requires both the ISL protocol and the use of routers that support that protocol.

Configuration Example

To illustrate the ease by which vLANs can be established across a Fast Ethernet backbone using the ISL protocol, let us return to Figure 7.1 and assume each switch is a Cisco Systems Catalyst 5000. At the time this book was prepared, each Catalyst 5000 switch was manufactured with five slots in which modules could be installed, with slot 1 always used for the supervisor module which includes a console port for switch management and two 100-Mbps Fast Ethernet ports. A variety of other modules can be installed in slots 2 through 5 to obtain 10-Mbps Ethernet and 100-Mbps Fast Ethernet support. Each port is identified by the expression X/Y, where X identifies the slot number used by a module, while Y identifies the port's position on the module. Assuming vLAN 1 on Switch A in Figure 7.1 is connected to port 1 on a module installed in slot 2, and vLAN 2 is connected to port 2, on that module you would use the Catalyst 5000's command port to configure the two vLANs by entering the following commands:

```
set vlan 1 2/1
set vlan 2 2/2
```

This first "set vlan" command creates vLAN 1 and assigns port 1 in slot 2 to it. The second command creates vLAN 2 and assigns port 2 in slot 2 to that vLAN.

To provide vLAN communications across the Fast Ethernet backbone requires the use of a trunk. When a Catalyst switch port is configured as a trunk, it automatically operates in ISL mode and uses the spanning tree protocol on all vLANs transported to ensure no closed loops occur. If we assume that port 1 on module 1 in switch A provides the trunk connection to switch B, you would enter the following trunk command to configure the port.

```
set trunk 1/1 1,2
```

Here the trunk command configures port 1 in slot 1 as a trunk and adds vLANs 1 and 2 to the trunk.

The previous commands only set up switch A. Thus, a similar series of commands would be required to be entered at the console of switch B to establish vLAN interoperability between switches. For example, assume vLAN 1 on switch B was connected to port 1 on a module in slot 3, while vLAN 2 was connected to port 2 on a module in slot 3. Then you would enter the following two commands into switch B:

```
set vlan 1 3/1
set vlan 2 3/2
```

Assuming that the Fast Ethernet backbone connection occurred on port 1 on the module in slot 1, you would then enter the trunk command as follows:

```
set trunk 1/1 1,2
```

Here the trunk command configures port 1 in slot 1 as a trunk and adds vLANs 1 and 2 to it, providing an ISL link to switch A. Thus, the entry of two series of three commands would provide vLAN interoperability between the two switches shown in Figure 7.1.

The 802.10 Security Protocol

Similar to the manner by which the ISL protocol was developed to provide vLAN connectivity across a Fast Ethernet backbone, Cisco Systems modified the IEEE 802.10 Security Protocol to convey interswitch vLAN communications across FDDI backbones. In doing so, the 802.10 standardized header was modified so that a 32-bit or four-byte vLAN ID field replaces a Security Association Identifier (SAID) field.

Through the use of a unique identification mechanism, vLAN information can be forwarded to switches and routers connected to one another via an FDDI backbone network. Once a packet arrives at a switch, its vLAN ID is noted as a mechanism to route the packet to an appropriate switch port, where its header is removed prior to the packet exiting the destination switch. Figure 7.3 illustrates the flow of the modified IEEE 802.10 Security Protocol between several Cisco Systems switches via an FDDI backbone network.

In examining Figure 7.3 it should be noted that several types of Cisco Systems switches are capable of supporting the

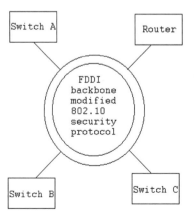

Figure 7.3   vLAN communications via an FDDI backbone.

modified 802.10 Security Protocol. In addition, since one Catalyst 5000 can be connected to another via an ISL link, it becomes possible to use both ISL and the modified 802.10 protocol to construct vLAN associations that cross both Fast Ethernet and FDDI backplanes.

The 802.10 Frame

The IEEE 802.10 standard was modified in late 1992 as a mechanism to support the security requirements of network users communicating within shared LANs, such as Metropolitan Area Networks (MANs). This standard includes both encryption and authentication which provides data confidentiality as well as the verification of the originator.

Under the 802.10 standard, a *secure data exchange* (SDE) *protocol data unit* (PDU) is defined. This SDE PDU represents a MAC layer frame with an 802.10 header inserted between the frame's MAC header and its information field. A special *integrity check value* (ICV) field is then appended to the end of the frame to protect against the unauthorized modification of the data in the frame. Figure 7.4 illustrates the IEEE 802.10 frame format header.

The header contains the destination and source address from the original frame as well as a length field whose value is

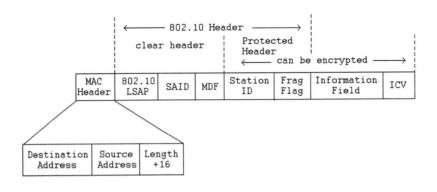

Figure 7.4 The IEEE 802.10 frame format.

incremented by 16. As indicated in Figure 7.4, the IEEE 802.10 header that follows the MAC header consists of clear and protected portions. The clear portion of the header contains three fields and is not encrypted, while the protected portion of the header also contains three fields that can be encrypted.

The first field in the clear portion of the header is the *logical SAP* (LSAP), which represents an address that defines the type of data carried in the frame. LSAPs are both administered by the IEEE and implemented by manufacturers for distinct frame transportation purposes. Examples of IEEE-administered LSAP addresses include 06 for the ARPANET Internet Protocol (IP), 42 for the IEEE 802.1 Bridge Spanning Tree Protocol, and AA for the Sub-Network Access Protocol (SNAP). Some examples of manufacturer-implemented LSAPs include 04 for IBM SNA Path Control (individual), 05 for IBM SNA Path Control (group), E0 for Novell NetWare, and F0 for IBM NetBIOS. In the modified 802.10 frame the LSAP is expanded to three bytes and has the hex value 0A-0A-03.

The Security Association Identifier (SAID) is four bytes in length. Under the IEEE 802.10 Protocol, it is used to provide secure data transfer across shared media, enabling the exchange of encryption keys via a lookup in a Security Management Information Base (SMIB). The SAID field is followed by a *management-defined field* (MDF), which is used to transport information that facilitates PDU processing and is dropped by Cisco.

The protected header replicates the source address in the original MAC frame's header. This action protects the real source of the frame from being altered and forms a mechanism to validate or authenticate the originator. In actuality the station ID field is eight bytes in length, with the first six representing the carnonical source address of the original frame. The last two bytes are flags that are undefined and are set to NULL. Following the station ID field is a *fragmentation flag*, which when set indicates the frame is a fragment. Under Cisco's implementation of the 802.10 frame for vLAN encapsulation, fragmentation is not supported, and this field is always set to NULL. The protected portion of the header is then followed by the information field of the frame, with an *integrity check value* (ICV) field appended to the end of the frame. Here the ICV is used as a mechanism to safeguard against unauthorized modification to the frame. To accomplish this, the protocol executes an algorithm that operates upon portions of the contents of the frame to create a binary value that functions similar to a check digit.

Cisco Systems Frame Modification

Recognizing that the IEEE 802.10 frame structure was already being routed by their products, Cisco Systems was able to easily modify the protocol to accommodate its use as a mechanism for conveying vLAN associations. To do so, the 802.10 four-byte SAID field is used as the vLAN ID. This enables any device that supports the clear header portion of the 802.10 frame to become capable of supporting Cisco's method of vLAN identification. However, when used in this manner the IEEE 802.2 LSAP is changed to indicate a 802.10 vLAN frame, and the security aspect of the protocol, which includes encryption, is not used by Cisco. Thus, although it may appear from vendor literature that this use of the 802.10 protocol represents a standards-based vLAN method, in actuality it does not, merely representing a proprietary extension of the protocol.

The frame format illustrated in Figure 7.4 is applicable for transporting IEEE 802.3, Ethernet 2, and Ethernet SNAP. When an 802.2 frame is transported on FDDI, or a SNAP frame originates on FDDI, the FC field of the FDDI frame is included in the MAC header as a prefix to the destination address field shown in Figure 7.4.

Through the use of a four-byte vLAN ID field an FDDI backbone becomes capable of supporting the transfer of information to and from billions of distinct virtual LANs, which probably exceeds by several orders of magnitude the ability of devices to support such numbers. For example, when a router or switch receives a 802.10 frame, it matches the vLAN ID against the vLANs it is configured to support. Thus, most devices have a finite and much smaller support capability than the number of vLANs that could theoretically be supported by a four-byte field.

When the modified 802.10 frame format is used, the contents of the header govern the forwarding of the frame. When a router or switch determines that it supports the vLAN ID in the four-byte vLAN ID field, it will remove the 802.10 header and forward the original frame to any or all ports that are associated with the virtual LAN. Similar to the use of ISP, the use of the modified IEEE 802.10 header requires a router to enable communications between vLANs.

DE JURE STANDARDS

There are two de jure standards that should be considered when discussing vLANs. The first de jure standard represents the use of switched ATM backbone for the connection of vLANs on legacy LANs. This standard is known as *LAN emulation* (LANE) and provides a transparent method of communications so that its effect is transparent to vLAN associations. The second de jure standard represents an ongoing effort of the IEEE to standardize virtual LANs. This effort involves a considerable examination of the technical aspects of vLANs and their operability within and between different types of LANs. Due to the scope of this effort, it may be several years until IEEE 802.1Q standards are actually finalized. Thus, we will focus on LAN emulation and then discuss the present state of IEEE vLAN standardization effort in the remainder of this chapter.

LAN Emulation

LAN emulation (LANE) version 1.0 was approved by the ATM forum in February 1995 as a mechanism to enable legacy LAN traffic to communicate via an ATM backbone. To accomplish this, LANE makes a switched ATM LAN appear to resemble a legacy local area network.

Rationale for the Process

To obtain an appreciation for the LAN emulation process, let us assume we have a network consisting of two Ethernet switches connected via an ATM switch. Figure 7.5 illustrates the configuration of this network.

In examining Figure 7.5, note that each Ethernet switch routes data based upon the use of MAC addresses to perform

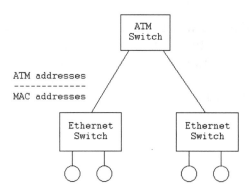

Figure 7.5 Using an ATM backbone.

bridging operations. Data flow on legacy LANs, such as an Ethernet LAN, is connectionless, meaning that no session is required to be established prior to data flow commencing. In comparison, ATM is a connection-oriented network that uses *virtual paths* (VPs) and *virtual channels* (VCs) imbedded in VPs to route data from source to destination. This means that the flow of information from an Ethernet network to another legacy network via an ATM backbone requires a mechanism to resolve addressing differences. Thus, LAN emulation provides a mechanism to resolve destination MAC addresses into ATM addresses so that 53-byte ATM cells can transport legacy LAN frames to their appropriate destination via an ATM backbone. To accomplish this address resolution required a client-server architecture to be developed. This architecture enables ATM cards in legacy LAN switches to work in conjunction with a *LAN emulation server* that provides the address translation. In addition, a mechanism was required to handle unknown destination MAC addresses as well as broadcast and multicast frames. Thus, another component of LANE involves a *broadcast and unknown server* (BUS).

Operation

To illustrate the operation of LANE, let's examine the function of the client and servers involved in the LAN emulation process.

LAN Emulation Client   The *LAN emulation client* (LEC) represents an interface through which an ATM endstation resolves address, forwards data, and provides other control functions. For the network configuration shown in Figure 7.5, the ATM adapter in each Ethernet switch would provide a LEC operational capability.

When a request is made to transport a frame beyond the local switch the LEC must establish a connection with an appropriate emulated LAN. To do so, it must first set up a connection with a *LAN emulation configuration server* (LECS).

LAN Emulation Configuration Server The LECS assigns LAN-emulated clients to different LANs by returning the ATM address of a LAN emulation server (LES) to the client. The LECS also returns the LAN type, LAN name, maximum message length, and timeout values associated with the LAN supported by the LES.

By appropriate configuration of the LECS, network managers and administrators can control which clients are combined to form different virtual LANs. In addition, clients can become members of multiple vLANs as the LECS can be configured to return the addresses of multiple LESs, one for each vLAN an ATM endpoint is configured for membership.

LAN Emulation Server The LAN emulation server (LES) is responsible for handling control protocol messages for all LECs. Once the client receives the ATM address of the LES, it joins the emulated LAN and registers its ATM address with that server. At that time, the LES also obtains the physical address (MAC) of the LEC. When the LEC needs the address of a new destination and queries the LES, the LES first checks its address tables and if a matching MAC address is encountered, returns the ATM address associated with the MAC address. If no match occurs, the LES transmits a multicast request to all other LECs in the network. The LEC that has the destination MAC address in its tables responds to the LES and the LES then broadcasts the response to all other LECs. The originating LEC recognizes the response which enables it to learn the ATM address of the destination switch. This enables the LEC to set up a switched virtual circuit through the ATM backbone to transport the frame as a series of ATM cells.

Broadcast Services Although broadcast messages have been included in LANs since their inception, ATM switches do not support this service. Thus, LANE includes a broadcast and unknown server (BUS) to facilitate the conversion of a legacy LAN broadcast or multicast frame into an appropriate number of ATM transmissions. In addition, the BUS is responsible for converting unicast address resolution requests from one LEC to all LECs. To convert broadcast or multicast LAN frames, the LEC sends a request to the ATM broadcast and unknown server. The BUS converts the broadcast or multicast frame such that one copy is sent to each registered LAN emulation client. The LES, LECS, and BUS are commonly implemented in firmware on an ATM switch.

vLANs and ATM Under LAN emulation devices register their presence on the network and become part of the same emulated LAN supported by a LAN emulation server. This action can be considered to form a MAC layer virtual LAN that defines a broadcast domain among endstations. Thus, all devices attached to an emulated LAN will appear as a bridged segment. As previously noted, by configuring the LECS to return the address of one LES for each vLAN an ATM endpoint is a member of, an ATM host can obtain membership in multiple vLANs.

In addition to operating at layer 2, LANE supports layer-3 operations. To illustrate this, consider an IP workstation that has to communicate with another IP workstation via an emulated LAN. The originating station will issue an IP Address Resolution Protocol (ARP) packet to determine the MAC address of the destination. That packet will be sent to the LANE broadcast and unknown server, which will broadcast the packet to all endstations on the emulated LAN. The destination station recognizes the ARP request and responds by transmitting its MAC address. Unfortunately, the return of the MAC address which flows to the LEC is not what the LEC needs to set up an ATM connection. Thus, the LEC must issue a MAC-to-ATM address resolution request to the LAN emulation server and the previously described emulation process is repeated. That process is referred to as *IP over ATM address resolution* and is discussed next.

IP over ATM Address Resolution

The actual transfer of IP over ATM is defined in RFC 1577, the title of which is "Classical IP and ARP over ATM." Here the term *classical* represents the manner by which IP networks are established in which clusters of nodes representing hosts and routers with similar subnet addresses are connected to devices outside their network by IP routers. Under RFC 1577 this "classical" view of IP was adhered to by the grouping of IP nodes into logical IP subnets (LIS). Thus, a LIS represents one or more nodes that share the same IP subnet and communicate with devices outside the subnet via an IP router.

When a LIS node is activated, it establishes a connection with another IP station or router configured to function as an ATMARP server. Since each node is configured with the ATM address of the ATMARP server, the LIS node knows where to send its request. The ATMARP server receives the LIS client request and notes its ATM address, but must learn the client's IP address to construct its tables. To do so the server transmits an inverse ARP request to the LIS client. Thus, as LIS clients become active, the ATMARP server can learn their ATM and IP addresses and store such information in its address table.

When the LIS client must communicate via IP, it knows the destination IP address but requires the ATM address. Thus, the client sends an ATMARP request to the server. The server responds to the request with an ATMARP reply if the ATM address associated with the destination IP address is in its address table. If not, the server returns a NAK (negative acknowledgment). Since LIS clients can become active and inactive throughout the day, RFC 1577 requires the ATMARP server to periodically send out inverse ARP requests to update its tables, which provides a mechanism to eliminate nonresponsive addresses from its table.

IEEE 802.1Q

Work on the IEEE 802.1Q standard began in March 1996 with the issuance of a Project Authorization Request (PAR) entitled "Standard for Virtual Bridged Local Area Networks." The PAR was assigned the 802.1Q project number and its scope was stated as follows:

> The formation of the IEEE 802.10 working group was accompanied by an initial effort which resulted in a preliminary explicit frame tagging format to provide a mechanism to identify frames that belong to different vLANs. The format was endorsed by Advanced Micro Devices, Inc., Agile Networks, Inc., Bay Networks, Inc., Cisco Systems, Inc., Digital Equipment Corporation, Fore Systems, Inc., Hewlett-Packard, Intel Corporation, Plaintree Systems, Inc., xpoint Technologies, Inc., and 3Com Corporation. Although several international meetings of the 802.10 working group occurred that resulted in several revisions to an 802.10 draft document, a considerable amount of work on the standard remains to be performed. In fact, the target completion data of the PAR is May, 1998.

At the time this book was prepared, the 802.1Q project was in its second draft stage. While a considerable amount of effort by members of the working group resulted in a comprehensive document, that document contained numerous sections that required further effort. Thus, readers should attempt to follow the efforts of the 802.1Q working group into 1998 as the continuing effort of the working group, through its project completion data, can be expected to fill in "to be determined" (TBD) sections as well as result in some revisions to the draft covered in this section.

Architecture

Under the 802.1Q draft standard, a three-level model framework for vLANs was proposed. Figure 7.6 illustrates the general format of the 802.1Q architectural model.

Configuration Layer The configuration layer of the vLAN model provides a mechanism for indicating the association of devices with different virtual LANs. The actual configuration process might occur via a variety of mechanisms, such as SNMP operating on a MIB, configuration files on a workstation, a server, and the use of a distribution protocol.

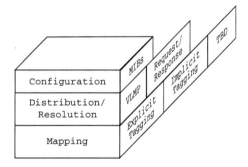

where:

```
MIB  Management Information Base
VLMP Virtual LAN Mapping Protocol
TBD  To be determined
```

Figure 7.6   vLAN Architectural Model.

Distribution/Resolution Layer   The distribution/resolution layer provides the mechanism which enables switches to determine the association between a packet and a vLAN. Thus, this layer is concerned with the distribution of vLAN association between switches. To accomplish this will require a virtual LAN mapping protocol (VLMP) to distribute vLAN associations as well as a request/response protocol to enable specific associations to be requested.

Mapping Layer   At the third layer, mapping provides the mechanism to associate packets with vLANs. As indicated in Figure 7.6, explicit and implicit tagging as well as some possible additional mechanism will be used to provide mapping.

   At the time this book was prepared, a considerable amount of effort of the 802.1Q working group had been accomplished at the mapping layer. Thus, in the remainder of this section we will primarily focus on tagging.

Frame Tagging

As mentioned in the introductory chapter in this book, there are two basic types of frame tagging—implicit and explicit. Implicit tagging enables a packet to belong to a vLAN based upon the receiving port of a switch or the content of the frame. Concerning the latter, implicit tagging can be based upon the MAC address, layer-3 protocol, layer-3 subnet address, and similar frame field contents. In comparison, explicit tagging requires each frame to contain an identifier that serves to classify the vLAN association of the frame.

Proposed vLAN Tagging

The explicit tagging of vLAN frames requires the addition of a header to each frame. Under the 802.1Q draft standard, that header is inserted immediately following the destination and source MAC addresses of a conventional frame.

The vLAN header consists of four fields; however, one field (user priority) remains to be defined and located in the header. Thus, the vLAN header which is shown in Figure 7.7 may be modified or, as an alternative, may have values assigned to one or more fields to encode up to eight priority states in the header.

VPID/SVPID Fields The virtual LAN protocol identifier (VPID) field is two bytes in length when an Ethernet version 2 protocol type is carried, and indicates the Ethernet protocol type

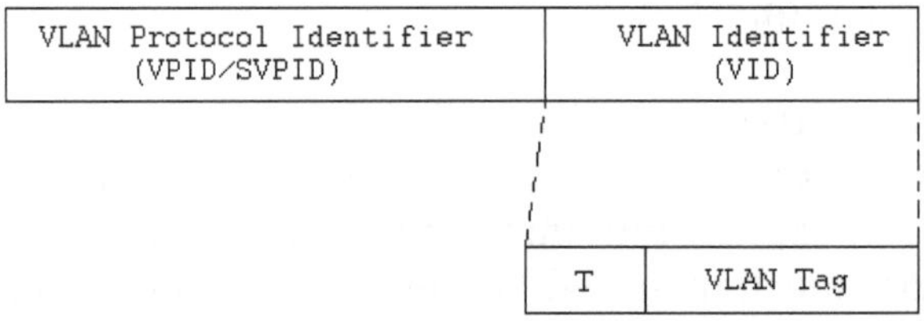

```
where   VPI is 2 or 8 octets in length based upon the media
        type carrying the frame. SVPID defines a SNAP encoded
        VPIP.

        VID is 2 octets in length with a one bit TR encapsu-
        lation bit.

        T is a Token Ring Encapsulation flag.

        Priority field (3 bits) remains to be located.
```

Figure 7.7   The proposed vLAN header.

transported. When a SNAP encoded vPID is transported, the field is expanded to eight octets. The first three contain the SNAP SAP header (AA-AA-03). This is followed by a three-byte OUI (00-00-00) and a two-byte vType field. Thus, the vType field in a SNAP-encoded VPID results in a prefix of the SNAP and OUI fields, with the resulting field having the acronym SVPID.

VID Field The virtual LAN identifier (VID) is two bytes in length. However, one bit, which while shown at the beginning of the field actually remains to be positioned in the field, is used to indicate whether the encapsulated frame is transported in a native Token Ring format. That is, when the bit is set to 1, this setting will indicate that data following the VID is in a Token Ring format. Through the setting of this bit, frames that originate as a Token Ring frame can be transported end-to-end in their native format within a vLAN tagged frame. Doing so ensures that Token Ring information is not translated while the frame flows across the virtual network, regardless of the type of media used to transport the vLAN frame. Although Token Ring information is not translated, the vLAN header will be translated, if necessary, when the vLAN frame flows from one medium to another. If the source address indicates that a routing information field (RIF) is present, the RIF will prefix the SVPID field. Otherwise, the source address field will be followed by either the VPID or SVPID field with the actual field based upon the type of media the frame is transported on.

Frame Formats

Figure 7.8 illustrates examples of vLAN-tagged Ethernet, LLC, and Token Ring frames transported on IEEE 802.31 Ethernet media. Note that the number of bytes for each field is indicated in parenthesis under the field abbreviation. When transmission occurs over FDDI or Token Ring media there are several changes to each frame. For example, vLAN-tagged Ethernet, LLC, and Token Ring frames transported on Token Ring media would use a SNAP-encoded VPID (SVPID), which is eight bytes in length, in place of the byte VPID. In addition, when Token Ring frames

1. vLAN-tagged Ethernet frame

DA (6)	SA (6)	VPID (2)	VID (2)	PT (2)	Data (48-1500)	CRC (4)

2. vLAN-tagged LLC frame

DA (6)	SA (6)	VPIP (2)	VID (2)	LN (2)	LLC (3)	Data (0-1497)	PAD (0-43)	CRC (4)

3. vLAN-tagged Token-Ring frame

DA (6)	SA (6)	VPIP (2)	VID (2)	LN (2)	LLC (3)	TRdata (0-1497)	PAD (0-43)	CRC (4)

Legend:

DA	Destination MAC address
SA	Source MAC address
VIPD	VLAN Protocol ID
PT	Ethernet Protocol Type
LN	Length Field (802.3 style)
LLC	Logical Link Control
VID	vLAN identifier
Data	Data in native format for the medium carrying the frame.
TRdata	Data in native Token-Ring format.

Figure 7.8 vLAN-tagged frame formats for IEEE 802.3 Ethernet media.

flow on a Token Ring network they can contain a routing information field which is never carried on an Ethernet media-based LAN. For comparison purposes, Figure 7.9 illustrates the format for three types of vLAN-tagged frames for transmission on Token Ring and FDDI media.

In comparing the transportation of vLAN-tagged frames on IEEE 802.31 Ethernet and Token Ring/FDDI media, note that the latter results in the prefix of each type of frame by a *ring control* (RC) field. That field is one byte in length and represents the Token Ring access control field when the medium is a Token Ring. In comparison, when the medium is FDDI, the RC field is expanded to two bytes, with the second field representing the FDDI frame control (FC) field.

1. vLAN tagged Ethernet frame

RC (1/2)	DA (6)	SA (6)	SVPID (8)	VID (2)	SPT (8)	Data (46-1500)	CRC (4)

2. vLAN tagged LLC frame

RC (1/2)	DA (6)	SA (6)	SVPID (8)	VID (2)	LLC (3)	Data (0-N)	CRC (4)

3. vLAN tagged Token Ring frame

RC (1/2)	DA (6)	SA (6)	Route (0-30)	SVPID (8)	VIDtr (2)	LLC (3)	TRdata (0-N)	CRC (4)

Legend:

RC	Ring Control field (AC Token Ring) and FC (FDDI)
DA	Destination MAC Address
SA	source MAC Address
SPT	SNAP encoded Ethernet Protocol Type
SVPID	SNAP encoded VPID (vLAN Protocol ID)
VID	vLAN Identifier
VIDtr	vLAN Identifier Token-Ring encapsulation
Route	Token Ring Source Routing Information
Data	Data in native format for the medium carrying the frame
TRdata	Data in native Token Ring format.

Figure 7.9 vLAN-tagged frame formats for Token Ring and FDDI media.

The Continuing Effort

Although a considerable amount of effort was expended defining explicit frame tagging required to identify vLANs, that effort was far from completed when this book was prepared. At that time, the IEEE 802.1Q working group had not decided where and how to incorporate user priority. In addition, there were a large number of issues remaining to be resolved. Some of those issues include the use of single or multiple spanning trees per set of vLANs, the number of vLANs handled per tree, how to handle a default vLAN, and methods to support multiple links between two points in a network. In addition, the method of explicit tagging by which frames expand beyond their original standard length may present a problem if and when standard-compliant switches are used in a legacy network. This is because although standard-compliant switches and routers can be expected to support the extended length of frames, legacy bridges, routers, and repeaters may not be capable of passing such frames. Due to this, proprietary implicit vLAN creation methods that work may continue to represent a viable alternative to a standardized explicit tagging vLAN creation method once such standards are promulgated.

Virtual Networking

8

In the preface to this book, it was mentioned that a virtual organization can be considered as one without boundaries. When this concept is extended to networking, the term *virtual networking* represents communications that occur without conventional boundaries. That is, instead of communications always flowing on a fixed path between two points, transmission occurs using a logical path established on a temporary basis based upon a variety of criteria. Such criteria can include the destination address of data, other activity occurring on a network, and the service or services requested.

When we refer to virtual networking we are actually referencing several concepts. First, virtual networking can be considered to represent the process by which virtual LANs are interconnected to one another. This process can occur locally with two or more vLANs on one LAN switch, or vLANs located on two or more switches directly or indirectly interconnected to one another or remotely, with routers employed to link switches geographically separated from one another. Second, the connection of both conventional and virtual LANs does not have to occur on the fixed paths predominantly used by corporations and government agencies to interconnect geographically separated locations. Instead, a more flexible network structure can be used whereby transmission occurs using the facilities of another organization. Through the use of those facilities, different transmission sessions between the same connection points can occur on different transmission paths, with the actual path used based upon a variety of factors. This second method of virtual networking has its roots in packet-switched services. Due to the growth of the Internet, that network of interconnected networks now represents a viable virtual networking facility many organizations may wish to consider using to replace conventional point-to-point transmission facilities that currently constitute the bulk of private networks. Thus, in this chapter we will focus on two types of virtual networking: interconnecting virtual LANs locally and using the Internet as a virtual network.

RATIONALE

The rationale for virtual networking varies based upon the type of virtual networking you wish to perform. For example, assume you are attempting to interconnect two or more vLANs on a common switch or located on local switches or routers to provide a virtual LAN that spans a wide area within a building or campus. Then the rationale is simply to extend your virtual LANs beyond a single physical location. If you are considering the use of the Internet as a virtual network to interconnect geographically separated locations, the rationale to do so involves considering reliability, economics, and the ability to integrate voice and data applications.

Reliability

From a reliability perspective, the Internet resembles a mesh network structure. This means there is normally more than one path between locations linking Internet Service Providers to the backbone networks used for the main transmission path between the networks linked to from the Internet. In comparison, due to cost constraints most corporate, government, and private networks are constructed using point-to-point transmission facilities. Thus, once traffic reaches an Internet Service Provider it is more than likely that communications will obtain a higher level of reliability than if traffic flowed on a private network where the flow of data primarily occurred on point-to-point transmission facilities that do not have redundant paths for alternate routing.

To understand how the Internet can provide a more reliable method of communications, consider the two networks shown in Figure 8.1. Those network diagrams provide a general comparison between the network infrastructure of a private three-node network and the backbone of the Internet used to connect three corporate locations via the Internet. In examining the private network structure at the top of Figure 8.1, note that any line failure automatically disables communications between two of the three corporate locations. In comparison, when each corporate location is connected to the Internet through a circuit routed from that location to an Internet Service Provider's Internet access point of presence, the failure of a circuit is far more limited. For example, the failure of the circuit linking corporate

Private Network

Internet

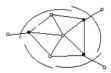

Legend: • Internet Service Provider Internet
              access point of presence.

Figure 8.1 Comparing network structures.

location A to an Internet Service Provider only affects transmission to and from that location. If a circuit failure occurs within the Internet "cloud," alternate routing may allow all sites to continue communicating since routers within the Internet may automatically switch transmission to alternate paths. Thus, the use of the Internet can be expected to provide a more reliable transmission service than that obtainable from the installation of point-to-point circuits commonly used to construct a private network.

Economics

Conventional point-to-point analog leased lines are tariffed based upon mileage. Digital leased lines are tariffed based upon the operating rate of the circuit and the mileage between interconnected locations. In comparison, most Internet Service Providers charge users a monthly fee based upon the operating rate of the connection. While the preceding comparison may not at first appear to be significant, let's consider a few examples to illustrate how using the Internet as a virtual network can result in significant economic savings.

First, let's assume a 500-mile distance between locations A and B and A and C, and that each pair of locations will be connected via a digital T1 line operating at 1.544 Mbps. Since the monthly cost of a T1 line is approximately $3.00 per circuit mile, the monthly cost for the private network shown at the top of Figure 8.1 would be approximately $3,000. Assuming that each corporate location is within a major metropolitan area, the connection of each location to the Internet via an Internet Service Provider can be expected to cost between $750 and $1,000 per month. At a monthly cost of $750, the use of the Internet could save the organization $750 per month, while a monthly connection cost of $1,000 would not produce any economic benefits.

Now, let's assume that locations A, B, and C represent New York City, Miami, and Los Angeles, resulting in the distance for the two circuits expanding to approximately 3,500 miles. At a monthly cost of $3.00 per mile for a T1 circuit, the communications cost of the private network will increase to $10,500. In comparison, since access to the Internet within major metropolitan areas is distance insensitive, the cost for using the Internet would remain the same as previously discussed, somewhere between $2,260 and $3,000 per month.

Based upon the two previous examples, we can make a general statement concerning the economics associated with replacing point-to-point private network communications circuits with the use of the Internet as a virtual network. That is, the greater the distance between locations to be connected, the greater the probability that the use of the Internet will result in economic savings in comparison to the construction of a private network.

Applications

In addition to traditional data communications, the Internet provides a potential mechanism for integrating voice, data, and fax. Although throughput delays and a lack of predictability upon occasion limit the transmission of voice over the Internet to having users speak "CB-style," the ability to use one common Internet connection, as well as the distance-insensitive tariff associated with using the Internet, makes it an attractive vehicle for integrating corporate communications. If backbone bandwidth continues to be enhanced, it's a distinct possibility that in the near future a variety of voice, data, and fax applications will be integrated for use on the Internet. Since there is a reasonable probability that the transmission of voice and fax via the Internet will reach a level acceptable to the corporate environment, let's examine how this can be accomplished.

Voice and Fax

In a traditional LAN internetworking environment routers are used to link corporate sites via the Internet. Since digitized voice and fax can be transported as data via a router, the key requirement for adding a voice and fax capability to LAN internetworking is to obtain appropriate hardware and software that digitizes voice and data for transport by a router. One product that was released in late 1996 that provides this capability and which warrants a description is Micom Communications Corporation's voice-over-IP (V/IP) equipment.

Micom's V/IP

Micom Communications Corporation's V/IP capability is based upon the use of the firm's V/IP cards installed in a server. Those cards enable a server to obtain a connection to a corporate PBX via a local wire pair that supports the simultaneous transmission of up to 24 voice conversations at a T1 line operating rate. The V/IP cards compress voice based upon the ITU-T G.729 voice compression standard, resulting in an 8-Kbps data stream instead of the conventional 64-Kbps data stream associated with Pulse Code Modulation (PCM) voice digitization. Although the conversion of digitized voice into IP packets would require a higher data rate of approximately 10 Kbps due to frame overhead, Micom's V/IP cards obtain a further reduction in the voice digitization rate by suppressing gaps in speech, resulting from silences inherent in voice conversations. Since human speech typically has 50 percent or more periods of silence, the actual bandwidth required to transport one voice conversation is reduced to an average of approximately 4 Kbps. Thus, a full complement of 24 voice conversations from a PBX would require an average bandwidth under 100 Kbps.

Figure 8.2 illustrates how a Micom server with V/IP cards could be used to add a voice and fax transport capability between corporate locations via the Internet. Fax transmission, which is analog and would normally require a 64-Kbps PCM signal to digitize, is handled differently by the Micom V/IP cards. Those cards, which have the ability to automatically detect a fax signal on a voice channel as well as its modulation scheme, enable the signal to be converted back into its digital format, resulting in a digitized fax signal that requires 9.6 Kbps or less bandwidth. When received at the destination, the signal is then remodulated for delivery to the receiving fax machine.

As bandwidth bottlenecks associated with the Internet are alleviated, the integration of corporate voice and fax as well as

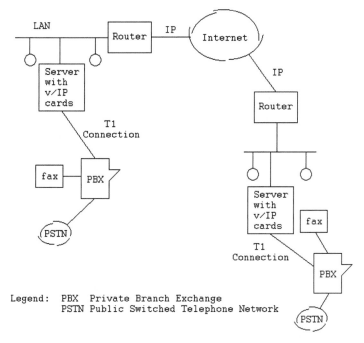

Figure 8.2   Adding a voice and fax transport capability via the Internet.

data for transport via the Internet offers the opportunity for significant cost savings. Even if not totally practical today, the use of the Internet should be considered as a backup facility for expensive private networks, especially those that include international circuits.

LOCAL VIRTUAL NETWORKING

Earlier in this chapter we noted that the interconnection of vLANs, either residing on the same switch or on different switches within close proximity of one another, can be considered to represent local virtual networking. In this section we will focus our attention upon this topic, noting how vLANs can be interconnected. In doing so, we will build upon information presented earlier in this book.

Inter-vLAN, Intraswitch Communications

The first category of communications between vLANs represents those domains established on the same LAN switch, a method I will refer to as inter-vLAN, intraswitch communications. As noted in Chapter 6, there are two basic methods you can consider to obtain an inter-vLAN, intraswitch communications capability. First, you can use multiple LAN adapter cards or multiple protocol stacks and a single adapter card. I will refer to this method as *creative communications*. The second method employs the use of a router.

Creative Communications

Figure 8.3a illustrates the use of multiple LAN adapter cards to obtain an inter-vLAN communications capability. Note that this method requires the attachment of the station to two or more LAN switch ports, with each port associated with a different vLAN. Since each adapter card has a distinct MAC address, this method of vLAN interconnection can be accomplished using either a layer-1 (port-grouping) or layer-2 (MAC-based) vLAN creation method. In comparison, Figure 8.3b illustrates how a dual protocol stack on a workstation or server can be used with a single connection to a LAN switch to obtain an inter-vLAN communications capability on the switch. In this example, multiple protocols are transmitted via a common switch port and each protocol stack provides a connection to a vLAN based upon a layer-3 protocol. Thus, this method of inter-vLAN communications is restricted to a layer-3 vLAN creation method based upon protocol. Although either method a or b in Figure 8.3 provides an inter-vLAN communications capability, both require the setup to occur at each station, which can result in a time-consuming process. In addition, connecting more than two vLANs together is usually difficult, if not impossible, due to hardware and software limitations associated with workstations. That is, many workstations may have neither a sufficient number of expansion slots for additional adapter cards nor sufficient memory to support additional protocol stacks.

Creative Communications

a. Layer-1/2 vLAN Creation

Workstation/Server

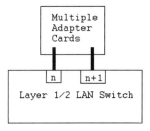

b. Layer-3 vLAN Creation

Workstation/Server

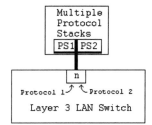

Using Routers

c. One port per vLAN.

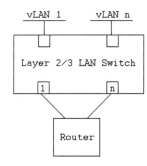

d. Using a global port.

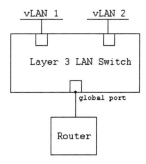

Figure 8.3 Inter-vLAN communications methods.

Using a Router

The second major method used to provide an inter-vLAN, intraswitch communications capability is through the use of a router. When using a router to connect vLANs on the same switch, the method of connection will be based upon the functionality of the switch and the router. When a layer-2 vLAN creation method is used by a switch, each router port contains a MAC address that is associated with a layer-2 broadcast domain. Thus, one port to router connection will be required for each vLAN requiring an inter-vLAN communications capability on the switch, resulting in traffic from one vLAN to another being routed by the router. This method of inter-vLAN communications is illustrated in Figure 8.3c.

If a layer-3 vLAN creation method is supported by the LAN switch, vLANs can be created based upon different IP subnets on IPX network addresses. Then, if the switch does not support a trunking capability, different switch ports can be grouped together by subnet or network address, resulting in predefined router ports being associated with a specific vLAN at layer 3. The router would then forward traffic from one vLAN to another based upon destination subnet or network address.

If a LAN switch has a trunking capability it becomes possible to use a single global port to connect the switch to the router to obtain an inter-vLAN, intraswitch communications capability. Figure 8.3d illustrates the hardware connection between a router and a global port on a switch. Here the term global port references a switch port that belongs to all vLANs configured on the switch, in effect resulting in the switch obtaining a trunking capability.

The configuration illustrated in Figure 8.3d is applicable only to certain switches and routers. When a router is used with a layer-3 switch, the router must be modified to perform, in effect, a routing trick to enable it to provide an inter-vLAN, intraswitch communications capability. For example, a RAD Network Devices router, referred to as Vgate, uses a different MAC address for each vLAN it provides connectivity for. One port on the Vgate uses a unique MAC source address for each IP- and IPX-defined vLAN. This action enables traffic generated by the Vgate to the switch to have a different source MAC address based upon the subnet the address is associated with, resulting in it being forwarded through the switch to other switch ports that belong to the virtual LAN. This technique enables a single connection between RAD's Vgate and a LAN switch to appear to the switch as multiple router connections. In comparison, a conventional router cannot support multiple IP subnets or IPX network addresses on a single port, making it incapable of providing routing via a trunk or global port connection.

Inter-vLAN, Interswitch Communications

A second type of communications between virtual LANs involves the situation where stations reside on different switches. I will refer to this type of communications as inter-vLAN, interswitch communications. Similar to our discussion of inter-vLAN, intraswitch communications, there are two basic methods that can obtain an inter-vLAN, interswitch communications capability—creative communications and the use of routers. In addition, a third method, via the use of backbone switches, may be possible if vendor equipment provides this capability.

Creative Communications

Figure 8.4a illustrates the use of multiple adapter cards in a LAN station to link vLANs on two switches together. As discussed earlier in this chapter, this method of linkage is applicable only for connecting a station to two or three vLANs due to hardware constraints. In addition, if the necessity arises to provide an interconnection capability to a large number of workstations and/or servers, the cabling and use of switch ports can result in a considerable expenditure of funds. For such reasons, this method of providing an inter-vLAN, interswitch communications capability should probably be considered only when very few network stations need this capability. For example, if two or three servers needed to become members of two vLANs on separate switches, you might consider this method for providing inter-vLAN, interswitch communications.

Using a Router

There are three basic methods by which routers can be used to provide inter-vLAN, interswitch communications. Two methods assume the lack of LAN switch support for trunking or global ports, while one method assumes LAN switches support this capability.

Single vLAN per Switch   Figure 8.4b1 illustrates the use of a router to link switches that are configured to support a single vLAN. In this example, either layer-2 or layer-3 vLAN creation

a. Creative communications.

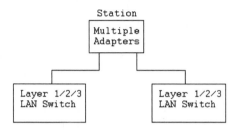

b. Using a router.

1. Single vLAN per switch.   2. Multiple vLANs per switch.

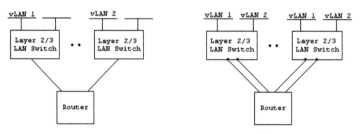

3. Multiple vLANs per switch using global ports.

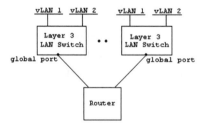

Figure 8.4 Inter-vLAN, inter-switch communications.

methods can be used by the LAN switches. When a layer-2 vLAN creation method is used, the MAC address of one router port is associated with the vLAN on one switch while the MAC address of the other router port is associated with the vLAN on the second switch. When a layer-3 vLAN creation method is used there are two methods by which vLANs can be created.

First, vLANs can be created based upon IP subnet or IPX network address. When this method of vLAN creation is used, the router simply examines the destination subnet or network address and routes data based upon the address. If a vLAN creation method based upon protocol is used, one port on the router could be configured to support a protocol used by one switch while the second router port could be configured to provide support for the protocol used on the second switch. This method of inter-vLAN, interswitch communications is much less common as it requires the router to perform protocol conversion and operate as a gateway. As an alternative, some routers can be configured to provide a translation bridging operation which allows operations to occur at the layer-2 level of the OSI Reference Model.

Multiple vLANs per Switch   When multiple vLANs are configured on LAN switches there are two methods you can consider to provide an inter-vLAN, interswitch communications capability. First, if the LAN switches do not support a trunking or global port capability, you can use multiple switch to router connections, with each connection joining one vLAN on a switch to the router. This method of connectivity is illustrated in Figure 8.4b2. Second, if the LAN switches support a trunking or global port capability, you can use a single connection between each LAN switch and a router. The topology associated with providing an inter-vLAN, interswitch communications capability when multiple vLANs are configured on LAN switches and the switches support a trunking or global port capability is illustrated in Figure 8.4b3.

Backbone Switching

A third method that can be considered to provide an inter-vLAN, interswitch communications capability can be obtained through the use of backbone switches. The topology associated with the use of a backbone switch would be similar to that shown in Figure 8.4b1 and 8.4b2, with the router replaced by a backbone switch. The backbone switch commonly represents a high-speed switch with a limited number of ports, such as a 100BASE-T,

FDDI, or an ATM switch. A "legacy" switch, such as a 100BASE-T or FDDI switch, would use bridging to provide communications between vLANs on different switches or multiple vLANs on the same switch. Since most high-speed backbone switches operate at the MAC layer, the use of backbone switching to provide an inter-vLAN, interswitch communications capability is normally limited to the use of layer-2 LAN switches.

ATM Considerations

The use of ATM backbone switches to interconnect Ethernet or Token Ring switches adds a layer of complexity that should be considered as it affects both vLAN creation and interswitch performance. To understand why this occurs, let us turn our attention to the method by which non-ATM connected endstations residing on Ethernet or Token Ring switches communicate with one another via an ATM backbone switch.

So-called "legacy" LANs, such as Ethernet, Token Ring, and FDDI, primarily operate using a connectionless technology where traffic is transmitted on a path and can be viewed by many stations prior to the destination recognizing its address in a frame and copying the frame "off the wire." In comparison, ATM is a connection-oriented transmission method in which a direct path or circuit is established between the source and the destination station. For connectionless traffic to flow through a connection-oriented network, the ATM network must emulate the broadcast nature of legacy LANs as well as provide a mapping or resolution process that converts MAC addresses to ATM addresses. Those functions are performed by an ATM Forum standard known as LAN emulation (LANE).

LAN Emulation Under the ATM LAN emulation (LANE) standard, a LAN emulation server (LES) is required to perform MAC to ATM address mapping or resolution in conjunction with LAN emulation clients (LECs). The actual resolution occurs as a client-server process; however, the client is commonly a non-ATM LAN switch, while the server function can be performed in an ATM switch, router, or a separate workstation.

Figure 8.5 illustrates the LANE process when the LES function is assumed to be incorporated into an ATM switch. Here the LAN switch in the lower-left portion of Figure 8.5 receives a frame (1) from a legacy endstation destined for another legacy endstation that is not connected to the local switch. Thus, the frame must traverse the ATM backbone switch.

Since the MAC address in the LAN frame must be converted into an ATM address, the LEC, which is assumed to reside in the LAN switch, transmits a MAC-to-ATM address resolution request to the LES, with the LES function assumed to reside in the ATM switch. Since the LES does not know where the destination MAC address resides, it must transmit a multicast request (2) to every LEC in the network other than the LEC providing the resolution request. In Figure 8.5 this results in the LES transmitting two requests to two LECs. Assuming the destination station is connected to the third LAN switch, that switch has the desti-

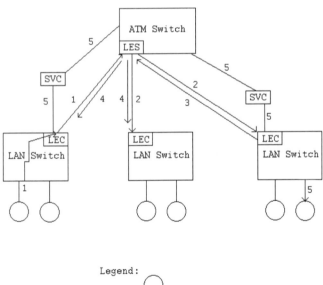

Figure 8.5   The ATM LAN emulation process.

nation MAC address in its address table and responds (3) to the LES query. The LES will then broadcast (4) the response received from the LEC to all other LECs in the network.

The LEC that originated the MAC-to-ATM address resolution request recognizes the broadcast as a response to its request, learns the ATM address of the destination switch, and sets up a switched virtual circuit (SVC) as indicated by the number 5 in Figure 8.5. The SVC transports the frame via ATM cells from the originating LAN switch to the destination LAN switch, where it is reassembled into a frame and delivered to the destination station.

In examining the use of ATM LAN emulation to interconnect legacy switches, note that the emulation process occurs from the LEC in the ATM interface of the LAN switch through the LES in the ATM switch to the LEC in the ATM interface in the destination LAN switch. That process is transparent to vLAN creation methods using MAC addresses and allows LAN switches to control whether frames from one switch should be destined via the ATM backbone to another LAN switch. If vLANs are defined by a port grouping method, each ATM interface on a LAN switch would be considered as just another LAN switch port. Thus, if ATM ports on each LAN switch are defined for inclusion in a LAN switch port-based vLAN, the vLAN can also span multiple switches.

Performance Issues Although most people consider the use of ATM backbone switches as a mechanism to enhance performance, in some situations the LAN emulation process may result in the throughput of a 155-Mbps ATM switch becoming less than that obtainable from the use of a 100-Mbps Fast Ethernet switch. This is because the LAN emulation process, as previously indicated, requires a considerable amount of LEC-to-LES interaction to obtain the MAC to ATM address resolution prior to a switched virtual call being able to be set up to actually transport the frame between switches.

Now that we have an appreciation for the concepts behind local virtual networking, let's extend the distance between switches so we can consider the use of the Internet as a mechanism for obtaining a virtual networking capability.

USING THE INTERNET

It was previously noted in this chapter that there are compelling economic and reliability reasons for considering the use of the Internet as a virtual network. Unfortunately, there are also a few compelling reasons some organizations may wish to bypass using the Internet as a mechanism to replace leased lines. Two of the more compelling reasons to bypass the Internet include security and performance issues. As we will shortly note, with the addition of appropriate hardware it becomes possible to overcome security problems associated with the use of the Internet.

Security Considerations

The connection of a corporate network to the Internet exposes that network to attacks from hackers, crackers, and other unscrupulous persons beyond the direct control of the manager of a private network. This situation is true regardless of whether your Internet connection is established to enable corporate employees to access the World Wide Web or to use the Internet as a virtual network. For either or both situations, there are several security mechanisms that can be used to obtain a significant barrier between the public Internet and corporate private networks to enhance corporate security. Those security mechanisms include the use of a firewall, encryption, a proxy server, and an authentication server. Since many recently introduced firewalls now include proxy and authentication server capabilities as well as the ability to encrypt data, we will primarily focus our attention upon the use of firewalls that include security features previously requiring their implementation on separate servers. In doing so, we will first examine the functionality of a basic firewall and then examine the operation and utilization of additional security features added to many vendor products.

The Basic Firewall

A basic firewall is a computer operating special software developed to provide a user-selectable barrier between two networks. Normally one network is a public network while the second network is commonly a private corporate network.

The firewall has its origin in the enhancement of routers to provide a filtering capability to selectively bar different types of predefined network traffic. In fact, a basic firewall is equivalent to the filtering capability included in many routers. Thus, network managers and administrators can consider using the filtering capability of a router as a substitute for obtaining the functionality of a standalone basic firewall. Although the filtering capability of many routers and firewalls is equivalent, their installation and use with respect to the topology or network structure slightly differs from one to another. Thus, an examination of firewalls should commence with an overview of how they are installed in comparison to the use of routers.

Installation   A firewall contains two or more interfaces that can include serial ports as well as different types of LAN adapter cards, such as Ethernet, Token Ring, or FDDI. The most common use of a firewall is as a barrier to control access from the Internet to a protected network. This method of utilization is illustrated by the schematic diagram shown in Figure 8.6.

When used as an access control device, the firewall performs filtering operations based upon predefined rules generally developed to prohibit certain vulnerable services and applications from entering or leaving a specific interface. In addition, the firewall may also perform encryption, authentication, and proxy services, two additional functions described in detail later in this section.

In examining Figure 8.6, the DMZ LAN represents a non-populated network whose sole connections are the router interface and one firewall interface. By excluding the connection of workstations and other networking devices, such as file servers, from the DMZ LAN, the ability of unauthorized or unwanted traffic to adversely affect internal network users is minimized since such traffic will be examined by the firewall prior to obtaining the ability to reach the populated LAN segments in the internal private network.

Information originating from the Internet destined to the corporate network is first received by the firewall via the DMZ LAN. If the predefined rules are not violated, the firewall will transfer information destined to hosts on the corporate network

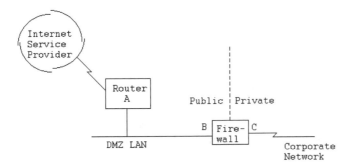

Figure 8.6 A firewall provides access protection between internal and external networks.

to the corporate network. Otherwise, information is placed in the great bit bucket in the sky where it can do no harm. In the reverse direction, rules can be established to bar access from hosts on the corporate network to different Internet applications or locations, such as www.playboy.com. Thus, firewall rules can be set up to be bidirectional. To differentiate directions, data flowing toward the corporate network from the Internet will be referred to as *inbound traffic* in this section, while data flowing in the opposite direction will be referred to as *outbound traffic*.

If a router's filtering capability is used in place of a basic firewall, the corporate network is placed immediately behind the router and the router in effect functions as a basic firewall. For either situation, the connection of geographically separated private networks via the Internet would require routers with filtering capability or firewalls at each connection point to provide protection to each private network.

Filtering Operations Most filtering operations are based upon the use of source and destination IP addresses and well-known port numbers. Under TCP, ports indicate the ends of logical connections used to transport long-term conversations, that is, specific types of applications. A port assigned by the Internet Assigned Numbers Authority (IANA) for a specific application is known as a *Well Known Port number*.

Numbers for Well Known Ports were originally assigned in the range 0 to 255 and were later expanded to the range 0 to

1023. Ports from 1024 through 49151 are referred to as *Registered Ports*. Although those ports are not controlled by the IANA, it registers the use of those ports. Registered Ports are used for a variety of purposes, ranging from network blackjack to Lotus Notes and individual use. A third type of port is the Dynamic or Private Port which ranges from 49152 through 65535. One common ersatz-security method some organizations employ is to attempt to "hide" a service by changing a Well Known Port number for a specific application, such as port 23 for Telnet, to a Registered or Private Port number, such as 2023 or 64023. While this action might cause a bit of inconvenience to a casual hacker, more sophisticated persons will more than likely use a script or port scanning program to probe for available ports being used.

Table 8.1 lists approximately 20 Well Known Ports and their assigned use. As we will shortly note, one of the decisions required to facilitate the installation and setup of a firewall concerns the services that will be permitted across the firewall as well as the systems in the form of IP addresses authorized to support such services.

In examining the firewall schematic illustrated in Figure 8.6, note the physical interfaces labeled A, B, and C. Each interface represents a network node which requires a distinct IP address, and the assignment of those addresses must be carefully considered to facilitate the installation and operation of a firewall.

The router's IP address, indicated by the letter A, is assigned from the block of addresses, such as a Class C address, provided by an Internal Service Provider (ISP) to an organization. Although there are no firm rules concerning the assignment of IP addresses, if your organization was assigned a Class C address you could consider the use of any IP addresses in the class with the exception of .0 and .255, since .0 represents the Class C network while .255 represents a broadcast address. Thus, you could assign any one of 254 out of 256 potential Class C addresses to the router. Of course, you must coordinate this assignment with your ISP to ensure that inbound traffic from the Internet can reach your router.

The IP address indicated by the letter B in Figure 8.6 repre-

Table 8.1 Representative Examples of Well-Known Ports

Port Number	Description
20	File Transfer (data)
21	File Transfer (control)
23	Telnet
25	Simple Mail Transfer Protocol
42	Host Name Server
43	Who Is
53	Domain Name Server
69	Trivial File Transfer Protocol
70	Gopher
79	Finger
80	HyperText Transmission Protocol (WWW)
109	Post Office Protocol—Version 2
110	Post Office Protocol—Version 3
111	SUN Remote Procedure Call
119	Network News Transfer Protocol (NNTP)
513	remote login (rlogin)
520	Routing Information Protocol (RIP)
540	Unix-to-Unix Copy Program (UUCP)

sents the firewall's external interface and should be an address that can be routed externally. That address should be an address in a network assigned to your organization by either your ISP or the InterNIC. If obtained from the latter, your ISP must be aware of that address and that address should be entered in their routing tables.

A word of caution is in order concerning IP addresses and your ability to use those addresses. Some Internet Service Providers will provide a requested number of IP addresses, such as several Class C addresses. However, unless specifically requested to activate those addresses, they will not be entered into the ISP's routing tables and will not be usable. Needless to say, a quick telephone check to determine your ISP's policy may save you several hours or more of effort in attempting to determine the reason for the inability of inbound data to reach the firewall.

The third address you will need when installing a firewall represents the internal interface of that device. Denoted by the letter C in Figure 8.6, that address should be on a different network address range from address B. The rationale for using a different network address range from address B is to enable the firewall to hide your internal firewall connection from the general public. If you just happen to have an unused IP address or an entirely different network address range from the address used for B, you're sitting pretty. However, if your organization is similar to others, IP addresses are rapidly becoming a scarce resource. Rather than use an address you might prefer to save, you can consider using an address from three blocks of IP address space reserved for private Internets. Those addresses are defined in RFC 1918. In fact, in addition to using an address from one of three blocks of IP addresses defined in that RFC for the firewall's internal interface, you can also use addresses from those blocks for other devices located within your internal network.

Under RFC 1918, the title of which is "Address Allocation for Private Internets," the IANA reserved the following blocks of IP address space for private Internets:

```
10.0.0.0 to 10.255.255.255
172.16.0.0 to 172.31.255.255
192.168.0.0 to 192.168.255.255
```

IP addresses within the three address blocks make it possible for organizations to use application layer gateways such as firewalls to connect their internal network to the Internet while enabling the internal network to use nonunique IP addresses.

Policy versus Rules Two key issues associated with the use of a firewall include an organization's network policy and the rules required to implement that policy. Concerning organization policy, that policy commonly includes the decision to filter certain protocols and network addresses. For example, trivial FTP on Well Known Port 69, which is used for booting diskless workstations, can also be used to read any file on a host under certain circumstances.

Similarly, rlogin service on Well Known Port 513 can provide unauthorized access to accounts when improperly configured.

Thus, common organization policies include blocking tftp and rlogin at a firewall. Other services, such as Telnet, FTP, and SMTP, operate on certain hosts. Thus, another common policy is to restrict access to certain services based upon the IP destination address of inbound traffic. Since some organizations may wish to allow access to certain services on their protected network based upon an originating host IP address, another common policy is to restrict access to some services based upon the IP source address of inbound traffic as well as the destination address of the traffic. Thus, filtering operations required to implement organizational policy can be based upon Well Known Port number as well as source and/or destination IP address.

Once your organizational policy is determined you can use that policy to plan the rules necessary to implement it. In doing so, it is important to review the design structure of the firewall as that structure will have a considerable effect upon the rules necessary to implement your policy.

Firewalls commonly follow one of two basic design structures—permitting any service unless it is explicitly denied or denying any service unless it is explicitly permitted. Needless to say, the rules you will develop to implement organizational policy will vary based upon the basic design structure of the firewall. Concerning those rules, which will be discussed shortly, a word of caution is in order. For some people, configuring a firewall can resemble one of my favorite scenes from the movie *The Lion in Winter*. In that movie, the king turns to the queen. As the camera pans into those beautiful eyes of Katherine Hepburn, the king says: "Know the facts," to which she retorts: "Which ones, there are so many."

Similar to the queen's predicament when facing a large number of facts, organizations installing firewalls may have to consider a large number of configuration options that can considerably vary between vendor equipment and even between equipment within a vendor's product line. Thus, the filtering illustrations presented later in this chapter should be viewed as representing a methodology that may have to be restructured for implementation on a specific vendor product.

To illustrate the establishment of an organization policy and filtering rules necessary to implement that policy requires a network to work with. Figure 8.7 illustrates a portion of a private network to be located behind a firewall.

Let's assume your organization has two private networks that will be connected via the use of the Internet. One network, partially illustrated in Figure 8.7, was assigned the block of IP addresses 123.45.67.XX, while a second network, which is not shown, was assigned the class C address 198.78.46.XX. At the first private network location, let's assume there are three computers that we wish to allow network users with the IP address block 198.78.46.XX to access. Those computers include a Telnet system whose IP address is 123.45.67.8, a Web server–based help desk whose address is 123.45.67.9, and an FTP server whose address is 123.45.67.10. Let's further assume that although any IP address in the Class C block 198.78.46.XX can access the Telnet and Web servers, only hosts with IP addresses 198.78.46.30 and 198.78.46.31 will be allowed to access the FTP server from the Internet. Thus, organizational policy would be to allow access to the Telnet and Web servers from any user on the public side of the firewall whose packet source address is in the Class C 198.78.46.XX address block while restricting access to the FTP server to hosts whose source addresses were previously mentioned. Otherwise, all other services and packets are to be blocked.

Figure 8.8 illustrates an example of the ruleset you would develop to implement the previously described policy for inbound traffic. The first rule allows TCP Telnet packets from any source address in the address block 198.78.46** (here the asterisks represent a don't care condition) to the host whose address is 123.45.67.8. TCP connections include a source and destina-

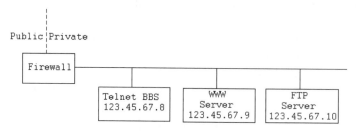

Figure 8.7 Private network resources.

| Packet | Address | | Port | | |
Type	Source	Destination	Source	Destination	Action
TCP	198.76.46.**	123.45.67.8	>1023	23	permit
TCP	198.78.46.**	123.45.67.9	>1023	80	permit
TCP	198.78.46.30	123.45.67.10	>1023	21	permit
TCP	198.78.46.31	123.45.67.10	>1023	21	permit
*	*	*	*	*	deny

Figure 8.8 Preparing an inbound traffic ruleset to implement packet filtering.

tion port, with a destination port of 23 representing the Well Known Port number for Telnet. Since TCP source ports are randomly selected at or above 1024, the firewall, if it supports source port filtering, must allow source ports greater than 1023.

The second rule enables inbound traffic to the Web server from any source address in the same Class C address block, while the third and fourth rules permit access to the FTP server from the indicated source addresses. The fifth rule, which is usually unnecessary, denies all other services and packets from entering the private network. Since most firewalls deny anything not specifically permitted, the last rule may not be necessary.

Some words of caution are warranted concerning filtering rules. First, most firewalls permit bidirectional filtering. Since a common default of *all services not explicitly permitted are denied* is associated with firewalls, this means you will usually have to develop a set of outbound traffic rules. Those rules must be carefully considered and should not simply represent enabling outbound traffic as the reverse or reciprocal of inbound traffic. For example, FTP uses port 21 for control purposes while port 20 is used for the actual transfer of data. Thus, bidirectional filtering must take into consideration the fact that the FTP server responds on port 20 to control requests received on port 21. A second important consideration is to carefully examine the services behind the firewall and the necessity for hosts on the public network to access those services. For example, DNS is transported by UDP. Thus, blocking all UDP would block access to your organization's DNS on the internal network. Another potential problem associated with implementing a ruleset concerns the order of the specified rules. Those rules are placed in a table in memory which the firewall usually checks against inbound and outbound traffic based upon table order sequence. Thus, moving the fifth rule in Figure 8.8 to position one in the ruleset would bar all inbound traffic, even if such traffic was permitted in a subsequent rule, since the first match would terminate further table searching.

Encryption

Since the flow of corporate data via the Internet makes such information vulnerable to being read by other organizations and individuals, many organizations will require firewalls to provide an encryption capability. Through encryption the information content of packets becomes unrecognizable, providing protection of information routed through the Internet. When packets are encrypted for transmission via the Internet, the term *encrypted tunnel* is often used to reference the transportation of such data. Here the term *tunnel* references the process of tunneling whereby information transported from one point to another is encapsulated in wrapper packets. In actuality, the term *tunnel* can be misleading as there are several methods by which firewalls can encrypt data. One method, in which the contents of entire packets originating on a public network are first encrypted and then encapsulated in new packets using the destination address of another firewall, is indeed tunneling. Another method, in which only the information field of a packet originating on a private network is encrypted, does not alter any control information in the packet header. Thus, this technique does not require the packet to be encapsulated for transmission and does not actually represent tunneling. Regardless of the method of encryption, both methods hide the contents of information carried through the Internet, providing a level of protection to the contents of packets.

Figure 8.9 illustrates the use of a pair of firewalls to provide an encrypted group tunnel through the Internet to link two geographically separated private networks. Although encryption safeguards the contents of packets from observation, by itself it does not verify the data originator nor provide a mechanism to limit the ability to restrict users on the Internet to subsets of services for which you want to provide access. Recognizing this limitation, many firewall vendors now incorporate authentication and proxy services within their products.

Authentication

Although packet filtering and encryption represent common functions performed by firewalls, two additional functions can be associated with this category of communications equipment that warrant discussion. Those features include authentication and proxy services.

Although passwords represent a form of authentication, they are only periodically changed and represent a vulnerability as their flow over the Internet can be monitored. Recognizing this problem, many firewalls now include an advanced authentication service which integrates onetime passwords in the form of tokens generated by a pseudo-random number generator with access to specific services behind the firewall. For example, a firewall may support the use of credit card–size numeric password generators which generate a new five- or six-digit code every minute. When a user attempts to access a specific service, he or she is prompted by the firewall's authentication program for the PIN number and numeric code displayed on his or her security card. The firewall uses the PIN to execute an algorithm associated with the PIN, producing a numeric code that is com-

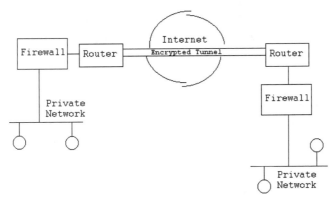

Figure 8.9 Using firewalls to create an encrypted tunnel.

pared to the received code. Since codes change on a short time basis, typically every 30 or 60 seconds, some authentication programs will compare the received code to a series of codes that could have been generated a minute before or after the code was received. Assuming the received code matches one of those generated codes, the remote user is authenticated and allowed access to the requested service. However, once passed through the firewall, a second level of security in the form of a Telnet or FTP server password request is commonly required to actually access the requested service.

Although it is possible to place individual authentication programs on separate servers, the use of a firewall simplifies administration as well as reduces the cost of authentication. For example, if your organization wanted to provide authenticated access to several Telnet and FTP hosts, you would require the installation of authentication software on each host as well as the distribution of separate token generating cards to authorized users of each system. Users requiring access to two or more hosts might then require multiple security cards unless authentication software on each host could be coordinated with the software on other hosts. In comparison, centralizing authentication at the firewall enables management of token generation cards to be simplified. Figure 8.10 illustrates the general operational steps performed by a firewall performing authentication for predefined host services.

In planning for firewall authentication you should examine the methods of authentication supported. Although most firewalls support several methods, selecting different methods for different users can considerably add to your administrative burden without enhancing the security of your private network. If you select a time-based token system where passwords or numeric codes change every 30 or 60 seconds, you should consider the fact that remote access to your firewall can result in transmission delays that can easily result in a mismatch between the entry of a valid token and its rejection upon arrival at the firewall. Thus, it is important to be able to set a comparison time variance that enables the firewall to compute valid tokens preceding and succeeding the token it generates at the time an incoming token arrives.

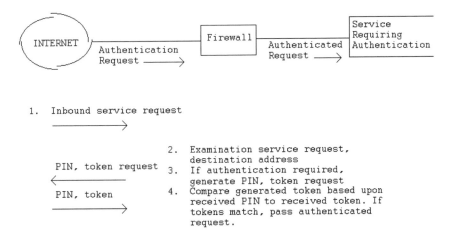

Figure 8.10 Firewall authentication process.

Proxy Services

While filtering and authentication are important tools to enhance security, by themselves they leave some gaps that you
may wish to close via the use of proxy services. A proxy service is
an application that mimics the underlying protocol for a specific
service and enables administrators to make rule-based decisions concerning whether to allow or disable commands supported by that protocol. For example, an FTP proxy might be
configured to allow users to download files but preclude their
ability to upload files.

Although many firewalls now include various proxy services,
other products do not. In the event you decide that a particular
firewall product has all the features you want except for one or
more specific proxy services, you may wish to consider supple-
menting that firewall with an application gateway. The latter
represents a host running one or more proxy services. When
using an application gateway you would configure your firewall
to redirect all inbound traffic for a specific proxy service, such as
FTP or Telnet, to the application gateway. The user requiring
access to a specific host application would be routed to the application gateway, which would check the user's source IP address
as well as commands the user attempts to perform, accepting or
rejecting those operations based upon predefined rules. Regard-

less of whether you intend to use a firewall with built-in proxy services or an application gateway, it is important to determine the rules or policies you wish to effect for those services that require restrictions. In addition, you should consider matching those rules or policies against the capabilities of the firewall or application gateway you intend to use. Doing so will ensure the communications equipment can provide the desired degree of protection your organization requires, or will alert you to a potential problem that may require additional effort to resolve. For example, an FTP proxy should as a minimum allow you to selectively block Get, Put, CD, Delete, List, and Rename commands. If for some reason one or more of those commands are not supported by the FTP proxy service of a firewall, you may wish to consider the use of a different product or the redesign of the storage structure of your FTP server.

A word of caution is in order concerning proxy services. Certain proxy services implemented either on a firewall or on an application gateway bar all services unless those services are enabled. This could result in an unintended problem when an employee dials into an ISP when traveling and attempts to access a service not previously enabled. If that employee just arrived at an overseas location, the administrator might receive a telephone call at a time when he or she is normally counting sheep, requiring a trip to the office. Thus, proper planning as well as the testing of a firewall prior to its installation into a production environment can alleviate many unanticipated problems.

Testing Considerations

The variance between the capabilities of different vendor products, as well as the differences associated with implementing rules on different products, can result in your best intentions going astray. To avoid potential embarrassments as well as security gaps, it is highly recommended that you consider installing a firewall on a network segment established to enable the testing of the firewall's configuration prior to it being placed into a production environment. Although doing so will usually result in the necessity to change a few IP addresses on the external side of the firewall from their intended addresses, the ability to significantly test the firewall can provide indications of configuration problems that can be corrected without seriously affecting the operational capability of your organization.

Performance Issues

As previously noted, there are considerable advantages in terms of reliability, economics, and application integration associated with the use of the Internet as a replacement or supplement for private analog and digital leased lines. Unfortunately, in addition to security you must also cope with performance issues that can place the proverbial "fly in the ointment" with respect to the use of the Internet as a replacement for private leased lines.

During 1996, the tremendous growth in World Wide Web traffic threatened to turn portions of the Internet into the Long Island Expressway at rush hour, in effect resulting in substantial bottlenecks that significantly degraded transmission performance. In fact, many pundits were predicting a catastrophic collapse of portions of the Internet due to the success of its unrestricted growth. What started as a mechanism for the exchange of text-based electronic mail messages has evolved into a transport mechanism for downloading weather maps and pictures of Madonna, accessing on-line magazines and even placing individual telephone calls. The 500-character email long ago was commonly replaced by the hundred-thousand-byte message including a 95 Kbyte picture of the author or an attached binary encoded document, while short interactive Telnet sessions with 2,000-byte screens have been, to a significant degree, replaced by Web surfing where downloading a page with imbedded graphics can result in the transmission of 200,000 bytes. At the same time transmission requirements were growing by several orders of magnitude, the number of Internet users was growing exponentially. Although the growth in content transmission and user population resulted in significant delays in many applications during 1996, from a personal perspective I believe that evolving and planned Internet backbone communications modifications can provide significant relief for performance bottlenecks. For example, some Internet backbone carriers during late 1996 upgraded their facilities from a T3 operating rate of approximately 45 Mbps to an ATM operating rate of 155 Mbps, with a further upgrade to 622 Mbps planned for implementation in the near future. This increase in Internet backbone capacity should alleviate many existing bottlenecks. In addition, the commitment of seven companies to continue to enhance the Internet backbone may enable capacity to eventually surpass demand. For example, through the use of wavelength division multiplexing, the transport capacity of fiber can be significantly increased, in some situations providing a 10-Gbps transmission capacity. Thus, as new capacity and new techniques are added to circuits used for Internet transmission, the Internet can be expected to evolve into a network capable of transporting corporate time-sensitive information in the form of voice, fax, and data. Thus, corporations may wish to periodically test the use of the Internet to ascertain its capability to serve as a replacement or supplement for the computer network. In the interim, time-insensitive information in the form of such diverse applications as electronic mail and fax should be considered for placement on the Internet if doing so can provide sufficient economic gains.

Index

4B5B coding, 64, 102–104
802.1Q standard, 277–283
802.10 security protocol, 269–273
100BASE-FX, 29, 64–65
100BASE-TX, 29, 64–65, 207
100BASE-T4, 29, 64–65
100VG-AnyLAN, 30

A
abort token, 66–67
access control field, 71–75
acknowledgement number field, 141
active monitor, 75, 86–87
Address Resolution Protocol. *See* ARP
allocation number field, 141
American National Standards Institute.
    See ANSI
ANSI, 16–17, 94
ARP, 145
Asynchronous Transfer Mode. *See* ATM
ATM
   ATM Adaption Layer, 116–117, 125
   ATM Layer, 117–118
   benefits, 113–116
   cell, 115–118, 122–125
   cell loss priority, 125
   cell switching, 126–128
   header error check, 125
   LAN Emulation, 128–131, 273–276,
      298–300
   network interfaces, 121–122
   operation, 118–121
   payload type identifier, 125
   permanent switched virtual circuit, 126
   protocol stack, 116–118
   switched virtual circuit, 126
   virtual circuit identifier, 123–128
   virtual path identifier, 123–128
authentication, 311–313

B
backbone switching, 297–298
backoff, 52–53
backpressure, 209–210
bandwidth utilization, 7
beacon frame, 88–89
BPDU, 171–172, 266
bridge
   blocking state, 168
   designated bridge, 170–171

filtering and forwarding, 161–162, 168
operation, 159–184
root bridge, 168–170
source route transparant, 164, 177–181
source routing, 164, 172–177
spanning tree protocol, 166–172
standby bridge, 171–172
table flushing, 10–11
table operation, 163–165
transparent operation, 159–165
translating operation, 159, 161–164
transparent operation, 159–165
utilization, 181–184
Bridge Protocol Data Unit. *See* BPDU
broadcast, 32
broadcast address, 42, 80, 136
broadcast and unknown server, 275–276
broadcast domain, 1–2, 4, 9, 240

C
checksum field, 134
collision detection, 51–54
connection control field, 139
connectionless service, 61–63
constant value field, 266

D
data field, 46
datagram, 144–145
datastream type field, 139–140
designated bridge, 170
destination address field, 41–44, 77–81,
    106–107
destination connection ID field, 140
destination network field, 136
destination node field, 136
Destination Services Access Point. *See*
    DSAP
destination socket field, 136–137
Differential Manchester encoding, 50–51,
    68–71
DMZ LAN, 302–303
DNS, 154–156
docking station, 247
Domain Name Service. *See* DNS
dotted decimal address, 151

downstream neighbor, 66
DSAP, 56–57, 59, 92–93, 107–108
dual attached stations, 99–101

E
encryption, 310–311
end-of-stream field, 64–65
Ethernet
    collisions, 52–54
    frame composition, 38–47, 179–181
    frame determination, 60–61
    full duplex, 194, 204–205
    hub operation, 186–189
    jam pattern, 51–52
    late collisions, 53–54
    logical link control, 39, 56–64
    media access control, 47–55
    NetWare 802.3 frame, 59–61
    SNAP frame, 58–59
    types of service, 61–63
    vLAN, 281–283
    wait time, 52–53
explicit tagging, 2–3, 262–269, 279–283
exterior domain, 224

F
failure domain, 88
Fast Ethernet, 29, 33, 64–65
fat pipe, 206–207
fax transmission, 289–291
FDDI
    bandwidth allocation, 108–113
    data encoding, 101–103
    802.10 security protocol, 269–272
    frame formats, 103–108, 180–181
    hardware components, 95–98
    network access, 99–101
    network advantages, 94–95
    topology, 98–99
Fiber Distributed Data Interface. *See*
    FDDI
filtering, 228–231, 303–310
firewall, 231, 301–310
flat network, 4
flooding, 175
frame, 24

frame check sequence field, 46–47, 84, 106–107
frame control field, 76–77
frame header, 35
frame operations, 37–131
frame status field, 84–85, 106–107
functional address indicator, 79–80

G
global port, 293–296

H
high-bits source address field, 266

I
I frame, 57–58, 91–92
IEEE, 16–18
IEEE 802 standards, 27–35
implicit tagging, 2–4, 8, 279
index field, 266
information field, 82–84
Institute of Electrical and Electronic Engineers. *See* IEEE
intelligent switches
  advantages of use, 194
  architecture, 203–204
  basic components, 192–193
  flow control, 209–210
  high speed port operation, 204–210
  latency, 196
  network utilization, 212–218
  switching techniques, 195–202
  Token Ring switching, 210–212
interdomain communications, 9
interior domain, 224
International Standards Organization. *See* ISO
International Telecommunications Union—Telecommunications standardization. *See* ITU-T
Internet, 286–290, 301–316
Internet Protocol. *See* IP
Internet Service Provider, 286–290
Internetwork Packet Exchange. *See* IPX
Inter-Switch Link. *See* ISL

inter-vLAN communications, 239–240, 247, 292–300
IP, 148–154
IP multicast, 10
IPX, 133–139
ISL, 261–269
ISO, 16,19
ISO Reference Model, 19–27
ITU-T, 16, 18–19

J
jabbering, 88
jam pattern, 51–52

L
LAN administration, 6–7
LAN Emulation, 128–131, 273–276, 298–300
LAN Emulation Client, 274–275, 298–300
LAN Emulation Configuration Server, 275
LAN Emulation Server, 275, 298–299
length field, 45–46, 134, 265
link state protocol, 227
LLC, 23, 30–33, 35, 39, 56–64, 91–93, 107–108
locally administered addressing, 42–44, 78–79
logical connection, 23
Logical Link Control. *See* LLC
logical SAP. *See* LSAP
LSAP, 271–272

M
MAC, 23, 30–32, 35, 85–91
MAC-based switching, 240–249
Manchester coding, 50–51, 69–70
Media Access Control. *See* MAC
Micom V/IP, 290–291
multicast, 32, 42, 151, 255–256, 264

N
name server, 156–157
NetWare, 133–143
NetWare Ethernet 802.3 frame, 59–60

network layer operations, 133–157
network standards, 15–36
nondata symbols, 69–71
NRZI signaling, 102–103
null address, 80

P
packet, 23
packet type field, 134–135
Physical Medium Independent. *See* PMD
PMD, 33–34, 96–97
port grouping vLANs, 233–240
port switching hub, 3–5
preamble field, 40
proxy services, 313–314
purge frame, 88

R
ring station, 66
RIP, 141–143, 226–227
root bridge, 168–170
root path, 170–171
router
    basic operation, 218–220
    communication protocol, 222
    filtering, 228–231
    inter-vLAN communications, 293–297
    networking, 221–229
    routing protocol, 222–228
    transport protocol, 222–223
    Vgate router, 294
routing information field, 81–82, 173–176
Routing Information Protocol. *See* RIP

S
S frame, 57–58, 91–92
SAP, 7, 42, 138–139, 141–142
security, 7–8
segment, 145
sequence number field, 140–141
Sequence Packet Exchange. *See* SPX
Service Access Points, 33, 56, 92–93
Service Advertisement Protocol. *See* SAP
shortest path first. *See* SPF
single attached stations, 99–101
SLIST command, 142

source address field, 44, 81–82, 106–107,
    265
source connection ID field, 140
source network field, 136–137
source node field, 137
source routing, 172–177
Source Service Access Point. *See* SSAP
source socket field, 137
spanning tree protocol, 166–174, 268
SPF, 227–228
SSAP, 56–57, 59, 92–93, 107–108
standby monitor, 75, 86–88
start-of-frame delimiter field, 40
start-of-stream field, 64–65
subnetting, 152–154
switching hubs. *See* intelligent switches

T
TCP/IP
    addressing, 148–154
    ARP, 145
    datagram, 144–145
    DNS, 154–156
    ICMP, 145
    IP, 148–154
    name server, 156–157
    subnetting, 152–154
    TCP, 145–146
    UDP, 147–148
token, 66–67, 105
Token Ring
    abort token, 65–67
    access control field, 71–75
    active monitor, 75
    destination address field, 77–81
    duplicate address test, 89
    frame control field, 76–77
    frame status field, 84–85
    full duplex, 194, 204–205
    hub operation, 188–189
    information field, 82–84
    logical link control, 91–93
    medium access control, 85–91
    monitor bit, 74–75
    priority bits, 71–73
    reservation bits, 71–73

standby monitor, 75
starting/ending delimiters, 68–71
station insertion, 89–91
transmission formats, 66–68
vLAN, 281–283
transport control field, 134
tunneling, 310–311
type field, 44–45, 264

U
U frames, 57–58, 91–92
UDP, 147–148
unicast, 32, 42
unipolar non-return to zero signaling,
50–51, 68–69
universally administered addressing,
42–44, 77–78
User Datagram Protocol. *See* UDP
user field, 264–265

V
vector distance protocol, 224–226
vectors, 85–87
Vgate router, 294
virtual circuit, 144–146
virtual networking, 285–316
virtual organization, 5–6
vLAN

awareness, 9
construction basics, 2–4, 233–260
802.1Q standard, 277–283
802.10 security protocol, 269–273
field, 266
inter-vLAN communications, 239–240,
247, 292–300
ISL protocol, 262–269
LAN Emulation, 273–276
LAN switch, 237–240
layer-3, 249–254, 257–260
MAC-based, 240–249, 257–260
multicast support, 255–257, 259
network issues, 8–11
overview, 1–4
port grouping, 233–240, 257–260
protocol-based, 251–254, 257–260
rationale for use, 5–8
rule-based, 254–257
standards, 261–284
subnet-based, 249–250
unaware, 9
wiring hub-based, 234–237, 257–260
voice transmission, 289–291

W
well known ports, 303–305, 308–309
wiring hub, 234–237